Mass Migration Under Sail

European Immigration to the Antebellum United States

Dr. Cohn provides an in-depth and comprehensive analysis of the economic history of European immigration to the antebellum United States, using and evaluating the available data as well as presenting new data. This analysis centers on immigration from the three most important source countries – Ireland, Germany, and Great Britain – and examines the volume of immigration, how many individuals came from each country during the antebellum period, and why those numbers increased. The book also analyzes where they came from within each country; who chose to immigrate; the immigrants' trip to the United States, including estimates of mortality on the Atlantic crossing; the jobs obtained in the United States by the immigrants, along with their geographic location; and the economic effects of immigration on both the immigrants and the antebellum United States. No other book examines so many different economic aspects of antebellum immigration.

Raymond L. Cohn is Professor of Economics at Illinois State University. Over the last twenty years, he has written for the following journals: *Explorations in Economic History*, the *Journal of Economic History*, *Social Science History*, and the *International Journal of Maritime History*. Dr. Cohn is also a member of the following associations, among others: the American Economic Association, the Economic History Association, and the International Maritime Economic History Association.

Mass Migration Under Sail

European Immigration to the Antebellum United States

RAYMOND L. COHN

Illinois State University

CAMBRIDGE
UNIVERSITY PRESS

CAMBRIDGE UNIVERSITY PRESS
Cambridge, New York, Melbourne, Madrid, Cape Town, Singapore, São Paulo, Delhi

Cambridge University Press
32 Avenue of the Americas, New York, NY 10013-2473, USA

www.cambridge.org
Information on this title: www.cambridge.org/9780521513227

First published 2009

Printed in the United States of America

A catalog record for this publication is available from the British Library.

Library of Congress Cataloging in Publication data
Cohn, Raymond L., 1950–
Mass migration under sail : European immigration to the antebellum United States /
Raymond L. Cohn.
p. cm.
Includes bibliographical references and index.
ISBN 978-0-521-51322-7 (hbk.)
1. European Americans – History – 19th century. 2. Immigrants – United States –
History – 19th century. 3. United States – Emigration and immigration – History –
19th century. 4. Europe – Emigration and immigration – History – 19th century.
5. European Americans – Economic conditions – 19th century. 6. Immigrants –
United States – Economic conditions – 19th century. 7. United States – Emigration
and immigration – Economic aspects – History – 19th century. 8. Europe –
Emigration and immigration – Economic aspects – History – 19th century.
9. Europe – Economic conditions – 19th century. 10. United States – Economic
conditions – 19th century. I. Title.
E184.E95C64 2009
304.873094–dc22   2008023219

ISBN 978-0-521-51322-7 hardback

To Scotti, who has always been with me

Contents

Contents   ix

List of Tables and Figures

Tables

Figures

Preface

The genesis for this book came from the many years I have spent investigating economic aspects of European immigration to the United States during the antebellum period. Although my initial interest concerned the mortality experienced by the immigrants on the voyage, soon I began working on broader topics. However, writing this book quickly convinced me how little I really knew about many aspects of antebellum immigration. I have increased my knowledge of the economics of antebellum immigration many times over because I have been required to address topics I had not previously considered. The result is a comprehensive economic analysis of European immigration to the antebellum United States. I consider the immigrants in the various European countries, on the voyage, and in the United States, as well as analyze the reasons that immigration occurred and its effects on the United States. Thus, although parts of this book repeat the findings in some of my earlier work, much of the material and explanations are new.

Although my ancestors arrived in the United States well after the antebellum period, the years before the Civil War have always fascinated me. Fundamental changes occurred in the economy, as Jefferson's dream of a country of gentlemen farmers was overtaken by the reality of the growth of manufacturing and large cities. Immigration certainly played a part in these changes, a part I believe has never been fully appreciated. The effects of immigration during the antebellum years were considerable because it was the first time the volume of immigration became large, a development explored in this book. During these years, people also came to live permanently in a new place. The thought of going back to Europe, although certainly possible, was not very practical given the many days required to travel between the United States and Europe on a sailing ship. The permanence of the move to the United States during the antebellum years made immigration quite different from that at later times – or during the present day – when many people came to work and planned on (or at least strongly considered) going back to their homes at some future date. It is the large volume of permanent immigrants arriving during the antebellum years that caused immigration to have widespread effects on the United States for the first time.

Two important features of this book deserve mention. The first is the emphasis on presenting and discussing the available data on antebellum immigration. Although some of the data presented are new, most are available in various government publications. However, I have attempted to present as much data as possible in a logical manner in an effort to provide a reference for anyone searching for numerical information on European immigration to the antebellum United States. Of equal importance, the book also provides an analysis of the data, both as to its quality and its accuracy, so that the reader can appreciate its shortcomings. The second feature of the book is that I have written it in a manner that is as non-mathematical and non-econometric as possible. Although economic models and reasoning lie behind the analysis in the book, no formal models are presented or tested. My reasons are twofold. First, I want the book to appeal not only to my fellow economic historians but also to as many researchers as possible in other fields. Second, much of the discussion of the data emphasizes the uncertainty and imprecision in many of the numbers that exist. Empirical tests of economic models are only as good as the available data, and a number of problems exist with those for the antebellum period. In writing the book in the manner I have, I hope to interest more researchers who work in economic history and other fields in the subject of historical immigration, with the hope that they will improve or expand upon the arguments presented here.

In writing a book, the author always incurs a debt to a number of individuals who provide assistance along the way. In my case, three economic historians read each chapter as it was written and provided me with invaluable feedback. I want to especially thank these individuals: Drew Keeling, Cormac Ó Gráda, and Simone Wegge. Their comments vastly improved this book and kept me from making a number of errors. I also wish to thank two individuals who read the entire manuscript for Cambridge University Press and provided me with numerous helpful comments. I would be remiss if I did not also thank Marianne Hinds Wanamaker and Joel Mokyr, both of whom read an earlier draft of this manuscript and provided me with helpful comments. I did not incorporate every comment provided by the readers, so none of the previously mention individuals should be held responsible for anything said in this book or for any remaining errors. However, I always appreciated each person's willingness to help as well as his or her time and effort. I also thank the interlibrary loan staff at Milner Library for procuring copies of numerous books that are cited in the manuscript and Illinois State University for granting me the sabbatical that allowed me to begin writing the book. Finally, thanks go to my wife, Scotti, whose love, encouragement, patience, and willingness to listen have always been highly appreciated.

A Unique Period for Immigration

On September 7, 1817, Edward Phillips of Shrewsbury in Shropshire, England, sailed from Liverpool on the *James Monroe*. He arrived safely in New York on October 17 and immediately headed for Philadelphia, where he found work. On March 18, 1854, Johann Bauer, born in Heidelsheim in Baden, Germany, left from Bremen for New York. He arrived safely on May 2, stayed with friends for two months, then left for Illinois, where he found work.[1] The voyages of these two individuals, which nearly bracket the period studied in this book, illustrate one important characteristic of immigration from Europe to the United States during the antebellum period. The immigrants arrived after a long voyage on a sailing ship. Phillips' trip was forty days and Bauer's took forty-five. Although Bauer left almost forty years after Phillips, they both experienced voyages of similar length. Given the long trip, an individual only made the voyage if he or she expected the move to be permanent. In fact, neither of these men ever returned to Europe. Until the 1840s, immigration was almost always a one-way trip because the sailing ship was the sole means of travel across the Atlantic Ocean. Only then did steamships begin crossing the ocean on a regular basis. Until steerage was widely introduced on steamships in the late 1850s, however, the only passengers carried by these vessels were those sufficiently wealthy to pay for a cabin. Thus, throughout the antebellum period, the voyage by sailing ship meant that immigration was usually a permanent move.

A second important characteristic of the antebellum period was that it was when mass migration began. In the colonial and early national

[1] Erickson, *Invisible Immigrants*, pp. 265–7; Kamphoefner, et al., *News*, pp. 149–53.

periods, the number of individuals coming to the United States was small, and the numbers remained small into the 1820s. During the late 1820s and early 1830s, however, well before the potato famine, the number of individuals migrating each year began to rise sharply. The potato famine then increased the volume of immigration even more, and the higher numbers of immigrants from Europe persisted until the United States imposed restrictions in the 1920s. As Phillips and Bauer illustrate, the migrants arrived from a number of different European countries.

Only during the antebellum years did both characteristics hold, that is, large numbers of permanent immigrants arrived in the United States from Europe on sailing ships. During earlier periods, all individuals who came to the United States from Europe traveled on sailing ships. The numbers, however, were usually small. After the Civil War, the annual volumes became even larger, but by 1870, most passengers arrived on steamships and many did not plan to stay in the United States.[2] It was the high volume of permanent immigrants arriving via the sailing ship that makes the antebellum period unique in the history of world immigration. Although these features suggest that immigration during the antebellum period deserves separate treatment, they do not imply that every aspect of the immigration occurring at this time was necessarily unique.

Besides possessing a combination of unique characteristics, antebellum immigration should be investigated for at least two other reasons. First, antebellum immigration provides a situation that is close to the classic theoretical migration model, where individuals are assumed to migrate to achieve economic improvement.[3] At least as a starting point, the classic model does not account for the possibility of return migration, and the antebellum period is unique in that little return migration occurred. The model also predicts specific consequences of the migration for the individuals and each country. Given the large volume of immigration during the antebellum period, the theoretical effects predicted by the classic immigration model should be readily apparent. The period examined in this book thus provides an excellent test of the predictions of the classic immigration model. Second, the United States experienced rapid economic growth during the nineteenth century. The century saw

[2] In 1870, 86% of the European immigrants arriving in New York City came on a steamship. The percentage in 1852 had been only 1%. See Cohn, "Transition," Table 1, p. 472.

[3] In this model, migration occurs because the economic return in the country of destination is larger than the economic return in the country of origin, after adjusting for the cost of migrating. See Chapter 3 for further discussion.

the United States move from being a fairly minor economic and political power on the world stage to being the country with the largest economy and one with a growing political clout.[4] Because of its rapid growth, the United States became the most important destination for immigrants as they sought to improve their standard of living. The large inflow of people, which increased over the entire century but first became sizeable during the antebellum period, in turn provided an important source of labor and other resources to the rapidly growing U.S. economy. A study of antebellum immigration thus sheds light on an important factor in nineteenth-century U.S. economic growth.

Structure of the Book

This book explores the economic causes and effects of European immigration to the United States during the period of mass migration under sail, or between about 1815 and 1860. The available data concerning immigration and an evaluation of those data are central features of the book. Essentially, the following chapters lay out what we currently know – and do not know – regarding the economic history of immigration during this important period. First, the book examines a number of aspects relating to the flows of antebellum immigration, including how many people came, where they came from, and why the volume increased at this time. Next, the immigrants are examined, including who they were, their trip from home to the arrival port in the United States, and their experience in the United States. Finally, the effects of European immigration on the antebellum United States are analyzed.

The entire period of mass European immigration to the United States occurred between 1815 and 1914, when 35 million people migrated. Somewhat more than 5 million of these individuals arrived before 1860. Although these 5 million individuals were the smaller part of the entire mass migration, the annual antebellum volume was much larger than in earlier years. Chapter 2 explores the volume and sources of immigration during the antebellum years. The available data are presented and critiqued, and the timing of the increase in volume is determined. In addition, the chapter explores where the immigrants came from within Europe and illustrates the changes in the European sources of immigration over the antebellum years. Chapter 3 then extends the analysis by explaining

[4] For a discussion of U.S. economic ascendancy during the nineteenth century, see Wright, "Origins," pp. 651–3.

the reasons that immigrant volume increased substantially around 1830. After discussing the economic theory of immigration, the chapter examines the factors that changed in Europe, the United States, and ocean travel that caused many more people to immigrate. Essentially, immigration became easier. Chapter 4 continues the discussion by analyzing the importance of push, pull, and other factors during the antebellum period. In particular, the chapter investigates both the potato famine and the relationship between downturns in the U.S. economy and downturns in the volume of European immigration.

Chapters 5 through 7 examine the European immigrants themselves. The higher volume of immigration during the antebellum period was associated with a fundamental change in immigrant composition, which is the subject of Chapter 5. Although most immigrants were positively selected before the early 1830s – they were more skilled than the underlying labor forces they left – the skill level of the immigrant stream declined during the antebellum period. Thus, the antebellum years not only saw more immigrants arrive, but also a substantial reduction in their "quality." Chapter 6 explores the trip undertaken by the European immigrants in moving to the United States. The routes and transportation modes the immigrants took within Europe to get to the embarkation ports are discussed. In addition, this chapter examines the conditions faced by the passengers in crossing the Atlantic by sailing ship, a trip that averaged more than six weeks, and provides an estimate of the mortality suffered during the ocean voyage. The outcomes achieved by the immigrants in the United States, both geographically and financially, are addressed in Chapter 7. After all, the fundamental economic goal for antebellum immigrants was to improve their economic well-being, and the United States was selected because of its rapid rate of economic growth. Essentially, the analysis shows that all the different immigrant groups achieved success in the growing U.S. economy, even given the discussion in Chapter 5 concerning the declining "quality" of the immigrant stream. The chapter also explores the attempts by various agencies in the United States to assist the arriving immigrants.

The economic and political consequences of immigration for the United States during the antebellum period are investigated in Chapter 8. A comparison of the skills of the immigrant stream and those of the native-born U.S. labor force is provided for 1850. The chapter investigates the broader economic and political consequences for the United States of the changes in the volume and composition of immigration. In particular, the connections between immigration and overall real wages, the relative wages of skilled and unskilled workers, developments in manufacturing and transportation, and the outbreaks of nativism are examined. Some of the benefits obtained by the United States from the large volume of immigration are also briefly addressed. Chapter 9 discusses how immigration changed after the Civil War and recaps the findings of the book.

Argument of the Book

This section provides an overview of the line of reasoning presented in detail in the remainder of this book.

Although small in volume, the immigrant stream before the 1830s was generally more skilled than the native-born labor force in the Colonies and then the United States (Chapter 5).[5] The exceptions might have been immigrants arriving as part of a religious flow. The method of transatlantic passage, the sailing ship, meant the journey was long and that virtually all of the immigration was permanent. The high cost of crossing the Atlantic mostly restricted travel to those who could afford to pay the passage fare and indentured servants, who paid their fare by working at reduced wages in the Colonies for a period of years. However, skilled labor was especially scarce in the Colonies, so more skilled individuals gained the most from migrating. Immigrants who were able to pay their own way must have had relatively high incomes, which meant they were more likely to be wealthy farmers, skilled workers, or entrepreneurs. Even the indentured servants experienced a larger gain in the New World if they were more skilled. The overall immigrant stream before the 1830s, therefore, had a relatively high skill level.

During the eighteenth century, the average yearly volume of immigration increased slowly, with the annual total usually being less than ten thousand (Chapter 2). Most immigrants came from Great Britain. After 1750, consistent population growth began to occur throughout Western Europe, which put increased pressure on the standard of living and caused emigration to increase from other European areas, such as Ireland and Germany (Chapter 3). During the first fifteen years of the nineteenth century, immigrant volume fell to very low levels due to the

[5] The discussion in the remainder of this section is carried out without footnotes. The reader is referred to the other chapters for further details and references. The chapter to consult is indicated as follows: at the end of some sentences is a chapter number in parentheses. The reader will find further detail on the material in that sentence in that chapter. Following sentences refer to the same chapter until the next sentence in which another chapter is referred to in parentheses.

Napoleonic Wars. After the end of the wars in 1815, the shipping market was disorganized and transatlantic fares were high, causing the volume of immigration to remain small. Throughout the 1820s, fares slowly fell as the shipping market improved in various ways. In addition, remittances and prepaid tickets became more common and European governmental restrictions on emigration declined. These factors combined to make the transatlantic crossing cheaper by 1830 and thus more affordable to a larger segment of the European population.

Industrial production in the United States did not grow rapidly during the 1820s, and this factor contributed to the low rate of immigration during this decade (Chapter 4). A much more rapidly growing U.S. economy during the early 1830s, in conjunction with the smaller costs of getting to the United States, led to a large increase in immigrant volume in 1831 and 1832 (Chapters 2 and 3). Between 1815 and 1860, a total of 5.2 million Europeans immigrated to the United States, with most arriving after 1830 (Chapter 2). Based on the previous discussion, it is apparent that "push" factors, "pull" factors, and other factors were all important to explain why immigration occurred (Chapter 4). In the antebellum years before the 1840s, the largest proportion of the immigrant stream came from southwest Germany and Ulster in northern Ireland (Chapter 2). These areas had two factors in common. Population densities were very high, which made it difficult to earn a living from agriculture. In addition, the possibility of earning some income in nonfarm activities while remaining on the farm were limited. Emigration was thus an attractive solution for individuals living in these two areas.

The large increase in volume was not the only fundamental change in immigration during the 1830s (Chapter 5). The composition of the immigrant stream also became less skilled, as a greater share of the European labor force could now afford to immigrate. The decline in skills occurred for each of the major source countries: Ireland, Germany, and Great Britain. Yet the German stream remained more skilled than the British, who were more skilled than the Irish. The discrepancies were due to differences in trip length, volume of remittances, and languages. After the early 1830s, the overall skill level of the immigrant stream was similar to that of the native-born U.S. labor force, although the former was relatively abundant in nonfarm unskilled labor and relatively scarce in farmers (Chapter 8). Another factor that could have affected immigration – mortality on the voyage – remained fairly constant over the antebellum period (Chapter 6). About 1.5 percent of those leaving European ports died during the voyage or shortly after arrival, with most deaths occurring on a small number of voyages where epidemics broke out.

Transatlantic passenger shipping routes were fairly specialized, with connections between specific European and U.S. ports (Chapter 6). Over time, however, an increasing percentage of the European immigrants landed in New York City (Chapter 7). This trend reflected advantages of the city as a port, the opening of the Erie Canal, the growing economic importance of the city, and the establishment of the Commissioners of Emigration of the State of New York in 1847. This agency provided some type of assistance to about one-third of the arriving immigrants. A key objective was to help the immigrants move elsewhere in the United States, with northern urban areas being an important destination. The Irish were more likely to remain in the Northeast, the Germans were more likely to move to the Midwest, and the British spread throughout the North. The locational pattern reflected differences in income and skill levels. The poorer and less-skilled Irish found it more difficult to move to the Midwest and were pulled toward the low-skilled factory and servant jobs that were most abundant in the Northeast. The more-skilled Germans were least likely to work in the factories and more likely to be merchants or farmers. The British had a sizeable presence in a wide variety of occupations, from farming to factories.

After the early 1830s, further improvements in shipping, increased remittances, continued population growth in Europe, and the spread of information caused an overall increase in annual volume and, especially, increased numbers from newer areas of Ireland and Germany (Chapters 2 and 4). Although the trend was upward, volume declined in certain years, sometimes because of downturns in the U.S. economy and sometimes because of other factors (Chapter 4). The outbreak of the potato famine in Ireland in 1846, along with other events in Europe, intensified the desire to emigrate. The U.S. economy grew substantially during these years, so the United States provided not only a refuge, but also a source of jobs for those fleeing Europe. Thus, the volume of immigration to the United States increased significantly beginning in 1846. During the peak volume years from 1850–1854, male immigration increased the U.S. male labor force by more than 4 percent per year (Chapter 8). The huge volume led to stagnation in real wages at this time and caused a huge increase in nativist sentiment. The 1854 off-year elections resulted in unprecedented electoral success for the nativists who, although always a presence during the antebellum years, had never achieved much success at the polls. The unexpected election results, in combination with improved conditions in Europe, caused immigrant volume to fall by half in 1855. With the outbreak of a depression in 1857 in the United States, immigrant volume did not surpass its 1854 peak until 1873, when almost all immigrants arrived on steamships.

Antebellum immigration had a number of effects on the U.S. economy (Chapter 8). The unskilled immigrant labor was important in building the antebellum transportation network, and thus they contributed to the decline in internal transportation costs. In addition, the early part of the antebellum period saw manufacturing production begin to shift to larger firms using less-skilled production methods. Skilled European immigrants who arrived before 1830 contributed to this change. Originally, manufacturers used native-born females and children as workers. The larger volume of lower-skilled immigrants arriving by the 1840s, however, provided a ready labor force for manufacturers and thus reinforced the trends in production methods. As a result of these changes, individual artisans lost a good deal of independence, although the latter part of the antebellum period saw skilled wages increase relative to unskilled wages. Besides the distributional effects, immigration raised the rate of economic growth in the antebellum United States in a variety of ways, from adding to the stock of labor to increasing entrepreneurship to adding to the capital stock.

The Current Migration Paradigm

At one time, immigration to the United States was regarded as permanent, unique, and a consequence of the modernization of Europe. An undifferentiated mass of immigrants was viewed as being uprooted from their European homes. Since the 1970s, this view has undergone significant change, mainly in response to an article written by Thistlethwaite.[6] Migrants are now viewed as having been rational decision makers who considered the benefits and costs of moving, factors that were strongly influenced by information available from previous migrants. As a consequence, migration is viewed as a regional phenomenon, where migrants traveled from a specific place in Europe to a place overseas where previous migrants from their village or area had settled. In addition, some individuals returned to their European homes. Thus, migration to the United States is no longer seen as unique because numerous individuals migrated to other places, and many did so before the Industrial Revolution. In sum,

[6] Thistlethwaite, "Migration."

migration is viewed as a consequence of individuals seeking to improve their economic well-being by moving within regional networks. Sometimes this led to a temporary move and other times to a permanent move, sometimes a move to the United States and sometimes to somewhere else, sometimes it involved a return to one's origins and sometimes not, and so on.

In fact, the preferred term is no longer "immigration" or "emigration" but "migration." The change is meant to emphasize that the movement of people was seldom permanent. For example, Walter Nugent titled his book, *Crossings: The Great Transatlantic Migrations, 1870–1914*, because he places migration to the United States in a broader context of transatlantic migrations.[7] Quotes from two other historians emphasize the same point. In one of his articles, Charles Tilly concludes that "(i)t is not very useful to classify migrants by intentions to stay or return home, because intentions and possibilities are always more complex than that – and the migrants themselves often cannot see the possibilities that are shaped by their networks."[8] In his masterly book on intra-European labor movements during the early 1800s, Jan Lucassen wrote, "The ties which bound the migrants to their... area of origin... were still very strong. In most instances, it is impossible to speak of permanent migration."[9] Although primarily discussing migrant labor within Europe, Lucassen later writes, "The difference between migratory labour and permanent resettlement, so clear-cut in past centuries, has grown vague."[10]

A culminating work along these lines is the book by Dirk Hoerder, *Cultures in Contact: World Migrations in the Second Millennium*.[11] As the title suggests, the book is a compendium of migrations over the last millennium that occurred for a variety of reasons. For example, between 1000 and 1500 CE, Hoerder discusses the Jewish Diaspora, the Muslim movement into Spain, the Crusades, early slavery, the migrations of the Normans and the Wends, and the movement of people for marriage, because of droughts and religious persecution, and as farmers, soldiers, pilgrims, prostitutes, traders, and workers. In this 700-page book, only about 40 pages address the immigration of Europeans to the United States between 1800 and 1920. Similarly, Leslie Page Moch writes, "... migrants to every sort of destination – from the regional capital to the mines of

---

[7] Nugent, *Crossings*.
[8] Tilly, "Transplanted Networks," p. 87.
[9] Lucassen, *Migrant Labour*, p. 122.
[10] Lucassen, *Migrant Labour*, p. 215.
[11] Hoerder, *Cultures*.

Missouri – were pushed by the same set of forces." A few sentences later, she says, "... overseas migration systems were intimately linked with those on the continent." In another article, Moch writes, "If we consider international migration, ignoring the regional and national moves created by the same economic and social situation... our understanding of migration will be impoverished."[12] Thus, the current view is that European immigration to the United States was not very different from a mass of other moves.

Given this body of recent work, how can a book that focuses on European immigration to the United States during the antebellum period, and generally ignores other migratory movements during the same period, be justified? I do not wish to argue that all aspects of the current migration paradigm are incorrect. Clearly, they are not. However, not all facets of the current migration paradigm accurately describe the unique case of European immigration to the antebellum United States. In a number of ways, the subject of this book is fundamentally different from intra-European migration or international migration after the Civil War.

A primary reason for the difference is that immigration to the United States was expected to be, and in virtually all cases was, permanent. Although a desire to increase one's income led to both seasonal migration within Europe and immigration to the United States, the first was temporary, whereas the latter was permanent. Immigration to the United States during the antebellum years required a six-week voyage across the Atlantic by sailing ship. The length of the trip made a return to Europe difficult. Thus, an individual did not view travel to the United States as a seasonal movement, but rather a one-time move. Although a few antebellum migrants eventually returned to Europe as visitors or to live permanently, the numbers were small. The best estimates of return migration during the period of sailing ship travel are by Kamphoefner for Germany. He concludes that return migration to Germany in the 1860s was about 2 percent, while for earlier periods, the rates were "consistently under 1 percent."[13] His calculations are based on records of return migration kept by a number of German states. In arriving at this figure, he notes that many previously higher estimates included individuals who returned

---

[12] Moch, "European Perspective," p. 133; Moch, "Dividing Time," p. 43.

[13] Kamphoefner, "Volume," pp. 297–301. In addition, see Harper, *Emigrant Homecomings*. Her book consists of twelve chapters, each by a different author who examines a particular case study of return emigration. Most of the authors use government documents or family letters to develop their arguments. All the case studies in Harper's book before the steamship, however, involve merchants or soldiers.

to visit or retrieve family members. Return migration to Ireland was similarly very small. Return migration to Britain may have been larger, but more of the British would have been merchants or otherwise involved with international trade. Overall, although some return migration obviously occurred during the antebellum period, the volume appears to have been very small.

In the sense that it was permanent, immigration to the United States during the antebellum period had some similarities to the settlement of about forty thousand Germans in the southern Ukraine between 1760 and the 1830s.[14] Few of these individuals expected to return to their last place of residence in Germany, and virtually none did. However, immigration to the United States was still different in that most of it occurred later in time, the volume was much larger, and the migrating individuals had to travel in a limited space on a sailing vessel. Immigration to the United States was also clearly different from the migration of Asian indentured servants around the world that began in the 1830s. Although many of these individuals ended up staying in the African, Caribbean, or South American countries where they were taken to work, all were guaranteed a return ticket as a condition of their indenture.[15]

Other factors that made European immigration to the United States during the antebellum period unique were its size and the fact that governments or charities did not assist most migrants. As noted earlier, more than 5 million people left Europe for the United States between 1815 and 1860. Only a small number of individuals permanently left Europe and went somewhere other than the United States, and these were generally assisted. The reason that individuals freely chose to immigrate to the United States during the antebellum period was its rapid economic growth. Moving to the United States held out the promise of improving one's economic condition. Beginning in the 1820s, Brazil received a few Germans but most of those who went did so as part of a sponsored group and did not achieve much economic success.[16] A number of people also went to Australia, although until the 1830s almost all were convicts sent there by the British government. Even after 1830, most or all of the cost of transporting voluntary migrants to Australia had to be paid by the government or other organizations, a sign that any expected economic gain from moving was not very large. It was not until the Victorian

[14] Hoerder, *Cultures*, pp. 284–7, 309–12.
[15] Northrup, *Indentured Labor*.
[16] Walker, *Germany*, pp. 38–41, 96–9.

gold rush of 1851 held out the promise of riches that non-assisted migration to Australia became an important part of the total.[17] Canada was another overseas destination, although it is well known that many of these migrants traveled on to the United States because the possibilities for improving one's standard of living in Canada were limited.[18] Thus, almost every individual or family who wanted to leave Europe during the antebellum period, and who was not assisted by government or charity in their travel, went to the United States, the primary non-European country where immigrants could realistically expect to improve their economic status.[19]

After the Civil War, the steamship quickly became the dominant means of travel across the Atlantic and led to revolutionary changes in European overseas migration.[20] The length of the voyage to the United States fell to about two weeks. Once the steamship made transatlantic travel quicker and safer, potential migrants could easily go to additional overseas destinations. Moreover, the possibilities for economic improvement in other overseas destinations improved. Thus, during the last thirty years of the nineteenth century, large numbers of Europeans began to travel without assistance to Argentina and Brazil, substantially lessening the percentage of the total who went to the United States. Many more migrants who went overseas also returned to Europe because steamship travel made doing so much easier. In fact, some Italians worked in Argentina part of the year and in Italy the other part.[21] By this point in time, a significant portion of overseas migration was similar to seasonal or temporary migration in Europe. It became much easier for migrants to travel to an overseas destination for a season or a period of years and plan on returning to Europe to buy land or retire. Thus, migrating to work in the United States could be considered simply as an alternative choice for an individual who otherwise could have moved within Europe or worked in another country.

---

[17] Richards, "Migration," pp. 153–61. Another factor to note is that the cost of transportation to Australia and the South American countries was higher than to the United States.

[18] McInnis, "Population," pp. 380–2.

[19] Bade says that 80% of European emigrants prior to 1850 went to the United States, although this figure would be higher if only non-assisted migrants were considered. See Bade, *Migration*, p. 93.

[20] Cohn, "Transition."

[21] Baily, *Immigrants*.

Virtually all of the studies that consider migration to the United States and contribute to part of the current migration paradigm – that migration can never be considered permanent – center on the period of steamship travel. To give a very small sample, studies have been done comparing Italians who moved to New York City with those in Buenos Aires, the migration of Poles to different places are compared, and so forth. Nugent's book comparing the great transatlantic migrations begins in 1870.[22] Generally, perhaps because it differs in fundamental ways, study of the permanent immigration of the millions of Europeans to the antebellum United States has been somewhat ignored by the proponents of the current migration paradigm.

In many ways, the analysis in this book agrees with the current migration paradigm. Almost all of the European immigrants to the antebellum United States were seeking to improve their economic well-being. The migration was regional in that the migrants did not come equally from all parts of Europe or, indeed, all parts of the major source countries, nor did the immigrants settle in the same parts of the United States. Yet the European immigration to the antebellum United States was also different from most previous and many later types of migration. Few individuals planned to return to their European homes when they moved. In addition, at the time no other major movement of individuals out of Europe occurred. Both of these factors were intimately connected to the existing means of ocean travel, the sailing ship. Thus, in important ways, the immigration examined in this book represents a unique case of migration.

[22] Baily, *Immigrants*; Morawaska, "Labor Migrations"; Nugent, *Crossings*.

2

The Onset and European Origins
of Mass Immigration

Critical to any economic analysis of antebellum immigration is data on the total number and geographic source of the European immigrants. In fact, the total number of immigrants who arrived during the antebellum period has been subject to a good deal of controversy. For example, Robert Swierenga, after comparing Dutch records to the U.S. records, concluded, "How nearly one of every two Dutch arrivals were omitted in the official U.S. immigration statistics is a mystery that demands further study. Should such underreporting apply to other immigrant groups the figures on total immigration in the nineteenth century would require drastic revision."[1] Actually, this chapter will show that the U.S. records for total immigration in most years are reasonably complete, although those for many individual countries are seriously flawed. One premise of this book is that mass immigration from Europe began during the antebellum period. Thus, an issue related to the total number of immigrant arrivals is when the sustained rise in the volume of immigration began, which is something also determined here. Finally, although the major source countries are well known, the geographic origins of the immigrants within these countries are often not clear. The evidence on both how many immigrants came from the major European source countries and where they came from within these countries is also investigated.

[1] Swierenga, "Dutch International Migration Statistics," p. 462. Swierenga makes a similar comment in his more recent book, *Faith*, pp. 302–3. Many researchers studying Scandinavian immigration have arrived at a similar conclusion. For example, see Olssen, *Swedish Passenger Arrivals*; Hvidt, *Flight*; and Runblom and Norman, *From Sweden*. For the postbellum period, the U.S. records are believed to be more complete. See Ferenczi, *International Migrations*, p. 194.

TABLE 2.1. *Average Yearly Immigration to the United States, 1700–1860 (not including slaves)*

Years	Average Yearly Immigration
1700–10	2,143
1710–20	5,211
1720–30	6,105
1730–40	8,316
1740–50	198
1750–60	6,469
1760–70	4,673
1770–80	1,496
1783–89	8,249
1790–99	9,790
1800–09	8,408
1810–19	12,668
1820–26	8,532
1827–31	22,946
1832–35	57,465
1836–45	77,697
1846–54	314,496
1855–60	175,111

Sources: 1700–80: Galenson, *White Servitude*, Table H.3, pp. 216–17. Nearly the same data also appear in Carter et al., *Historical Statistics*, Series Ad17. 1783–1819: Calculated from Grabbe, *Vor der großen Flut*, Table 13, p. 93. 1820–60: Calculated from Carter et al., *Historical Statistics*, Series Ad1.

Determining the Beginning of Mass Migration

The existing estimates of non-slave immigration to the United States from 1700 to 1860 are shown in Table 2.1 and Figure 2.1. Because the information for the eighteenth century is sparse, the figures in Table 2.1 are given as the average *annual* volume in each decade.[2] Beginning in 1820, yearly estimates of immigration are available and these are shown

---

[2] Estimates for colonial immigration are also given in Gemery, "White Population," Table 5.8, p. 171. Gemery's figures are found as a remainder after estimating birthrates, death rates, and population growth. For one decade, estimated immigration is negative and huge positive figures result for the 1780–90 period. Gemery even comments on the questionable nature of some of his results. Wokeck, *Trade*, provides estimates of German and Irish colonial immigration but these cannot be used because they do not include British immigration, which accounted for more than one-half of the colonial total. Thus, the estimates provided by Galenson appear to be the most accurate available.

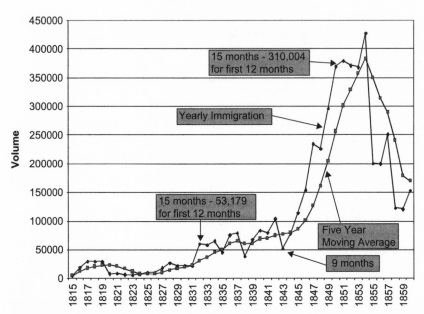

FIGURE 2.1. Immigration to the United States, 1815–1860. *Sources:* 1815–1819: Hansen, *Atlantic Migration*, pp. 79–103. 1820–1860: Carter et al., *Historical Statistics*, Series Ad1.

in Figure 2.1, along with estimates for the 1815–19 period.[3] In addition, to show the trend more easily, a five-year moving average is included.

The estimates in Table 2.1 and Figure 2.1 show much fluctuation and some disagreement, but also show a slight upward trend in immigrant volume before the 1830s. Immigration increased between 1710 and 1740, and was high again during the 1750s, presumably before the outbreak of the Seven Years' War in 1756. After the conclusion of the war in 1763, volume again increased. It fell during the American Revolution, but then rose again after that war's conclusion. Overall, between 1783 and 1826, immigration was generally about ten thousand immigrants per year,

---

[3] Annual estimates are also provided in McClelland and Zeckhauser, *Demographic Dimensions*, Table A-24, p. 113. They adjust the figures from the Passenger Lists in a variety of ways, and use a complex demographic model as part of their estimation procedure. See the discussion on pp. 32–38 of their book. Their estimates also appear in Carter, *Historical Statistics*, Series Ad17, p. 1–545. Although McClelland and Zeckhauser perform many of the same adjustments that I do in the remainder of this section, I am able to rely on somewhat better information than they had available. In any case, using their figures would not fundamentally change any of the findings of this section.

double the four to five thousand average before 1780.[4] Only during the last half of the 1810s, however, did the average annual volume exceed ten thousand.[5] The major reason for the higher volume of immigration in the last half of the 1810s was the 1815 eruption of Mount Tambora, a volcano on Sumbawa Island in the eastern end of the Indonesian archipelago. This event is estimated as the second greatest volcanic eruption in history. Its effect was to throw ash and dust in the atmosphere, with the result that the world's average temperature fell by 1 degree Celsius during 1816.[6] This year became known as "the year without a summer." Crops failed in both Europe and the United States, resulting in a substantial, although temporary increase in the numbers leaving Europe.[7] Hansen estimates that 115,000 immigrants arrived between 1815 and 1819.[8] By the first part of the 1820s, immigrant volume had fallen to more typical historical levels.

The sustained rise in immigrant volume to the United States began during the last years of the 1820s. Between 1827 and 1831, the volume rose to more than twenty thousand immigrants per year. Then in

---

[4] In Table 2.1, the average of the figures from 1700–80 is 4,326, and from 1783–1826, it is 9,685.

[5] Others have estimated average annual immigration during the 1780s at twenty thousand. See the discussion in Gemery, "White Population." These figures contrast with Grabbe's estimate shown in Table 2.1 of 8,249 per year for the 1783–9 period.

[6] Winchester, *Krakatoa*, p. 292. See the discussion of the connection between volcanic eruptions and temperature in Post, *Last Great Subsistence Crisis*, pp. 2–6.

[7] See Post, *Last Great Subsistence Crisis*, pp. 6–24, for a discussion of conditions throughout the United States, Canada, and Europe. The United States experienced frosts that harmed crops in June, July, and August as far south as southern Ohio and Richmond. The United States also suffered through a drought that summer. In Europe, the summer was also very cold and flooding rains occurred. Conditions were even worse in Canada. Besides the volcano, other factors also may have contributed to the dire conditions, such as a postwar depression in Europe and the demobilization of huge armies. See Skeen, "Year."

[8] Hansen, *Atlantic Migration*, pp. 79–103. Hansen's annual estimates are provided throughout these pages. Although old, the estimates may be fairly accurate. Grabbe, the current authority on the 1783–1820 period, estimates total immigration of 126,700 between 1810 and 1819. His yearly estimates of the number of immigrants from the United Kingdom, Germany, and Switzerland who arrived in the Delaware region indicate that about 91% did so between 1815 and 1819, inclusive. If the same percentage were applied to Grabbe's total immigration, then immigration between 1815 and 1819 would have been more than 115,000. See Grabbe, *Vor der großen Flut*, Table 13, p. 93. Both Hansen's and Grabbe's totals are higher than the figure of 91,254 for 1815–19 given in McClelland and Zeckhauser, *Demographic Dimensions*, Table A-24, p. 113. I have chosen to use Grabbe's figures for two reasons. The first is they were developed after the book by McClelland and Zeckhauser. The second is they are based on information derived directly from a number of ship lists.

1832, according to the official figures, immigrant volume jumped to more than fifty thousand immigrants, at least five times its historical yearly average.[9] In reality, this large increase was probably spread out over two years. For 1831, Erickson found the U.S. arrival records are missing for April, May, and August.[10] It is not likely these records were collected at the time and have since been lost. Instead, the official U.S. figures for 1831 seem to reflect the returns from only part of the year because the total number of Irish and British passengers leaving for the United States recorded by the UK returns is substantially higher.[11] If the UK total were added to the non-UK total recorded for 1831 by U.S. officials, the total for 1831 would rise to more than thirty thousand immigrants.[12] This figure is at least as high as those for any year during the late 1810s. Thus, the higher numbers arriving during the late 1820s rose to unprecedented levels, probably first in 1831 and then very obviously in 1832.

The increase in 1831 and 1832 was not temporary. In only two years after 1832 did the volume fall below fifty thousand immigrants and in those years only slightly. Figure 2.1 clearly shows the jump in the early 1830s. If annual estimates existed back to 1700, the break in the figure would be even more impressive. Annual volume would almost never reach twenty thousand immigrants between 1700 and 1826, and would fluctuate up and down, with only a slight upward trend. After 1832, the next year in which the annual volume was lower than forty-five thousand immigrants was *1932*, which was in the depths of the Great Depression and after the United States adopted policies that restricted immigration from Europe. Although others have recognized this increase in trend, its significance has often not been appreciated. One reason is that the official figures begin in 1820, therefore the long period with little upward trend

---

[9] The increased numbers traveling to the United States were a major factor in causing total European immigration to the Americas during the 1830s to slightly exceed that of Africans for the first time. Before the 1830s, migration flows to the New World had been dominated by the movement of Africans. See Eltis, "Free and Coerced Transatlantic Migrations," pp. 255–6.

[10] Erickson, "Uses," p. 322.

[11] See the discussion in Erickson, "Uses," pp. 323–4.

[12] The UK returns recorded 23,418 passengers for the United States. The official U.S. returns recorded 8,247. However, as discussed later in this chapter, in many years a large number of passengers did not have their country of origin specified. In 1831, 7,397 passengers were in this category. If these passengers were all from the United Kingdom, then the difference between the figures from the two countries becomes 7,774, a reasonable number for the three missing months. Adding the latter figure to the U.S. total for 1831 yields an estimate of 30,407. This figure would still be too small because it ignores arrivals during the missing three months from countries other than the United Kingdom.

is not directly apparent. A second reason is the outbreak of the potato famine in Europe during the last half of the 1840s. As a result, yearly immigrant volume rose into the hundreds of thousands. In hindsight, it is easy to misinterpret the potato famine as the event that first caused immigrant volume to increase, but it was not.

The break in trend had already occurred in the late 1820s and early 1830s. The data presented for the period beginning in 1820 originate in the U.S. Passenger Lists, ship manifests filed by the captain with U.S. port authorities upon arrival. These manifests provide virtually all of our detailed knowledge concerning antebellum immigration because few European data sources exist for this period. German authorities at the ports of Hamburg and Bremen collected data on outgoing passengers beginning in 1832. Although summary information exists for both ports, the original records survive only for Hamburg and these are not complete.[13] More than half of the German emigrants at this time, however, did not leave from either of these ports, therefore the German port records are of limited use as an indicator of overall U.S. immigration from Germany.[14] For the rest of mainland Europe, good records exist for Dutch and Scandinavian emigrants, but these countries provided only a small portion of total U.S. immigrants. Turning to the British Isles, the official British records did not distinguish between British and Irish passengers until 1853. Although these records contain data on the port of embarkation, such information is of little use because many of the Irish left from the British port of Liverpool. In addition, ships carrying fewer than twenty passengers or leaving from some smaller ports were not included. Baines suggests that the British records missed more than half of the British emigrants before the early 1850s.[15] For Ireland, the Emigration Commissioners published data on emigrants to the United States, but Ó Gráda explains these were largely based on informed guesswork.[16] Thus, for the antebellum period, most researchers have little choice but to rely on the data originating in the U.S. Passenger Lists.

The U.S. Passenger Lists were the result of a law passed on March 2, 1819, which mandated the collection of passenger ship manifests

[13] Ferenczi, *International Migrations*, pp. 693–6. Wegge, "Hesse-Cassel Emigrants," p. 361. Wegge's work uses data on German emigrants collected by the government of Hesse-Cassel. Although some other German regional governments also collected emigration records, most did not.

[14] Ferenczi, *International Migrations*, Table IV, p. 696. The European ports of embarkation are discussed in more detail in Chapter 6.

[15] Baines, *Migration*, pp. 47–8. Also, see the discussion in Carrier and Jeffery, *External Migration*, pp. 17–19.

[16] Ó Gráda, "Note," p. 143.

beginning October 1 of that year. Apparently, the large immigration of the preceding few years convinced Congress that better information was needed. Each manifest recorded the following information: the ship name, ship captain, port of embarkation, date of arrival, and a list of passengers. For each passenger, the manifest recorded his or her name, age, gender, occupation, "country to which they severally belong," "country of which they intend to become inhabitants," and a column was available to indicate if the individual died on the voyage.[17] From this information, immigration was determined by deleting from the total those passengers who were U.S. citizens, those who died on the voyage, and the Europeans who did not intend to stay in the United States. Quarterly summaries of the information from the lists were transmitted to the State Department, which periodically submitted the information to Congress. It is the data compiled from these lists that are given in *Historical Statistics*, and that are the basis for the numbers shown in Figure 2.1.[18]

One issue of interpretation concerning Figure 2.1 needs to be addressed. Before 1832 the totals are for the fiscal year, running from the previous October 1 through September 30. Thus, the 8,385 passengers listed as arriving in 1820 arrived between October 1, 1819, and September 30, 1820. The total for 1832 is for fifteen months because the fiscal year was changed to correspond with the calendar year. This change is not the cause of the sharp increase in immigration during 1832, because the summary information provides a figure of more than fifty-three thousand immigrants for the period October 1, 1831, through September 30, 1832. The figure for 1843 is for nine months because the fiscal year was moved back to the preceding period. Then in 1850, the adjustment converted back to the calendar year, therefore the total for this year is also for fifteen months.

A key issue is whether the antebellum figures for *annual* immigration can be believed. In reality, the Passenger Lists have five known deficiencies that cause the information derived from them to be less than accurate.[19]

---

[17] Who filled out the lists is not clear. Clerks in the embarkation ports apparently filled them out in some cases. In other cases, the ship captains did. See the discussion in Olssen, *Swedish Passenger Arrivals*, pp. xii–xiii. Interested readers can search for specific individuals in these records at www.castlegarden.org.

[18] See Carter et al., *Historical Statistics*, Table Ad1–2, pp. 541–2. Virtually all of the data cited in this book that are in this most recent edition of *Historical Statistics* are also in the older edition. See U.S. Bureau of the Census, *Historical Statistics*. A contemporary discussion and presentation of the data are given in Bromwell, *Immigration*.

[19] Much of this discussion follows Hutchinson, "Notes." See Swierenga, *Faith*, pp. 293–309, for a critique of the Passenger Lists in relation to the Dutch records. Also, see the discussions in Erickson, "Uses," and Gould, "European Inter-Continental Emigration."

First, although the summary statistics do not include U.S. citizens, they do include foreigners who did not intend to stay in the United States, contrary to the intentions of the law. Thus, the totals are estimates of foreign *passengers*, that is, they include foreign tourists, merchants and others on business, and those in transit. It is thought that no more than 2 percent of all foreign passengers fell into these categories, although the percentage is certainly greater if only the British are considered.[20] In some years, passengers traveling in cabins may have been excluded, and most of these would have been non-immigrants, but it is not clear whether and when this was done. Second, again contrary to the intentions of the law, the totals generally do not exclude deaths on the voyage. As detailed in Chapter 6, these numbers were small in most years. Third, the totals do not exclude return migrants although, as discussed in Chapter 1, the numbers in this category were also quite small during the antebellum years.

Fourth, the totals include only a few immigrants to the United States who first landed in Canada. Only those who traveled from Canada on a ship, and thus arrived at a U.S. port, are included.[21] Most migrants who landed at a Canadian port (which was primarily Quebec) traveled overland to the United States and do not appear in the U.S. records. Although the total number of such individuals can never be known with complete accuracy, a lower bound estimate exists. Marvin McInnis, in estimating immigration to Canada, subtracts out those individuals who upon arrival said they were planning to travel directly on to the United States.[22] A. C. Buchanan, the British agent at Quebec, developed these figures by questioning newcomers at arrival concerning their intentions. Although crude, Buchanan's reports provide a figure of about two hundred thousand individuals between 1830 and 1860.[23]

The fifth known deficiency of the Passenger Lists concerns questions of completeness. The major port of arrival for immigrants was New York

[20] Hutchinson, "Notes," p. 971. His sources for this estimate were U.S. Treasury, *Special Report*, Table 2, and the 1891 version of U.S. Treasury, *Arrivals*.

[21] Besides those landing at a U.S. coastal port on a ship from Canada, during some years arrivals from Canada at a few inland ports were also included in the totals. Other individuals entered the United States via land from Mexico, although less is known concerning this flow.

[22] McInnis, "Population," pp. 380–2.

[23] McInnis, "Population," pp. 380–2. The exact figure calculated from McInnis's Table 9.2 is 200,409. This figure includes some number of individuals, fewer than nine thousand, who died from cholera in 1832 and 1834, although it does not include an estimated sixteen thousand individuals who died on ship or after arrival during 1847. The total also does not include an uncertain number of individuals who arrived at the Canadian Maritime provinces and traveled on to the United States by land.

City, which accounted for almost three-quarters of total arrivals between 1820 and 1860, although just more than 50 percent during the 1820s.[24] Although returns from New York were included in each year's total, it is not clear whether the port authorities collected lists from every ship, especially during the early years. One author, writing near the end of the antebellum period, suggestĕd that thirty thousand individuals arrived at New York alone in 1830, although that total may include U.S. citizens.[25] Another aspect of the possible incompleteness of the Passenger Lists is that the totals for some years do not include returns from every port. In particular, the estimates for 1828–30 are based on substantially fewer ports than the other years. This problem is minor for the most part. For example, the 10 ports that provided returns in 1827 but not in 1828 accounted for a total of 145 passengers in 1827, and many of these passengers might not have been immigrants. In *every* year, returns are included from all of the major ports. The single period where the lack of port data would be important is the last quarter of 1832, which includes arrivals only at New York and Boston/Charlestown (Mass.).[26]

Correcting for the first four known deficiencies would have no major effect on the *trend* in immigrant volume. In contrast, accounting for the issue of completeness might have a small effect, because this factor points to the estimates for the 1820s as being somewhat too small. In fact, an alternative estimate for the 1820s that adjusts for immigration through Canada and many of the other issues discussed finds a total of 205,000 immigrants.[27] Thus, the actual increase in immigrant volume may have been less sharp than is shown in Figure 2.1. Perhaps the most accurate conclusion is to say that, during the years from 1827 through 1832, the existing pattern of fluctuations with a slight upward trend was broken. The increase during this period is clear in the data in Table 2.1. Overall, even if more complete returns for the 1820s existed, they would still show that immigrant volume underwent a substantial increase during a fairly

---

[24] Discussion of the changing arrival percentages at U.S. ports is provided in Chapter 7.

[25] Tucker, *Progress*, as quoted in Hutchinson, "Notes," pp. 977–8.

[26] In addition, recall the previous discussion that the lists are missing for April, May, and August in 1831. On this point, see Erickson, "Uses," p. 322.

[27] McClelland and Zeckhauser, *Demographic Dimensions*, Table A-24, p. 113. They attempt to correct for many of the problems with the Passenger Lists. After doing so, their figures still show a jump occurred in the total volume of immigration during the late 1820s and early 1830s. Hutchinson, "Notes," p. 978, cites a contemporary estimate of two hundred thousand for 1820–30.

short period of years, and that the increase occurred well in advance of the potato famine.

The European Countries of Origin

The establishment of the timing of the increase in immigrant volume brings forth a number of questions concerning the European countries of origin of the immigrants. Which European countries did the immigrants traditionally come from? When the volume increased, was it due to a relatively equal increase from the traditional emigrant countries, or was the increase primarily due to increased volumes from specific countries? Finally, within the major countries of origin, how did the volume of immigration vary across the regions of these countries? The remainder of this chapter addresses these questions.

The most important country of origin for colonial immigration was England, with sizeable minorities arriving from Germany and the other parts of the British Isles. The exact percentages from each country have generated some controversy. Probably the best evidence comes from the first U.S. Census taken in 1790. Although these figures are not without controversy, this census showed that 59 percent of the white population was English, 17 percent were Irish or Scotch-Irish, 12 percent were German, and 9 percent were Welsh or Scottish.[28] Thus, individuals from England dominated while 85 percent of the white population in 1790 had their origins somewhere in the British Isles.[29] These population figures are only estimates of the relative importance of the countries in immigration, because immigrants from the different countries might have had different birthrates in the United States, and thus the (known) population figures would differ from the (unknown) immigration figures.[30]

---

[28] Calculated from Menard, "Migration," Table 2.2, p. 65. Menard also provides a discussion of the issues involved in determining the European backgrounds of the U.S. population based on the census.

[29] An estimate given in a popular textbook is that 75% of the white population were from the British Isles. See Hughes and Cain, *American Economic History*, p. 45. Of the entire U.S. population in 1790, African Americans accounted for 19.3%.

[30] A general idea of the importance of immigration from various countries in the eighteenth century comes from Wokeck, *Trade*, Tables 2 and 4, pp. 45–6, 172–3. She estimates that 111,000 Germans arrived between 1700 and 1775 and 51,000 Irish arrived between 1730 and 1775. The estimates from Galenson shown in Table 2.1 yield a total immigration of 346,000 between 1700 and 1780. Thus, the German total is 32% and the Irish total 15%, although note that Wokeck's estimates are for a shorter period than Galenson's.

TABLE 2.2. *U.S. Immigration, by Country and Time Period (in thousands)*

Country	1820–60	1820–26	1827–31	1832–35	1836–45	1846–54	1855–60
England	303	8	8	6	10	137	134
Scotland	48	2	2	2	1	23	19
Wales	8	–	–	–	–	3	4
Ireland	1,957	22	38	66	322	1,239	269
Other UK	436	4	6	22	113	212	79
TOTAL BRITISH ISLES	2,751	36	55	96	446	1,614	505
Germany	1,546	3	7	43	212	905	376
Netherlands	22	–	1	–	3	11	7
Belgium	10	–	–	–	1	4	4
France	208	3	8	16	51	105	25
Switzerland	38	1	2	3	5	15	11
Denmark	6	–	–	–	1	1	3
Norway/Sweden	36	–	–	–	6	23	8
Spain	16	2	1	1	2	5	6
Italy	14	–	–	2	1	4	7
Other Europe	6	–	–	1	1	1	2
TOTAL CONTINENT	1,901	10	20	67	283	1,073	449
Not Specified	186	10	30	55	10	54	26
TOTAL EUROPE	4,838	56	104	218	739	2,742	979
China	41	–	–	–	–	13	28
Canada	117	1	1	4	21	57	33
Mexico	18	–	5	4	4	2	2
West Indies	40	2	4	4	12	13	6
Other Non-Europe	8	–	1	1	1	4	2
TOTAL	5,062	60	115	230	777	2,830	1,051
Yearly Average	123	9	23	58	78	314	175

Notes: "Other Europe" includes the European countries not specifically listed in the table, including Russia. "Other Non-Europe" includes India, Other Asia, South America, Central America, Atlantic Islands, and Africa. "Not Specified" is listed in the source as "All other countries and countries not stated." Dashed lines indicate fewer than 500 immigrants. Row and column totals may not add up due to rounding.

Source: Calculated from Ferenczi, *International Migrations*, pp. 377–83.

Given that birthrates were large across the board during the Colonial period, however, it is likely that the immigration shares would be fairly close to the population shares.

    The accepted data concerning the country of origin of the immigrants to the United States between 1820 and 1860, taken from the Passenger Lists, are shown in Table 2.2. The most apparent fact is that Ireland and Germany were the two dominant source countries. Thus, Great Britain was a less important source of immigration during the antebellum period than the Colonial period. In fact, if the numbers are accepted at face value, then Ireland and Germany accounted for 69 percent of the U.S. total between 1820 and 1860. However, two data issues raise important questions concerning the accuracy of much of the information provided in Table 2.2.

The first data issue concerns the 186,000 passengers listed in Table 2.2 with country "Not Specified." Although *Historical Statistics* lists this entry separately from those for Europe, and labels it as "Other or unknown," most of these passengers were not actually from other countries; instead, most appear in this category because the "country to which they severally belong" column was left blank on the original Passenger List.[31] It is a virtual certainty that, during the antebellum period, these individuals were from Europe. For example, almost fourteen thousand individuals in 1830, more than twenty-three thousand individuals in 1832, and more than twenty-six thousand immigrants in 1833 did not have a country listed. These individuals must have been from Europe, and probably mostly from Ireland, Germany, and Britain, because the United States was not receiving a sizeable flow of immigrants from anywhere else. Thus, the "Not Specified" category is listed as part of the European total in Table 2.2 rather than separate from Europe as is done in *Historical Statistics*. Adjusting the Passenger Lists to account for some of the five known deficiencies discussed previously then yields an estimate of approximately 5.2 million for total immigration (actually, total passengers) from Europe to the United States between 1815 and 1860: the 4.84 million listed in Table 2.2 (which includes the "Not Specified"), the 200,000 who came through Canada after 1830, the 115,000 who arrived between 1815 and 1819, and an unknown number of immigrants who came through Canada before 1830.[32] When immigration from all countries is considered, the total rises to about 5.4 million immigrants.[33]

---

[31] Carter et al., *Historical Statistics*, Table Ad90–97, pp. 555–7. Note the individuals listed in column Ad97 as "Other or unknown" are explicitly not counted as being from Europe. See also Table Ad106–120.

[32] This total does not adjust for passengers not staying in the United States, deaths on the voyage, and return migration, factors that make the total too large as an estimate of immigration. However, the total also does not account for arrivals at West Coast ports, the undercount in the 1820s, and the partially missing figures for part of 1831.

[33] This total is similar to that given in McClelland and Zeckhauser, *Demographic Dimensions*, Table A-24, p. 113. They adjust for many of the same issues discussed here and derive an estimate of 5.425 million for the entire 1800–60 period, and 5.318 million for the 1815–60 period. Note that their "total" immigration number of 7.4 million for 1800–60 in Table A-14 on p. 101 includes the U.S.-born children of immigrants who arrived between 1800 and 1860, and is not an estimate of total immigration.

TABLE 2.3. *Immigration from the United Kingdom, 1825–1846*

Year	England	Scotland	Wales	Other UK	Total Britain	Ireland	Percent Irish
1825	1,002	113	11	969	2,095	4,888	70.0
1826	1,459	230	6	624	2,319	5,408	70.0
1827	2,521	460	–	1,205	4,186	9,766	70.0
1828	2,735	1,041	17	1,559	5,352	12,488	70.0
1829	2,149	111	3	916	3,179	7,415	70.0
1830	733	29	7	384	1,153	2,721	70.2
1831	251	226	131	1,867	2,475	5,772	70.0
1832	944	158	–	4,229	5,331	12,436	70.0
1833	2,966	1,921	29	–	4,916	8,648	63.8
1834	1,129	110	1	9,250	10,490	24,474	70.0
1835	468	63	16	8,423	8,970	20,927	70.0
1836	420	106	2	12,578	13,106	30,578	70.0
1837	896	14	6	11,302	12,218	28,508	70.0
1838	157	48	–	5,215	5,420	12,645	70.0
1839	62	–	–	10,209	10,271	23,963	70.0
1840	318	21	–	2,274	2,613	39,430	93.8
1841	147	35	55	15,951	16,188	37,772	70.0
1842	1,743	24	38	20,200	22,005	51,342	70.0
1843	3,517	41	–	4,872	8,430	19,670	70.0
1844	1,357	23	3	12,970	14,353	33,490	70.0
1845	1,710	368	11	17,121	19,210	44,821	70.0
1846	2,854	305	147[a]	18,874	22,180	51,752	70.0

[a] Ferenczi lists 187 passengers here, but Bromwell, *History*, p. 132, lists 147.

Sources: Cols. 1–6: Ferenczi, *International Migrations*, pp. 377–83. Column 5 is also the sum of columns 1 through 4. Columns 5 and 6 also appear in Carter et al., *Historical Statistics*, Series Ad107 and Ad108. Col. 7: Calculated as column 6 divided by the sum of columns 5 and 6.

The second data issue concerns those listed in Table 2.2 as arriving from "Other UK." In *Historical Statistics*, these individuals are combined with those from England, Scotland, and Wales to provide a figure for "Great Britain." The process used to develop these estimates is shown for the years 1825 through 1846 in columns 1 through 5 of Table 2.3. In addition, the entry for Ireland in *Historical Statistics* says that it "(c)omprises the entire island of Ireland, 1820–1924."[34] It appears that migrants from the island of Britain and those from the island of

34 See Carter et al., *Historical Statistics*, Documentation for Series Ad108, p. 1–564. Also, see U.S. Bureau of the Census, *Historical Statistics*, pp. 105–6. For "Great Britain," see series C91, which is the total of England, Scotland, Wales, and Other UK given in Ferenczi, *International Migrations*, pp. 377–83. For "Ireland," see series C92 and the footnote pertaining to that column, which says the figures "comprise Eire and northern Ireland."

Ireland have been separated. This conclusion is, however, incorrect. The last column of Table 2.3 shows the percentage of Irish immigrants in total British Isles immigration during the 1825–46 period. In *every* year but three, the percent Irish equals exactly 70 percent![35] In 1830, the percentage would equal exactly 70 percent if the Irish total were 2,712 instead of 2,721, and the extra 9 individuals added to the British. In 1840, the Irish percentage would equal exactly 70 percent if the Irish total was 29,430 instead of 39,430, and the extra 10,000 added to the British. The third year, 1833, is conspicuous in being the only year in which no entry appears for "Other UK." Obviously, according to the current annual estimates, the Irish comprised exactly 70 percent of total immigration from the British Isles for twenty-one consecutive years!

In fact, the original compilations by the State Department as shown in Bromwell did not include a classification called "Other UK." Instead, Bromwell had a category labeled "Great Britain and Ireland" that included all those whose country of origin in the British Isles was not clear.[36] The numbers in this category are larger than those shown in Table 2.3 as "Other UK." The impetus for the change from the original numbers to the current numbers was apparently the move of the collection of the immigrant statistics from the State Department to the Treasury Department's Bureau of Statistics. This change occurred about 1870.[37] The new numbers for Ireland and Great Britain appear for the first time in the Bureau of Statistics 1872 publication, *Special Report on Immigration*. The same basic footnote appears to two tables, one reporting the number of immigrants from each country during each year and the other by each decade. The first footnote says, "The natives of Ireland are partly estimated on the basis of data obtained by the commissioners of emigration of New York, who have made careful inquiries on this subject. The total from the British Isles, given above, is from official returns to the Bureau of Statistics."[38] The "careful inquiries" apparently consisted of assuming the Irish constituted exactly 70 percent of all immigrants from the British Isles for twenty-one consecutive years! The Treasury

35 Erickson, "Uses," pp. 323–4, discusses this 70/30 breakdown for her two sample years of 1831 and 1841 and uses it to question the validity of the U.S. estimates. To the best of my knowledge, however, she did not examine the breakdown in other years.

36 Bromwell, *History*, Table IV for each year.

37 Hutchinson, "Notes," pp. 964–5, says the State Department series was supposed to continue until 1874 but apparently did so only to 1870. The Bureau of Statistics began publishing reports in November 1866 and continued to do so until replaced by the Bureau of Immigration in the 1890s.

38 U.S. Treasury, *Special Report*, p. xi.

Department then simply classified a sufficient number of the individuals in the "Great Britain and Ireland" category as Irish to make the Irish percentage exactly 70 percent of the total from the British Isles.[39] The remainder was then placed in a new "Other UK" category, eventually to be combined with those from England, Scotland, and Wales to form the "Great Britain" figure currently in use.

The numbers in the 1872 Treasury Department report were then repeated in subsequent official publications, and eventually in *Historical Statistics*.[40] Thus, the division of the Irish from the British immigrants as shown in *Historical Statistics* is not accurate, at least until 1847.[41] Beginning in that year, the Irish percentage varies each year but remains above 70 percent until 1854, when it declines to under 65 percent through 1860. Presumably, better data became available beginning in 1847.[42] At some time in the future, perhaps when all the Passenger Lists are computerized, one of the first orders of business should be to reexamine the lists for "Ireland and Britain" with the goal of trying to better distinguish between the Irish and British immigrants. In summary, the annual data shown in *Historical Statistics* for the number of immigrants from Great Britain and Ireland before 1847 are not accurate and should not be used by researchers.

Besides the British Isles, it is also likely that the numbers for many other countries are also inaccurate. This conclusion is based on an examination of the 1860 U.S. Census of Population, which surveyed the U.S. population concerning nativity.[43] Table 2.4 presents the census data on the

---

[39] For 1833, the entire amount in the "Great Britain and Ireland" category was added to the Irish total, but a sufficient number did not exist to raise the Irish percentage to 70%.

[40] Carter et al., *Historical Statistics*, p. 1–542, cites the 1903 U.S. Treasury publication *Monthly Summary* as its source. The old edition of *Historical Statistics* cited the 1926 Bureau of Immigration, *Annual Report*, as its source. See U.S. Bureau of the Census, *Historical Statistics*, source note for Series C89–119, p. 98. These reports, however, simply repeated the same numbers as in the 1872 report. For earlier publications repeating the 1872 numbers, see U.S. Bureau of Immigration, *Annual Report*, Table 74, pp. 170–75; U.S. Treasury, *Monthly Summary*, p. 4338; U.S. Treasury, *Arrivals*.

[41] The figures for 1820–4 are also suspect. In 1820, the percent Irish is exactly 60%. It is exactly 65% in both 1822 and 1824, although the percentage is different in both 1821 and 1823.

[42] Starting in 1852, the "Great Britain and Ireland" totals become much smaller, and the entire amount began to comprise the "Other UK" category. The reason for the better data is probably the establishment of the Commissioners of Emigration of the State of New York in 1847. This agency is discussed in Chapters 6 and 7. See their *Annual Reports*.

[43] U.S. Bureau of the Census, Eighth (1860), *Population*, pp. 620–3. The 1850 census also contains data on nativity. See U.S. Bureau of the Census, Seventh (1850), *Seventh Census*, Table XV, p. xxxvi.

TABLE 2.4. *U.S. Immigration and the Foreign-Born 1860 Population*

Country	1860 Census Population (thous.)	Immigration from Passenger Lists, 1820–60 (thous.)	Ratio (col. 2/col. 1)
England	432	303	0.70
Scotland	109	48	0.44
Wales	46	8	0.17
Great Britain[a]	586	795	1.35
Ireland	1,611	1,957	1.21
Germany[b]	1,276	1,546	1.21
France	110	208	1.89
Switzerland	53	38	0.72
Netherlands	28	22	0.79
Belgium	9	10	1.11
Denmark	10	6	0.60
Italy	11	14	1.27
Norway & Sweden	63	36	0.57
Spain	4	16	4.00
TOTAL EUROPE[c]	3,805	4,838	1.27

[a] For the "Population" column, the sum of the figures for England, Scotland, and Wales is used. For the "Immigration" column, the sum of the figures for England, Scotland, Wales, and "Other UK" is used.

[b] Does not include Austria.

[c] Includes the "Country, Not Specified" individuals listed in Table 2.2 in the immigration totals and the other European countries not listed separately in the table. Does not include estimates of immigrants arriving through Canada.

Sources: Col. 1: U.S. Bureau of the Census, Eighth (1860), *Population*, pp. 620–3. Col. 2: Table 2.2.

number of people who said they were born in each European country alongside the number of passengers from each country after 1820 as recorded in the Passenger Lists. In column 3, the ratio of passengers to foreign born in the U.S. population is presented. It is not clear what value to expect for this ratio. Presumably, the ratio should exceed unity for three reasons: some passengers were merchants or tourists who planned to return to Europe, some passengers were traveling through the United States to other countries, and some passengers died before the census was taken.[44] For example, the very high ratios for Spain and

---

[44] Two factors could raise the population figure above the U.S. immigration figure. A number of Irish and Germans arrived between 1815 and 1820, and a number also came through Canada. Only a portion of the first group would still have been alive in 1860, reducing the practical importance of this factor.

perhaps France may be due to some combination of the first two reasons. For Germany, Ireland, and Great Britain, however, the deaths of earlier immigrants are probably the main reason for the ratio being larger than unity.

According to the information in Table 2.4, the Passenger Lists undercounted arrivals from England, Scotland, Wales, Norway and Sweden, Denmark, the Netherlands, and Switzerland. If, however, all those in the "Other UK" category are included with the British countries, as *Historical Statistics* does, then the British ratio in 1860 (row 4) is similar to that for Ireland and Germany. Although it appears that the existing country information available from the Passenger Lists is broadly inaccurate in many cases, such a conclusion may not be warranted for the total if those in the "Not Specified" category are included. The ratio in the bottom row of Table 2.4 appears reasonable and provides some confidence in the accuracy of the 4.84 million individuals derived from the Passenger Lists for direct immigration from Europe between 1820 and 1860. It may be that a more accurate job of determining country of origin, including attempts to discover the origins of the 186,000 in the country "Not Specified" category, might yield more accurate estimates of immigration by country.

In fact, the data in Table 2.4 suggest the possibility that all or most of the "missing" immigrants from Norway and Sweden, Denmark, the Netherlands, and Switzerland might be among the 186,000 individuals recorded in the Passenger Lists without a country of origin. If the overall ratio of 1.27 is applied to the 1860 U.S. Census population from these countries, then the Passenger Lists should have recorded 196,000 immigrants from these countries instead of the 102,000 actually recorded. The extra 94,000 are slightly more than half of the 186,000 who are currently in the "Country Not Specified" category. This factor may solve Swierenga's "mystery" cited in the first paragraph of this chapter.

Overall, although the total numbers derived from the Passenger Lists appear to be fairly accurate, the figures for many individual countries are deeply flawed. Thus, the U.S. Census data shown in column 1 of Table 2.4 likely provide a more accurate idea of the antebellum origins of the European immigrants than the data in Table 2.2 do.[45] The census data indicate the Irish comprised 42 percent and the Germans 34 percent

---

[45] The census data shown in Table 2.4 provide an exact measure of the country origins of the immigrant stream only if the census was completely accurate and death rates did not differ among the immigrant streams from the various countries.

of total European immigration. The English comprised 11 percent and Great Britain as a whole comprised 15 percent of the total. The only other sizeable group was the French, who comprised 3 percent. The importance of French immigration may surprise many readers. One reason is that *Historical Statistics* includes French immigration as part of a more general category, "Other Northwestern Europe." In addition, relatively few studies have been done on French immigration, presumably because the large French population caused the percentage of the entire population that immigrated to be small.[46] Instead, some of the best studies of European immigration examine the Netherlands and the Scandinavian countries, where the rates of immigration were larger.[47] However, according to Table 2.4, only about 2.5 percent of total antebellum immigration originated in the Netherlands and Scandinavia combined. Overall, the basic conclusion obtained when data from the Passenger Lists were examined does not change. Antebellum immigration from Europe was dominated by Ireland and Germany, with a sizeable contingent coming from Great Britain. As a final point, although the country of origin data from the Passenger Lists cannot be trusted, immigration from these three countries was also the likely source of the increase in immigration that occurred during the late 1820s and early 1830s.[48]

In summary, if European immigration during the antebellum period is viewed from the perspective of the United States, Ireland and Germany were the most important source countries. British immigration was of some importance and all other countries of much less importance. The three primary source countries combined accounted for about 92 percent of immigration from Europe during the antebellum period. An examination of the features of the immigrant stream, which is done in Chapters 3 and 5, is therefore mostly dependent on the characteristics of the immigrants from Ireland, Germany, and Great Britain, and not on those in the fine studies of Dutch and Scandinavian immigration. Of course, it should be realized that Germany was not yet a country but a general area at that time. In addition, immigration was not equal from all parts of Germany, Ireland, and Britain, an idea that is now discussed in more detail.

[46] Zolberg, "International Migration Policies," pp. 261–4, provides some discussion of French immigration. He points out that perhaps twenty thousand left France each year during the first half of the nineteenth century. Of course, many of these individuals would have gone somewhere other than the United States.

[47] See Hvidt, *Flight*; Swierenga, *Faith*; and Runblom and Norman, *From Sweden*.

[48] A definitive statement cannot be made because large numbers of individuals are in the country "Not Specified" category during the critical period of the early 1830s.

Immigration from Germany

At the time, no country with the name "Germany" existed, but the term
was used to apply to the area that became Germany after the Franco-
Prussian War in 1870. The boundaries of that area differed somewhat from the current boundaries of Germany, particularly in the east.
Although some boundary changes occurred between the end of the
Napoleonic Wars in 1815 and the year 1870, the changes were not major.
The largest state was Prussia, which controlled the eastern areas of Germany, parts of central Germany, and (to complicate matters) a large part
of western Germany. Most importantly, the latter area contained Westphalia in the northwest and the Rhineland Palatinate in the southwest,
which were both regions of sizeable emigration. For the purpose of our
analysis of the regional origins of the German immigrants, the country is divided into four areas: 1) North and East Germany, comprised
of eastern and central Prussia, Saxony, Hanover, Mecklenburg, and Hol-
stein; 2) Central Germany, comprised of the Hessen states and Thuringia;
3) Northwest Germany, comprised of Westphalia and Hanover; and 4)
South and Southwest Germany, comprised of the Rhineland Palatinate,
Baden, Württemberg, and Bavaria.

The book by Mack Walker probably contains the most complete narrative discussion of German immigrant origins.[49] During the latter part
of the 1810s, immigrants left primarily from southwest Germany, especially Baden, the Palatinate, and Württemberg. These were also the areas
from which most of the eighteenth-century German colonial immigrants
came.[50] In addition, the flow also included people from Switzerland and
Alsace (in France).[51] During the period between 1830 and about 1844,
immigration continued from the same areas of Germany but also became
larger in the northwest and central areas, such as Hesse, Westphalia,
and Hanover. Before about 1845, few immigrants came from the north
and east areas of Germany.[52] In the period after 1845, when the outflow became very large, immigration became common from all areas of

[49] Walker, *Germany*. Also, see the discussion in Hansen, *Atlantic Migration*.
[50] See Doerries, "German Transatlantic Migration," pp. 116–17, and Köllmann and
Marschalck, "German Emigration," p. 513. Wokeck, *Trade*, Table 2, pp. 45–6, estimates that about 111,000 Germans immigrated between 1700 and 1775.
[51] Walker, *Germany*, pp. 1, 7, 33.
[52] Walker, *Germany*, pp. 46–7, 55–6. Also, see Marschalk, *Deutsche Überseewanderung*,
Table 5, p. 38, which provides partial figures on the changes over time in the origins of
the German emigrants.

TABLE 2.5. *Antebellum Immigration from the German Regions*

Region	Based on 1870 Census	Based on Adjusted 1860 Census
South and Southwest	46%	54%
Central	12%	16%
Northwest	20%	15%
North and East	22%	16%
Total Listed (Not Specified)	1,690,410 (243,692)	1,276,075 (511,376)

Note: All percentages are of the total excluding those "Not Specified."
Source: Table A2.1, columns 2 and 3.

Germany. In particular, Saxony, eastern Prussia, and Mecklenburg experienced a sizeable outflow for the first time.[53] Thus, over the antebellum period, the sources of immigration broadened from southwest Germany in the late 1810s to include all areas of Germany after 1845.

The Passenger Lists are of little help in determining the percentages of the German immigrants from each area. Although some of the lists specify the German state or city in the column "Country to which they severally belong," most of the time "Germany" is simply listed. Fortunately, an effort at determining the origins of the German immigrants can be made based on U.S. Census data. In both 1860 and 1870, the census records the nativities of the foreign-born U.S. population. Because no country called "Germany" existed when either census was taken, many of the foreign born listed the particular German state of their birth. The complications with using these data arise from two factors. First, those born in Prussia have to be allocated to the very different sections of Germany and, second, a number of individuals are simply recorded as having been born in "Germany." The appendix to this chapter describes the procedures used to deal with these issues. The resulting regional estimates, one based on the 1870 census data and one on adjusting the 1860 census data with data from the 1870 census, are shown in Table 2.5. It should be emphasized that the percentages refer to the German immigrants who were alive at the time of each census.

Although the method of calculation cannot provide exact percentages, the procedure yields results in line with the discussion of Walker. Taken at face value, the percentages in Table 2.5 indicate that about half of the antebellum German immigrants alive at the time of each census came

[53] Walker, *Germany*, pp. 74, 143, 165–6.

from the areas of the South and Southwest, confirming the narrative history of the importance of these areas.[54] With a total German immigration between 1820 and 1860 of about 1.6 million (Table 2.2), approximately 800,000 came from South and Southwest Germany. This area accounted for about one-seventh of *all* immigrants to the antebellum United States. Because the origins of the German immigrants became more dispersed over the antebellum period, a large majority of the immigrants from Germany before 1840 must have come from South and Southwest Germany. Thus, developments in this area are of great importance when the factors that caused the increase in immigrant volume in the early 1830s are examined in Chapter 3. Each of the other three regions of Germany contributed between 15 percent and 20 percent of the German total by 1860 or 1870, with the total from the Central region perhaps being somewhat smaller. These percentages emphasize that by the end of the antebellum period, substantial immigration was occurring from all regions of Germany.

Immigration from France (and Switzerland)

Before turning to the British Isles, immigration from France and Switzerland will be considered briefly. The importance of south and southwest Germany as a source of immigrants may explain why a sizeable number of immigrants came from these other two countries. Switzerland is located just south of southwest Germany. Thus, many of the conditions that caused large-scale immigration from southwest Germany may have also led to immigration from Switzerland.[55] Similarly, much of the immigration from France may have been from provinces contiguous to the German border, such as Alsace.[56] One factor consistent with this idea is that the main embarkation port in France was Le Havre, which

---

[54] Partial information on the origins of German emigrants is available in Köllmann and Marschalck, "German Emigration," Table III, p. 520. Their data imply that 39% of the German emigrants between 1830 and 1859 came from part of what I have defined as the south and southwest. The difference may be because of somewhat different areas, their lack of data for the 1820s (when the south and southwest were the major origins of immigrants), and the difference between emigration from Germany and German immigration to the United States. Also, see Marschalk, *Deutsche Überseewanderung*, Table 5, p. 38.

[55] On Swiss emigration, see Schelbert, "On Becoming an Emigrant."

[56] Although not reported by U.S. port authorities before 1860, some immigrants left from Austria. The 1860 U.S. Census lists twenty-five thousand individuals as having been born in Austria. See U.S. Bureau of the Census, Eighth (1860), *Population*, p. 621.

is on the northwest coast of France. German immigrants were the major group leaving through Le Havre, and their travel through northern France may have spread the idea of immigration to these areas.[57] If these suppositions are correct, then a large portion of the immigrants to the antebellum United States from the European continent, especially before the 1840s, came from the west central part of the continent, encompassing south and southwest Germany, eastern France, and Switzerland.

Immigration from Ireland

A variety of attempts has been made to estimate the regional origins of immigration from Ireland before 1860. In contrast to the Germans, the U.S. Census is of little use, because the country of origin is listed simply as "Ireland." The Passenger Lists are of some use, although here also most Irish were listed simply as coming from "Ireland." A few efforts have been made to estimate the regional origins of the Irish based on U.S. data other than the Passenger Lists. Besides estimates based on U.S. information, researchers have also provided estimates based on Irish census data. This latter work yields an estimate of total emigration from Ireland. Instead of immigrating to the United States, however, many Irish went to Canada and Great Britain, and some traveled to Australia. Because each group traveling to different destinations almost certainly differed in their regional origins, the material on the sources of overall Irish emigration can only be suggestive of the origins of the Irish emigrants who went to the United States. This fact is reinforced by the earlier discussion that many Irish emigrants sailing to Canada intended to continue on to the United States, and did so. Yet even if the exact regional origins of Irish immigration are not known, the various material is sufficient to provide some general conclusions.

Typically, most discussions of the regional origins of Irish immigration center on the four different provinces. The province of Ulster covers most of northern and northeast Ireland.[58] This province historically was the wealthiest and contained the most manufacturing, much of which was weaving and spinning linen in households. The province also contained the most non-Catholics, mainly Presbyterians who emigrated from

---

[57] See Chapter 6 for a discussion of the movement of Germans to the European ports of embarkation.

[58] The present-day country of Northern Ireland is composed of much, but not all, of the province of Ulster.

lowland Scotland in the late seventeenth and early eighteenth centuries. In the United States, the Presbyterian immigrants from Ulster have been called the Scotch-Irish. The other three provinces were predominantly Catholic. Leinster covers the east and southeast and includes the city of Dublin, Ireland's largest city. Historically, Leinster was probably second in wealth to Ulster. The other two provinces were Connacht, in the west and northwest, and Munster in the south and southwest. People living in these provinces were generally poorer.

The first large-scale Irish immigration to North America in the nineteenth century occurred between 1803 and 1805.[59] Researchers are in agreement that these Irish immigrants predominantly came from Ulster. Ó Gráda provides estimates of the origins of 3,215 immigrants during this period, and these are shown in column 3 of Table 2.6.[60] The dominance of Ulster is apparent. The next period of Irish immigration was in the last half of the 1810s. Similar to Germany, Ireland was also affected by the "year without a summer." Around thirty-five thousand individuals immigrated to North America from 1816 through 1818.[61] Yet even though conditions were unfavorable throughout Ireland, the North American immigrants still came predominantly from Ulster, where famine conditions were not as severe as elsewhere. Irish individuals from some of the other provinces, however, did migrate to England to find work.[62]

Estimates of total emigration from Ireland after 1820, including non-seasonal migration to Britain, have generally been based on Irish census data for different years.[63] Although a number of censuses were taken before 1861, the most accurate ones were completed in 1821, 1841, 1851, and 1861.[64] Total emigration is estimated as follows. The change in total population between each set of contiguous census years is calculated for each province. These numbers are then compared to a hypothetical

---

[59] Wokeck, *Trade*, Table 4, pp. 172–3, estimates that a total of fifty-one thousand Irish immigrants arrived between 1730 and 1774.

[60] Ó Gráda, "Across the Briny Ocean," p. 89.

[61] Adams, *Ireland*, pp. 70–1, 92. Although many of these individuals sailed to Canada, Adams estimates that 67–90% went on to the United States.

[62] Adams, *Ireland*, p. 123. Post, *Last Great Subsistence Crisis*.

[63] The first researcher to use this approach was Cousens in the 1960s. See Cousens, "Regional Variation"; Cousens, "Regional Pattern"; and Cousens, "Emigration." Some Irish worked in Britain on a seasonal basis, while others did so, more or less, permanently. The former presumably appeared in the censuses taken in Ireland, while the latter did not. Cousens, "Regional Variation," p. 18, also criticizes the even earlier attempts by Adams, *Ireland*, to estimate total emigration from parish reports. The criticism centers on the incompleteness of those reports.

[64] See the discussion in Cousens, "Regional Variation," p. 15.

TABLE 2.6. *Antebellum Emigration and Immigration of the Irish (percent of the total)*

Province	Percent of Irish Population in 1841	Emigration from Ireland: 1841–51	Immigration to North America 1803–5	Immigration to New York Based On:				
				U.S. Passenger Lists			NY Emigrant Savings Bank	
				1820–34	1835–46	1847–8	Before 1846	1846–52
Ulster	29%	28%	79%	39%	37%	41%	35%	20%
Leinster	24%	16%	13%	39%	39%	22%	30%	29%
Munster	29%	32%	3%	15%	12%	14%	20%	37%
Connacht	17%	24%	6%	7%	13%	24%	15%	14%
Sample Size	entire population	entire population	3,215	2,314	6,092	2,742	1,105	3,113

Sources: Columns 1, 7, and 8: Ó Gráda, "Famine," Table 4. Column 2: Calculated from Ó Gráda and O'Rourke, "Migration," Table 6, p. 14. Columns 3–6: Ó Gráda, "Across the Briny Ocean," Tables 4.9 and 4.10, p. 89.

population in the later year determined by applying "typical" provincial population growth rates to the earlier-year population and adjusting for provincial differences in death rates. Because outmigration occurred from all of Ireland, the latter number is higher than the former number, and the difference between the two is a measure of total emigration.[65] The estimates for 1841–51 have been redone by Ó Gráda and O'Rourke and are shown in column 2 of Table 2.6.[66] The results, however, indicate nothing about where the migrants went.

Between 1821 and 1861, economic historians believe that emigration spread to more regions of Ireland.[67] These areas included the northeast counties of Connacht, those close to Ulster, and a number of counties in Leinster, many of which were also close to Ulster. In general, before the famine, emigration was centered in Ulster and the north central counties of Ireland. The famine caused emigration to increase by such a large amount from Munster and Connacht, areas where the famine hit the hardest, that these areas became overrepresented in the emigrant stream relative to the population (compare columns 1 and 2 in Table 2.6). Emigration from Ulster and Leinster became less important in percentage terms because the effects of the famine were less in these areas. Total emigration increased so much, however, that the actual numbers leaving the traditional areas did not decline. Although famine conditions disappeared after 1851, the south and the west areas of Ireland remained the major sources of emigration through the 1850s. Thus, before the famine, emigration was slowly expanding from its historical origins in Ulster. The famine led to a fundamental change in the regional origins of Irish emigrants, such that those who left after the famine were more likely to come from Munster and Connacht.[68]

When the discussion is limited to just those Irish immigrants who came to the United States, the information is more limited. Large numbers of Irish emigrated to Britain, Canada, and Australia, therefore the

---

[65] See Fitzpatrick, "Emigration," pp. 565, 608. This method also records those Irish living in Ireland outside their home area as "emigrants." Fitzpatrick shows this group was a small part of the total.

[66] Ó Gráda and O'Rourke, "Migration." Provincial estimates of the percentage of young cohorts who were missing between the census years, along with rates of emigration from Irish ports, are given in Fitzpatrick, "Emigration," p. 608. No provincial percentages are available for the 1821–41 and 1851–61 periods.

[67] The discussion in this paragraph is based on Fitzpatrick, "Emigration"; Ó Gráda and O'Rourke, "Migration"; Cousens, "Regional Variation"; and Cousens, "Emigration."

[68] Ó Gráda, "Some Aspects."

provincial origins of the Irish emigrant stream could have differed substantially from the provincial origins of the Irish who came to the United
States.[69] Cousens provides a little data from Irish records for the 1831–41
period. Of those traveling to the United States, 58 percent left directly
from Ireland, and "two-thirds went from Ulster and Munster." For those
sailing through Liverpool, more came from "Ulster and Leinster."[70]
Ó Gráda provides more precise data from his examination of the New
York Passenger Lists between 1820 and 1848. These figures are shown
in columns 4–6 in Table 2.6. If the estimates are taken at face value, then
Ulster continued to be an important source of immigrants to the United
States into the early famine years. The major change is a decline in the
share from Leinster and an increase in the share from Connacht.

Another attempt to use U.S. data to estimate the regional origins of
immigration employs the records of the Emigrant Industrial Savings Bank.
This bank was established in 1850 in New York City to serve Irish immigrants.[71] The account records of this bank include information on name,
date of arrival, and county of origin of the depositors. The regional origins before and after 1845 are summarized in columns 7 and 8 of Table 2.6. These estimates partially support the large change in regional
origins found in total Irish emigration. Ulster became a less important
source of emigration after 1845, although Leinster did not. In turn, Munster, rather than Connacht, became more important. Overall, the Savings
Bank estimates in Table 2.6 indicate substantially more immigrants to the
United States from Leinster and fewer from Connacht than in the total
emigration data. The differences could be due to a number of factors. Not
all of the Irish emigrants came to the United States. Not all of the Irish
immigrants to the United States lived in New York City. Moreover, not
all of the Irish who lived in New York City opened accounts at the Emigrant Industrial Savings Bank. Leinster immigrants, for example, came
from a richer part of Ireland, and may have been more likely to have a
savings account. Similar criticisms also apply to the estimates from the
New York Passenger Lists discussed earlier.

Immigration from Ireland has some broad similarities to that from
Germany. In both cases, early immigration was centered in one region of

---

[69] Fitzpatrick, "Emigration," pp. 568–9, 609, indicates that, until the late 1840s, fewer
Irish lived in the United States than in Britain. Even in 1861, only 56% of the Irish living
outside of Ireland were in the United States.

[70] Cousens, "Regional Variation," p. 18.

[71] Ó Gráda, "Famine." For an attempt to infer regional origins based on the last names of
the Irish, see Ferrie, "New View."

the country. In both cases, immigration spread over time to most or all of the other regions in each country, and immigration continued from the earlier areas. The evidence specific to U.S. immigrants is more confusing, although at least one of the provinces – Ulster in one set of estimates and Leinster in the other – that was an early source of immigrants declined in relative importance. Thus, one of the other provinces became a more important source of immigrants over time, although again the two sources differ on which province. In summary, a good deal of work remains to be done in determining the regional origins of Irish immigrants to the United States.

Immigration from Great Britain

An approximate idea of the origins of the immigrants from Great Britain is given in Table 2.4, because the nativity information is provided separately for England, Scotland, and Wales. According to these data, immigrants from England accounted for 74 percent of the total from Great Britain during the antebellum period. Immigrants from Scotland comprise 19 percent and those from Wales 8 percent of the total. If Scotland is viewed as a separate country, then as many immigrants came from there as from France, and many more came from either country than from Switzerland or Norway/Sweden or the Netherlands or Wales. Thus, this section examines the regional origins of immigration from England and Scotland.

Very little consistent data exist on the regional origins of British immigration. As noted earlier, the British emigration statistics do not even provide the *country* of origin for the emigrants before 1853, and the later statistics are incomplete for a number of years.[72] A limited amount of data is available from one of the English censuses but these do not distinguish among countries of destination. In addition, a few efforts have been made to gather data on regional origins from the U.S. Passenger Lists, but these efforts run into the same issue that was discussed for Germany and Ireland. The Passenger Lists generally just list "England" or "Scotland" or, as was discussed earlier, "Great Britain" or "Great Britain and Ireland." Only a very limited number of lists provide more detailed information on the county of origin within each country.[73] Similarly, the

---

[72] See the discussion in Jones, "Background," pp. 24–5.

[73] For example, Van Vugt, *Britain*, pp. 29–30, 165, 169–70, is able to use the U.S. Passenger Lists to provide information on the city size background of 646 immigrants who arrived in 1851, and county of origin information for 169 preindustrial immigrants and 114

U.S. Census records only the number from each of the British countries, and not from the individual counties within each country.

When the regions of origin of the British immigrants are examined, the following regions are usually discussed. England is divided into a large number of counties. Instead of discussing these, the tendency is to divide the southern areas of England – which were almost totally oriented toward agriculture – from the northern areas – in which the Industrial Revolution was more apparent. Within the north, however, were also large numbers of individuals who were farmers. The division still makes sense because not many individuals made large internal moves within England, therefore the labor markets appear to have been mainly separate. Because individuals in northern agriculture had more non-agricultural opportunities and earned higher wages than did those in southern agriculture, immigration from the two areas can be viewed separately.[74] Scotland is easier to divide into regions. Typically, two regions – the Highlands and the Lowlands – are distinguished. The Highlands comprise the northern and western areas of Scotland, while the Lowlands are in the south and east. Wales is typically treated separately, but will be ignored in the following discussion due to the small number of its immigrants. Thus, our discussion of the regional origins of British immigrants will center on two regions each in England and Scotland.

No sustained heavy outflow of emigrants from England and Scotland occurred before the 1840s.[75] Even after 1845, emigration from Britain never became the mass movement it did in Ireland and Germany. Before 1848, a large majority of the emigrants went to the United States. Where these individuals came from is in doubt. Jones claims that most of these individuals were from the southern agricultural areas of England. In addition, the Scottish Highlands saw a high rate of emigration, acting perhaps in concert with Irish emigration, although the actual numbers were not large and much of it was to Canada. In years when the industrial sector was in depression – such as 1816, 1819, 1826–7, 1830–1, and 1841–2 – the typical outflow was supplemented with skilled workers from the northern urban areas in England and the Scottish Lowlands. Yet, in

English farmers. Erickson, "Emigration in 1831," p. 193, has found county of origin data on 435 individuals in 1827 and 678 in 1831. In general, the U.S. Passenger Lists do not do a good job of even dividing among the English, Scots, and Welsh until at least 1875. See Jones, "Background," p. 31.

74 The north-south division of agricultural wages is apparent in the data given for 1851 in Erickson, "Who," Table 11, p. 375.

75 The discussion in this paragraph follows Jones, "Background," pp. 28–46, 82–5.

Jones's view, even in the depression years, workers with rural origins dominated. The 1841 British census shows a total of 9,569 emigrants from England and 8,572 emigrants from Scotland. About one-fourth of the English were from industrial counties and, at most, industrial workers accounted for a slim majority in that severe depression year. The eastern, non-industrial part of the region stretching north from London saw few emigrants.[76]

In a series of articles based on samples from the Passenger Lists, Erickson and Van Vugt have challenged Jones's view concerning English immigration. In their view, immigration from England had much more diverse origins. What these origins were depended on the year. In 1827, the vast majority were from high-wage industrial counties, whereas in 1831, more were from agricultural areas.[77] Although less information on county origins is available for 1841, Erickson criticizes the use of the British census data. The census collected data on emigrants only for the first five months of the year, a period in which Erickson finds that emigration was particularly large among those with an agricultural background. Later in the year, she shows that many more industrial workers immigrated.[78] In 1851, Van Vugt finds that individuals leaving agriculture were a more important part of the total than in 1841 but still not a majority. The origins of the immigrants were found to be quite diverse.[79] For all the years, the size of the samples used is quite small, not surprising given that the Passenger Lists generally recorded only the country of origin. In addition, some questions have been raised with the representativeness of Erickson's and Van Vugt's samples, an issue that is addressed in more detail in Chapter 5. In summary, sufficient data are not available to draw any firm conclusions concerning the regional origins of the British immigrants to the United States and whether these origins changed over time.[80]

---

[76] Jones views emigration from the Scottish Lowlands as being similar to and affected by the same factors as that from the area of England north of London.

[77] Erickson, "Emigration in 1831," Table 18, p. 193.

[78] Erickson, "Emigration in 1841: Part II," pp. 25–6.

[79] Van Vugt, *Britain*, Table B6, and pp. 29–30, 169–70; Van Vugt, "Running," Table 5, p. 422.

[80] Baines, *Migration*, has investigated the origins of English and Welsh emigrants for the period from 1861 through 1900. His conclusion (p. 281) is that the "majority of emigrants must have come from places that were in the mainstream of economic change, not, for example, from the remote areas that had benefited less from the industrialization of the country." One factor that emigration from a county was related to was found to be previous emigration from that county. It is unclear how much importance Baines's results should be given in the present case, because Baines examines only the English and the Welsh and is considering emigrants to Australia and Canada as well as the

Summary

A good deal of concern has been expressed about the accuracy of the antebellum U.S. immigration statistics. Most of the concern has arisen from a comparison of the existing records of departures for the United States from an individual European country to the U.S. record of arrivals from that country. However, much of this unease is misplaced. As a measure of total immigration, the U.S. records appear to be quite accurate, at least once the individuals are included who did not have their country of origin listed. In fact, it is the apparent nonrecording of the origin of many individuals from the Netherlands, Scandinavia, and so forth that have caused historians of specific European countries to find more of their individuals left for the United States than are listed as arriving from that country. Once these individuals are included – along with an estimate for arrivals through Canada – approximately 5.2 million Europeans arrived in the United States between 1815 and 1860.

After undergoing a very slow increase throughout the Colonial and early national periods, the volume of European immigration to the United States began rising rapidly during the late 1820s and early 1830s, well before the outbreak of the potato famine. The major sources for immigration before the 1840s were Ireland and Germany, especially from two general areas: southwest Germany – including Switzerland and, perhaps, northeastern France – and the province of Ulster in Ireland, with perhaps some contribution from the Scottish Highlands. A small but significant flow also came from somewhere in England. By 1860, the regional sources of immigration were much less specific. Immigrants came to the United States from all parts of Germany and Ireland, and it is likely that the Scottish Lowlands and more parts of England were also sources.

Appendix 2.1
Estimating the Origins of the German Immigrants

Table A2.1 presents three estimates of the origins of the German immigrants based on the 1860 and 1870 U.S. Census data. The estimates in column 1 depend entirely on the 1860 census. This publication provided both a breakdown by state of origin of German immigrants living in the United States and a breakdown of emigration from Prussia between 1844

United States. Baines also investigates internal migration within England, a factor that complicates this analysis because it makes unclear whether a "county of origin" listed on a passenger list was the county of birth or the one of current residence.

TABLE A.2.1. *Estimates of Immigration from the German States*

Region or State	Based On:		
	1860 Census Data	1870 Census with 1860-Based Division of Prussia	1860 Census Adjusted by 1870 Proportions
South and Southwest	411,801 (61%)	662,303 (46%)	411,801 (54%)
Palatinate[a]	67,466	176,879	67,466
Baden	112,834	153,355	112,834
Württemberg	81,336	127,955	81,336
Bavaria	150,165	204,114	150,165
Central	116,442 (17%)	175,339 (12%)	121,068 (16%)
Hesse (incl. Nassau and Frankfurt[a])	116,442	168,639	116,442
Thuringia (incl. Weimar)	????	6,700	4,626
Northwest	66,117 (10%)	296,620 (20%)	113,167 (15%)
Westphalia[a]	66,117	173,298	66,117
Hanover (incl. Brunswick, Oldenburg, and Bremen)	????	123,322	47,050
North and East	83,333 (12%)	312,456 (22%)	118,663 (16%)
Other Prussia[a]	83,333	219,427	83,333
Saxony	????	45,254	17,186
North Germany (incl. Mecklenburg, Hamburg, and Lubeck)	????	47,775	18,144
Germany, not specified	598,382	243,692	511,376
TOTAL LISTED	1,276,075	1,690,410	1,276,075

Notes: All percentages are of the total excluding "Germany, not specified." Note the calculations determine the regional origins of antebellum German immigrants who were alive at the time of each census.

[a] Areas included in Prussia.

Sources: Calculated from U.S. Bureau of the Census, Eighth (1860), *Population*, pp. xxiv, 621, and U.S. Bureau of the Census, Ninth (1870), *Population*, pp. 338–9. See the text of appendix for the method of calculation.

and 1859 based on official Prussian sources derived from passports issued to those leaving.[81] Given that some of the previous immigrants would

[81] U.S. Bureau of the Census, Eighth (1860), *Population*, pp. xxiv, 621. The census also says that "... many others are known to have migrated without passports." For the estimation in Table 2.5 to be accurate, it must be assumed there was an equal tendency,

have died and a few would have left, the total in column 1 of Table A2.1 seems reasonable in light of the information in Table 2.2 that 1.6 to 1.7 million Germans immigrated between 1820 and 1860.[82] However, the problems with using the 1860 census data are also apparent. Almost one-half list their place of birth as "Germany." In addition, the census does not list any immigrants from a number of German states. These totals are presumably included in the "Germany, not specified" total. Because the latter total would also include individuals from all parts of Germany, the only conclusion from column 1 that seems reasonable is that the 61 percent found to have come from South and Southwest Germany likely represents an upper bound for this region, because all the other regions contained at least one state with data subsumed in the "Germany, not specified" total.

Column 2 uses the 1870 census data as a starting point. As can be seen, this census provides a more complete breakdown by German state. Another 724,000 Germans immigrated between 1860 and 1869, however, and immigrants came from all areas of Germany during this period, whereas the origins were more concentrated before 1845.[83] Thus, the 1870 census breakdown would be biased as a reflection of pre-1860 German immigration. On the other hand, the data are "cleaner" in that a much smaller percentage of the total is listed as "Germany, not specified." Given the small numbers and the better coverage, it makes sense to allocate the "not specified" individuals proportionately across the German states, therefore the percentage from each area does not change.[84] The remaining issue is the division of the Prussian data. Column 2 allocates the Prussian total based on the official Prussian statistics in the 1860 census. Although Prussia annexed some smaller states between 1860 and 1870, it is unlikely that the individuals in the United States from these areas would have listed their birthplace as "Prussia" instead of the older name, although what the census takers did is not clear.[85]

---

as a proportion of total immigration from each area throughout Prussia, for individuals to migrate without passports. This assumption is probably reasonable because the main reason for doing so was to avoid military service.

[82] The Passenger Lists show 1.55 million arriving from Germany. To this number must be added some Germans who came through Canada and others currently in the "Not Specified" category. Any estimate in the 1.6 to 1.7 million range seems reasonable given the nativity data in Table 2.4.

[83] The total number who immigrated between 1860 and 1869 is calculated from Carter et al., *Historical Statistics*, series Ad111.

[84] For the few states not listed, I followed Kamphoefner, *Westfalians*, p. 207, and allocated 3.9% of the "Germans, not specified" to these states.

[85] See the discussion in Kamphoefner, *Westfalians*, pp. 207–9.

Because the sources of immigration between 1860 and 1870 were different from the pre-1860 period, a further adjustment to the estimates is needed. Assume that within each of the four regions, the proportions from each state remained constant between 1860 and 1870. This assumption is supported by the earlier narrative discussion of the sources of immigration, which showed that immigration spread over time from what has been defined as South and Southwest Germany into Central and Northwest Germany and finally to East and North Germany. Then, 1860 estimates can be calculated for each major state. For example, in column 2, immigration from Hanover was 71 percent as large as from Westphalia (= 123,322/173,298). An estimate for immigration from Hanover in 1860 is then 47,050 (= 0.71 × 66,117).[86] Repeating this procedure for all of the states with missing data in 1860 yields the estimates in column 3.

Table 2.5 in the text reproduces the percentages from columns 2 and 3 of Table A2.1. The accuracy of these estimates is not clear. On the one hand, the procedure uses (probably fairly accurate) U.S. Census data. On the other hand, a large number of immigrants remain in the "Germany, not specified" category.

---

[86] Except for the Palatinate, this procedure would work fairly well for the states in south and southwest Germany, if any data for 1860 for these states had been missing.

3

The Jump in Immigrant Volume Around 1830

One unique aspect of the antebellum period was the jump in the average annual volume of immigration, which Chapter 2 stated occurred around 1830. This chapter explains why the annual volume suddenly increased at this time, although a few of the supporting details are deferred to Chapter 4. The related issue of why the early immigrants came predominantly from southwest Germany and Ulster is also examined. Both issues involve sustained population growth throughout Europe, differential opportunities for individuals in different parts of Europe, changes in the shipping industry, and changes in the ability of individuals to immigrate. By 1830, these factors led to many more Europeans being willing and able to immigrate across the Atlantic Ocean. At about the same time, economic opportunities for the immigrants in the United States rose, an aspect of the story investigated in greater detail in Chapter 4. The result of all these factors was a substantial increase in the volume of immigration during the late 1820s and early 1830s.

The Theory of Immigration and the Rise in Volume

To understand why immigrant volume increased, it is first necessary to understand the motivation for why individuals immigrate. As mentioned in Chapter 1, economic factors were paramount by the antebellum period, with individuals moving to a situation they expected to be better.[1] Thus, individuals or families compared their expected economic situation in the United States with their current one in Europe. If the former was better

[1] For a survey and evaluation of theories of migration, see Massey et al., "Theories."

than the latter, and the difference more than compensated for the costs of immigrating, the individual or family might move. "Might" because individuals could forgo the potential gain for two reasons. First, they might not want to leave their family. Second, they or their family might not have the funds needed to immigrate and remain alive until an income-producing job could be found in the United States. In fact, the difficulty of funding the trip sometimes caused family members to immigrate at different times. Often a male would immigrate first, get a job in the United States, and use his earnings to pay the cost of bringing over other family members or friends. In other cases, the individual or family might decide not to move because they did not have good information on their potential situation in the United States or the costs of immigrating. Overall, then, immigration is a function of the economic situation in each country, the costs of migrating, family considerations, and information flows.[2] Finally, the basic theory assumes there were no government constraints that would inhibit immigration.

The increase in immigration during the second quarter of the nineteenth century was due to changes in a number of the aforementioned factors. Beginning in the last half of the eighteenth century, economic conditions in Europe began to be pressured by rapid population growth. The desire on the part of many individuals to leave Europe was hindered, however, by the unsettled conditions resulting from the American Revolution, the French Revolution, and the Napoleonic Wars, the latter of which increased local demand for people to serve in the armies and constrained the available shipping. To some extent, the opposition of existing European governments also kept people from leaving Europe. When the Napoleonic Wars ended in 1815, transportation facilities were disrupted and existing transatlantic fares were high. Only the extreme conditions of the "year without a summer" led to the large numbers leaving during the last half of the 1810s. Otherwise, volume probably would have been as low as it fell to during the early 1820s. From 1815 to 1830, transportation

---

[2] The general approach used here broadly follows the discussion in Sjaastad, "Costs," and Wegge, "Chain Migration," p. 960. Baines, "European Emigration," pp. 526–33, distinguishes between the "relative income hypothesis" favored by economists and the "information hypothesis" favored by historians. Yet surely both factors were important in explaining immigration flows. In addition, some factors may have been more important during some periods or for some countries and other factors more important during other periods or for other countries. Thus, the approach taken in this chapter is very general. In another publication, Baines asks why even more Europeans did not leave, given the potential gain in income. Certainly part of the answer must be family considerations and, possibly, the lack of information in some areas. See Baines, *Emigration*, p. 25.

facilities improved, fares declined, remittances from previous immigrants became larger, and information improved as detailed in subsequent sections of this chapter. During the same period, government constraints on emigration diminished. All of these changes worked to lower the costs of migrating.

Conditions in the United States were also important. The general assumption is that U.S. economic conditions influenced the timing of immigration but not the underlying decision to immigrate.[3] In a longer-term sense, labor in the United States was scarce relative to land and other resources. Thus, the returns for laborers were generally higher than in Europe, so that many individuals could improve their well-being by immigrating to the United States. Over the shorter term, however, the volume of immigration was sensitive to U.S. business conditions, because these affected the likelihood of finding immediate employment. This relationship is discussed in greater detail in Chapter 4. At this point, we can note that economic opportunities in the United States for immigrants were not very extensive throughout the 1820s, but this situation changed rapidly in the early 1830s. By this time, the costs of immigrating had fallen substantially, as discussed in the remainder of this chapter. Thus, a large increase in the demand for labor in the United States occurred at a time when the costs of immigrating had declined. The result was a substantial increase in the volume of immigration in a short period of time.

Conditions in Europe Before the Potato Famine

The most important factor leading to a deterioration of economic conditions in Europe was the sustained growth of population after 1750. Before this time, population had grown haphazardly. Then, from a base of 120–40 million in 1750, population increased to about 187 million in 1800 and 266 million in 1850.[4] The growth in population occurred across Europe (Table 3.1). Between 1618 and 1648, the Thirty Years' War was fought in central Europe. The war was especially hard on the German states, which lost at least one-third of their 16 million population in 1600. Even after a period of fewer troubles during the last half of the seventeenth century, the German population had only recovered to

---

[3] Baines, *Emigration*, p. 21, distinguishes between two decisions: first, whether or not to leave, and second, when to leave.
[4] Armengaud, "Population," p. 28.

TABLE 3.1. *Population of Europe, by Country, 1750–1850 (in millions, except percentages)*

Country	1750	1800[a]	1850	Percentage Increase, 1750–1800	Percentage Increase, 1800–1850
Germany[b]	18.4	24.5	31.7	33%	29%
Ireland	2.4	5.0–5.2	8.2[c]	108%	58%[c]
Great Britain	7.4	10.9	20.9	47%	92%
Norway and Sweden	2.5	3.2	5.0	28%	56%
Denmark	0.7	0.9	1.6	29%	78%
Switzerland	1.4	1.7–1.8	2.4	21%	33%
Netherlands	1.9	2.1–2.2	3.1	11%	41%
Belgium	2.2	2.8–3.0	4.3	27%	43%
France	24.5	26.9–29.0	36.5	10%	26%

[a] Different population figures are provided in different sources. The percentage increase from 1750 to 1800 is calculated based on the smaller figure, while the increase from 1800 to 1850 is calculated using the larger one.

[b] These figures are for the 1914 boundaries of Germany, not including Alsace and Lorraine.

[c] Population in 1841 and percentage increase 1800–41.

Sources: All estimates for 1750: Anderson, *Population Change*, p. 23. 1800 and 1850 for Ireland: Ó Gráda, *Ireland*, pp. 6, 178. Other countries for 1800 and 1850: Armengaud, "Population," p. 29. A convenient summary is in Moch, *Moving Europeans*, pp. 65, 109.

14 million by 1700 and 16 million in 1750.[5] Using the 1914 boundaries of Germany provides a higher figure for the 1750 population of more than 18 million (see Table 3.1), which grew to more than 24 million in 1800 and almost 32 million in 1850. Even more rapid population growth occurred in Great Britain and especially in Ireland. Irish population doubled between 1750 and 1800, attaining a level of about 5 million in the latter year. The increase continued until the Irish population reached a level of about 8.5 million in 1845, just before the potato famine.[6] The British population rose from about 7 million in 1750 to 11 million in 1800 to 21 million in 1850. The huge increases in population among these three countries, and elsewhere in Europe, occurred despite the large emigration that occurred between 1815 and 1860.

Population increased without encountering a sustained food crisis because of changes in agriculture. On the Continent, the old three-field

[5] Benz, "Population Change," pp. 42–3, 58.

[6] For a discussion of Irish population growth before the famine, see Guinnane, *Vanishing Irish*, pp. 79–85. A comparison between Irish and English population is shown on p. 5 of Guinnane's book.

system, where one-third of the land lay fallow each year, began to change as much of the fallow land was brought under cultivation.[7] New fodder crops were introduced, such as clover and turnips, which provided some income and helped to restore the fertility of the land. With more land under cultivation each year, more people could be supported. Another important development was the introduction of the potato. In years of normal yield, the potato was highly productive, allowing people to be able to produce enough food to survive even on a small plot of land. As population grew in Ireland, the potato crop spread after its introduction around 1600. In southwest Germany, the potato was rapidly adopted in the years after 1815.[8] These developments, along with other technological ones, allowed food production to generally keep pace with the rising population. For example, England tripled its food production between 1700 and 1870.

The effect of the population growth on farm size depended on the inheritance system. In Ireland, a system of partible inheritance prevailed, where a family's land was divided among the children. Conditions became particularly marginal for the Irish peasants, who rented from landlords in most places.[9] Before 1815, a male usually received a small plot of land when he married. The land came from subdividing the family's previous rental holding. Thus, with the growth of the Irish population, plot size fell over time, in some cases to an extremely small size. In fact, the situation worsened after 1815, because Irish landlords became interested in converting cropland to pastureland to take advantage of higher relative prices for livestock. The conversion required removing many of the peasants from the land. As a consequence, the number of landless peasants increased. One estimate is that the number of farm laborers and farm servants rose from 665,000 to 1,300,000 between 1831 and 1841. For every ten agricultural workers in 1841, there were only three farms in Munster, four in Leinster, and five in Connacht.[10]

The inheritance system differed throughout Germany. In southwest Germany, the arrangement was similar to that in Ireland, except that the Germans were more likely to own their land than the Irish. As population

[7] Much of the discussion in this paragraph follows Moch, *Moving Europeans*, pp. 108–9. See Hochstadt, "Socioeconomic Determinants," p. 149, for a discussion of Germany. See Guinnane, *Vanishing Irish*, pp. 34–8, for an overall discussion of the Irish economy before the famine.

[8] Walker, *Germany*, p. 71.

[9] Much of the discussion in this paragraph follows Blessing, "Irish Emigration," pp. 14–16.

[10] Ó Gráda, "Demographic Adjustment," p. 189.

grew, the family's land was split equally among the sons and daughters, although the latter often received their share in the form of a dowry.[11] Thus, the average-size farm owned by each individual in these areas declined over time. In the Prussian areas, even those in the west of Germany, a system of impartible inheritance prevailed, where all of the family's land went to one child.[12] In certain areas, such as Hesse-Cassel, some villages practiced one form of inheritance while some villages practiced the other. The situation was different in the eastern sections of Germany.[13] These areas were less populated and Junker families owned much of the land in large estates. Increases in population in these areas did not, therefore, cause a division in the established estates. The estate owners, in exchange for the workers' occasional labor services, gave some individuals small plots of land. Others in the east became landless and worked as day laborers. Thus, the growth of population led to a decline in individual farm size in the areas of partible inheritance in southwest Germany, as it did in Ireland, but not in the areas where an impartible system prevailed or in the eastern sections of Germany.

The effect of the inheritance system on the incentive to immigrate has been the subject of some controversy.[14] A partible system makes it more difficult to earn a living in agriculture because the size of the farm declines. Thus, an individual might choose to sell his or her land and emigrate. On the other hand, ownership of land conferred a certain amount of prestige. An individual might want to hold on to his or her land, especially if some method existed that allowed the farmer to supplement his or her farm income. The possible adjustment mechanisms will be discussed shortly.[15] Under an impartible system, however, the non-inheriting siblings would be forced to find another occupation. Given that these individuals would almost certainly end up working outside of agriculture and competing with many other individuals in the same situation, emigration was also a realistic alternative in this situation.

As a consequence of the population growth, therefore, either farm size had to decline or people had to find non-agricultural jobs or both

---

[11] Benz, "Population Change," p. 48.
[12] In reality, even under an impartible system, the family might provide assistance for the other children in the form of cash, training, and so forth. In turn, under a partible system, some individuals might sell their land to one sibling and emigrate. See the discussion in Wegge, "To Part," p. 34.
[13] See Hochstadt, "Socioeconomic Determinants," p. 143.
[14] Much of this paragraph follows Wegge, "To Part," p. 31.
[15] For a formal discussion of this issue, see Berkner and Mendels, "Inheritance Systems," pp. 209–16.

occurred. In Ireland, the number of jobs outside of agriculture did not change much as producers of Irish manufactures came under increasing pressure from the British after the establishment of peace in 1815. Between 1831 and 1841, for example, non-agricultural jobs increased by only 3 percent in Munster, Leinster, and Connacht.[16] Good alternatives to working the land in Germany did not exist until the last part of the nineteenth century. In some areas, guild restrictions made it difficult, if not impossible, to enter many artisan occupations, at least without moving to the larger cities.[17] In addition, German manufacturing firms faced the same competition from the lower-cost British as did the Irish producers. Thus, both in Ireland and Germany, opportunities outside of agriculture were limited.

Given the lack of non-agricultural opportunities in Ireland and Germany, individuals in areas of partible inheritance sought to remain on the land. They could do so if they found a way to supplement the reduced income from the farm.[18] One method of doing so was to work part-time on the farm and part-time at some nonfarm tasks. In particular, the late eighteenth and early nineteenth centuries saw the expansion of protoindustry in which farm families worked at industrial tasks in the household. In many areas, these tasks involved some aspect of textile production. In Westphalia, for example, the major household task was linen production. In southwest Germany, production was more varied, involving aspects of cotton production and rural crafts.[19] Overall, however, the southwest areas of Germany contained relatively little protoindustry compared to the northwest, Rhineland, and Silesia.[20] An additional method of supplementing one's income from the farm was to spend some days or seasons working for someone else. In many areas of Europe, Lucassen has shown that large-scale seasonal migration systems existed during the early nineteenth century. Males traveled up to 250 kilometers to work for part of the year, leaving their farms in the hands of their wives or children.[21]

---

[16] Blessing, "Irish Emigration," p. 14.

[17] One area where guild restrictions were important was Hesse-Cassel. See Wegge, "Occupational Self-Selection," p. 383.

[18] Hochstadt, "Socioeconomic Determinants," p. 153, cites an estimate that two-thirds of rural workers in early nineteenth-century Germany needed to earn money outside of their farm. Adams, *Ireland*, p. 39, discusses the need for Irish small farmers to earn income from outside employment.

[19] See the list and discussion in Ogilvie, "Beginnings," pp. 266–74.

[20] Hochstadt, "Socioeconomic Determinants," p. 145. Most of the eastern parts of Germany saw little protoindustry because feudal relationships still held.

[21] Lucassen, *Migrant Labour*, p. 112.

Thus, despite the decline in farm size, many individuals were able to maintain their farms by finding a method of supplementing their farm income.

None of this background material directly addresses why south and southwest Germany and Ulster were the major areas of immigration to the United States in the early part of the nineteenth century. A first point is to note that both areas had been primary sources for immigration during the eighteenth century.[22] As discussed in the last chapter, most of the immigrants coming from Ulster were Scotch-Irish. Their families had lived in Ulster only a generation or two, with their ancestors having moved from Scotland. Both Scotland and England had been important sources of immigration to the colonial United States, and thus the Scotch-Irish in Ulster often had relatives or family acquaintances already in the United States. As to Germany, the fact that a number of immigrants during the eighteenth century had come from south and southwest Germany meant that potential immigrants during the early nineteenth century also had contacts in the United States. Thus, as it became easier and cheaper to cross the Atlantic Ocean after 1815 (see the next sections), immigration resumed from the traditional areas.[23] The antebellum volume was, however, higher because continued rapid population growth caused the relative economic conditions in Europe to worsen from the outbreak of the American Revolution to the end of Napoleon.

The fact that immigration during the first part of the nineteenth century came from the same European areas as during the eighteenth century still begs the question of why these areas first saw emigration to the United States. After all, population growth occurred at a high rate throughout Ireland and Germany. In addition, although both Ulster and southwest Germany were areas of partible inheritance, the previous discussion makes it uncertain whether this system or an impartible one had a greater effect on emigration.[24] Although the complete answer to the

[22] Ó Gráda, *Ireland*, pp. 74–5; Doerries, "German Transatlantic Migration," pp. 116–18. Wokeck, *Trade*.

[23] The routes taken by the immigrants in the nineteenth century were, however, not the same as those in the eighteenth century. In the earlier period, the Germans moved down the Rhine River and many left from Rotterdam or Amsterdam. See Wokeck, *Trade*, p. 60. In the nineteenth century, the routes out of southwest Germany were different, as is discussed in Chapter 6.

[24] In fact, Wegge, "To Part," finds for Hesse-Cassel in Germany, an area where both systems existed, that an impartible system actually led to a greater propensity to emigrate. Kamphoefner et al., *News*, pp. 2–3, also explicitly downplays the importance of inheritance systems in explaining German immigration.

early location of the immigrants is not clear, the areas did have two features in common. First, each area was one of large population density. In Germany, conditions were most crowded in the western and southwestern areas, where population densities during the early nineteenth century generally exceeded seventy-five people per square kilometer. In contrast, in vast areas of eastern Prussia, the densities were under twenty people per square kilometer.[25] In Ireland, Ulster had the highest population density.[26] Second, each area probably had less access to seasonal migration income than did other areas in Europe. The large-scale seasonal migration regions Lucassen found on the continent for the early nineteenth century are shown in Figure 3.1. Note that individuals in most parts of Western Europe were in an area where seasonal migration was common. The area on the continent where this fact was not true was south and southwest Germany, where the demand for seasonal labor was limited.[27] Something similar appears to have existed in Ireland. Although seasonal migration to England was an option for the Irish, most was from the western Catholic parts of Ireland.[28] If Protestants from Ulster sought seasonal work in England, they would have been competing with the poorer Catholic Irish, which was not a very promising option.[29] Indeed, as shown in Figure 3.1, a few of the Scotch-Irish were able to find seasonal work in Scotland, but the demand there was small as emigration from Scotland was also occurring.

Overall, both Ulster and southwest Germany were densely populated areas where the options for seasonal work were limited.[30] Thus, individuals in both areas would have had an early interest (and need) in permanently moving a long distance in order to try to increase their standard of living. By the early nineteenth century, individuals in both areas probably had family or friends or contacts already in the United States to help pave the way. In other areas of Germany, individuals had

[25] Sieglerschmidt, "Social and Economic Landscapes," pp. 28–9.

[26] Mageean, "Nineteenth-Century Irish Emigration," p. 49.

[27] Seasonal migration did not occur in Eastern Europe at this time, as the mobility of the peasants was limited by the remnants of serfdom. See Lucassen, *Migrant Labour*, pp. 125–7. Lucassen determined the major seasonal migration systems in the early nineteenth century primarily based on data gathered when Napoleon was in power.

[28] Ó Gráda, *Ireland*, p. 79. Kerr, "Irish Seasonal Migration," p. 371.

[29] Ó Gráda, *Ireland*, pp. 74–5.

[30] Wokeck, *Trade*, pp. 1–35, discusses reasons for emigration from southwest Germany during the eighteenth century. She cites high population growth as well as economic and political instability that led to individuals moving not only overseas but to other parts of Europe.

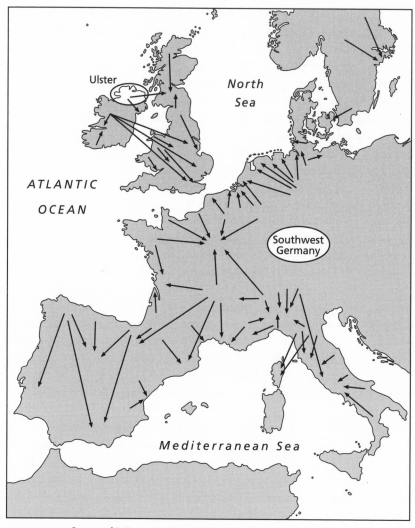

FIGURE 3.1. Seasonal Migration Areas in Europe Around 1800. *Source:* Lucassen, *Migrant Labour*, as reproduced in Moch, *Moving Europeans*, p. 77. Bubbles for southwest Germany and Ulster have been added.

more options to earn income from nonfarm activities. Money could be made by engaging in protoindustry, traveling to seasonal labor jobs or, by the second quarter of the nineteenth century, working in the growing manufacturing sector of the Ruhr. For example, individuals from north- west Germany had worked seasonally in Holland since before 1700.[31] In areas of Ireland outside of Ulster, individuals had the option of working

[31] Jackson and Moch, "Migration," p. 61; Hochstadt, "Migration," p. 457.

as seasonal labor in England. Large-scale immigration began to occur from wider areas of Germany and Ireland only after transatlantic travel became easier, information improved, and, in the latter case, the potato famine left few alternatives to leaving.

The third important source country for antebellum immigration to the United States was Great Britain. Here, the same issues discussed in Chapter 2 complicate the analysis. Some portion of the British immigrants came from the southern agricultural areas, while others came from the more industrial north. Whatever the proportions among the various areas, however, the tripling of British population between 1750 and 1850 was the likely underlying cause of the immigration. As new industries developed in Britain, workers who used the older methods were forced to seek other jobs. As population increased and Britain began to import more food, fewer of these jobs were in agriculture. The pressures were intensified during depression periods. Although it is unclear who exactly immigrated to the United States from Britain, all studies find that farmers and traditional craft workers were important components of the total.

It has become standard in many recent descriptions of the causes of European emigration during the first half of the nineteenth century to stress the importance of the decline in protoindustry.[32] The argument is that increased competition from British manufacturers after 1815 caused many individuals engaged in household manufacturing to lose their supplemental income, leaving the alternative of emigration. Although this development was almost certainly important in leading to emigration from specific areas, it is not clear how important it was in general, at least before the middle of the century. The specific case usually cited is Westphalia, which was a center of linen weaving.[33] As the low-cost British took the linen market away from German manufacturers, many Westphalians suffered a drop in income and looked to emigrate. Yet, as shown in Chapter 2, immigrants from northwest Germany comprised only about 15 percent of all German antebellum immigrants, and those specifically from Westphalia only about two-thirds of that. In addition, immigration from Westphalia only became significant after 1830. Linen production was important primarily in the Prussian parts of western Germany. The southwest, in particular, did not have much rural industry.[34]

---

[32] For example, see Kamphoefner, *Westfalians*; Moch, *Moving Europeans*, pp. 115–20; and Guinnane, "Population," p. 47.

[33] Kamphoefner, *Westfalians*.

[34] Hochstadt, "Socioeconomic Determinants," p. 145. Parts of Hesse-Cassel also had linen weaving, but immigration from this area was not large until after 1840 and was never a huge part of the German total. See Wegge, "To Part," p. 53.

In Germany as a whole, rural industry continued to expand until about 1850.[35] Only after this time did a general decline in rural industry add to the pressures to emigrate from most areas of Germany. Thus, at least until the 1840s or, perhaps, the 1850s, the decline of rural industry was an important factor in immigration only from areas of Germany that comprised a small part of total immigration.

On the other hand, one of the reasons for immigration from Ulster during the first part of the nineteenth century was the pressure of British manufacturers on Irish household linen production. It is difficult to know, however, the importance of this factor relative to others. Adams suggests that a portion of the early nineteenth-century emigrants had been displaced by the decline in household linen weaving, although he also says the industry survived under government protection until 1830. In addition, he finds the majority of immigrants to the United States before 1830 were farmers, some unknown number of whom would have been engaged in protoindustry.[36] On the other hand, Ó Gráda finds that most immigrants before the famine were laborers. For example, only 12 percent of those going to New York between 1820 and 1846 were textile workers, and another 14 percent were farmers. Not all the farmers would have been engaged in protoindustry, but some of those classified as laborers may have been.[37] In addition, although protoindustry was in decline in Ireland throughout the antebellum period, a substantial number of individuals continued to supplement their income from this source.[38] Before the late 1840s, therefore, it is unlikely that much importance should be given to the decline in protoindustry relative to the effects of the rapid population growth on increasing the population density in connection with the lack of seasonal migration work. After this time, all factors discussed became important and immigration to the United States became significant from many more parts of Germany and Ireland.

Another factor often advanced as important in increasing immigration was the reduction in government restrictions. During the seventeenth and eighteenth centuries, governments equated a larger population with a healthier country. For example, Britain refused to allow skilled artisans to emigrate from the United Kingdom. Many of the large emigrant movements that did occur at this time were because of religious differences.

---

35 Hochstadt, "Socioeconomic Determinants," p. 154.
36 Adams, *Ireland*, pp. 34, 41, 48–53.
37 Ó Gráda, "Across the Briny Ocean," pp. 83–5.
38 Ó Gráda, "Demographic Adjustment," pp. 184–5.

In the early part of the nineteenth century, the government restrictions began to disappear as a more liberal philosophy took hold. In 1819, for example, a British select committee concluded that government should subsidize the emigration of paupers. In 1824, the British ban on the emigration of artisans was removed. By 1827, all British emigration restrictions had been removed.[39] In Ireland, the situation was similar in that only the British-imposed restrictions on emigration existed. In fact, as landlords tried to consolidate land holdings, their interest in promoting immigration increased. Various Irish bodies thus helped a small number of those leaving.[40] On the continent, Prussia abolished personal serfdom and forced service in 1807.[41] The official restrictions that remained for a number of years in other German states began to be ignored. Local officials, who had to directly deal with the surplus population, allowed people to leave despite official policy and, in fact, sometimes subsidized a few of the emigrants.[42] In general, too much is probably made of changes in government policy as a reason that emigration increased. It is much more likely that the direction of causation was the opposite, that is, the rapidly growing population led to potential problems that may have become real ones for the government had emigration not been allowed. Government policy changed to reflect the new reality.

In summary, the major underlying European factor leading to individuals desiring to immigrate to the United States was rapid population growth. Living standards were pressured. Surviving solely through farming became much more difficult. Population densities were the largest in southwest Germany and Ulster. Individuals in these areas also had few methods of supplementing their income in order to remain on the farm. A viable option was to immigrate. Over time, immigration spread to other areas when individuals' economic positions were threatened by the continued rise in population and the expansion of low-cost British manufacturing. Even without many previous immigrants from these other parts of Germany and Ireland, by the late 1830s and 1840s, the reality

---

[39] Zolberg, "International Migration Policies," pp. 247–53.

[40] Fitzpatrick, "Emigration," p. 599, estimates that only 5% of Irish emigrants between 1810 and 1870 received government or private assistance. The 5% figure has been generally accepted. Recently, however, Norton, *Landlords*, pp. 308–9, has criticized the 5% figure. He uses historical records from an Irish land agency of the time to argue that the true percentage helped – through direct emigration assistance or by being paid to leave their land (money that often was used to fund emigration) – may have been substantially higher.

[41] Osmond, "Land," p. 97; Torpey, *Invention*, p. 59.

[42] Walker, *Germany*, pp. 16–20, 75, 93; Torpey, *Invention*, p. 65.

of immigration had become evident, as had the means to do so. Thus, European immigration spread more easily into newer areas.

Developments in Shipping

The population growth and other developments throughout Western Europe had occurred even during the Napoleonic War era. When the wars ended in 1815, therefore, the potential demand to immigrate to the United States was high. However, the shipping situation was not favorable. Although there had been a substantial increase in the registered tonnage of U.S. shipping during the preceding twenty-five years, little of it was oriented toward carrying passengers. Most passengers coming to the United States traveled either on small trading vessels or on British Post Office ships.[43] As a result, the cost of transatlantic travel was quite high, essentially out of range for many individuals given their income. During the last half of the 1810s, for example, a steerage ticket without provisions from Liverpool to New York cost seven to twelve pounds.[44] Even sailing from Belfast to Quebec cost a minimum of six pounds.[45] These fares comprised an exorbitant portion of a laborer's annual earnings, which has been estimated at ten to fifteen pounds in Ireland before the potato famine.[46] Prices were also high from the Continent, with fares of fifteen to twenty-five pounds for the trip from Holland to Philadelphia between 1815 and the early 1820s.[47] Thus, many Germans fleeing in 1816 could not afford the passage and became stranded in the Netherlands.[48] Some Germans were so anxious to travel during this period that the indentured servant system was revived for a short time. Under this system, which had carried perhaps half of the German passengers to the United States during the 1700s, individuals would sell their labor services for a period of years in exchange for passage across the Atlantic Ocean.[49] Not many

---

[43] Hutchins, *American Maritime Industries*, p. 233. During the eighteenth century, merchants in Rotterdam, along with their contacts in England and the United States, began to specialize in the movement of immigrants across the Atlantic Ocean. See Wokeck, *Trade*. The Napoleonic War period disrupted the eighteenth-century transatlantic transportation system. In Bremen and Hamburg, recovery of shipping after 1815 was slow. See Mustafa, *Merchants*, pp. 181–227.

[44] Jones, "Background," p. 16.

[45] Adams, *Ireland*, p. 93.

[46] Ó Gráda, "Across the Briny Ocean," p. 87.

[47] Grubb, "The Long-Run Trend," p. 184.

[48] Walker, *Germany*, pp. 28–29, estimates that 50,000 individuals from Baden attempted to leave, but only 15,000 actually succeeded. Most of the remainder returned to Germany.

[49] Galenson, *White Servitude*.

captains carried poorer people who wanted to indenture themselves or a member of their family, however, when carrying capacity was limited and many paying passengers were available in 1816 and 1817.

In the immediate aftermath of the Napoleonic Wars, government restrictions on who could trade between countries also inhibited shipping. These began to change very quickly, however. The United States signed a Reciprocity Treaty with Britain in 1815 and with many countries on the Continent during the first half of the 1820s.[50] Each treaty allowed ships from both countries to trade between the two. These treaties were a potential boon to the United States because the country had a comparative advantage in building ships due to its plentiful supplies of lumber. After the American Revolution ended, however, Great Britain imposed restrictions on the importation of U.S. lumber. Instead, the British began to import lumber from their colonies, especially Canada, as British sources of timber were exhausted. Two consequences resulted. First, the cost of British shipbuilding rose relative to that in the United States. Hutchins estimated that the cost of building a ship in the United States during the antebellum period was only about half that in Britain.[51] The British began to specialize in producing high-quality ships (including warships) and small coastwise vessels. Neither of these types of vessels provided much competition for the U.S. companies, which built ships for transatlantic trade and travel. Nor did British or European shipping companies buy many U.S.-built ships, because the countries also provided protection for domestic shipbuilders. Thus, U.S.-owned shipping companies dominated the basic trade between Europe and the United States.[52] Second, the ships arriving from Canada with timber were available to carry passengers back to Canada, because these ships did not usually go to the United States. Due to the available space, passage costs to Canada began to fall relative to those to the United States. In the early 1820s, an individual could travel from Ireland to Quebec for two to three pounds, although rates through Liverpool to New York were still five to seven pounds.[53]

[50] Hutchins, *American Maritime Industries*, pp. 252–3.
[51] Hutchins, *American Maritime Industries*, pp. 170–1, 202, 221.
[52] Hutchins, *American Maritime Industries*, pp. 203–6.
[53] Jones, "Background," p. 16; Adams, *Ireland*, p. 154. Edward Phillips, one the immigrants introduced in Chapter 1, paid slightly more than thirty-one pounds in 1820 to bring over his wife and five younger children, and comments the total was the "cheapest passage I could get." If the child fare was one-half the adult fare, then the adult fare would have been just under nine pounds. In an 1821 letter to his brother, he comments that his brother could send his young son for three pounds, and their other brother could come for six pounds. See Erickson, *Invisible Immigrants*, pp. 265–9. Phillips's nephew, also named Edward Phillips, did in fact immigrate to the United States in 1821.

Between 1818 and 1830, a number of developments occurred that resulted in an increased supply of passenger shipping to the United States. The first was the founding of the sailing-packet lines, shipping companies that sailed on a set schedule. Before the development of these companies, a passenger had to find a ship and wait until it was ready to leave port. Because most ships primarily carried freight, the wait usually depended on the captain getting a full cargo of freight. The desires of passengers were secondary. The first successful packet line was the Black Ball Line, which began operations between New York and Liverpool with four ships in January 1818.[54] The owners gambled that shippers of products would be attracted by fixed sailing dates, and this effect would outweigh any losses from the ships leaving occasionally without a full cargo. In fact, the line became sufficiently successful that they increased their sailings in 1822, and two additional New York to Liverpool lines soon began operations. Other new packet companies began service to Le Havre in 1822 and London in 1824. By 1825, twenty-eight ships were being used in the various packet lines.

The development of the packet companies may have assisted passenger travel more indirectly than directly. A fixed sailing date lowered the cost of travel for passengers, because they would spend less time and money finding a ship and waiting for it to leave port, so the packets were certainly attractive to passengers. The companies, however, were not much interested in steerage passengers. Their profits lay in attracting "fine freight, cabin passengers, mail, and specie."[55] Steerage passengers would occupy the same space as the more profitable fine freight. Thus, the packet lines only carried a limited number of steerage passengers. For example, in 1826, there were forty-seven packets and sixty-three nonpackets that arrived in New York. The packets carried 454 cabin passengers and 295 in steerage. In contrast, the nonpackets carried 131 cabin passengers and 2,032 in steerage.[56] The only packet companies that carried large numbers of steerage passengers in the 1820s were the Le Havre lines, presumably because less fine freight left from that port. On the routes to the other ports, therefore, the packets primarily increased space for steerage passengers indirectly. The packets took

---

[54] The discussion in this paragraph and the next follows Albion, *Square-Riggers*, pp. 15–46. A few earlier attempts had been made to establish packet lines. See Hutchins, *American Maritime Industries*, pp. 233–4.

[55] Albion, *Square-Riggers*, p. 28. "Fine freight" at this time was mainly cotton and woolen goods and manufactures.

[56] Albion, *Square-Riggers*, p. 248.

freight and cabin traffic away from the nonpackets, which led to the latter ships carrying more steerage passengers in order to remain in business.[57]

In total, the 1820s saw a large increase in the number and size of ships that could carry passengers. Between 1818 and 1832, seventy-six ships were built for the New York packet lines. Although passengers were not their first choice of cargo, the increased number of ships sailing between Europe and the United States would have led to more instances when passengers were carried. In general, the American shipbuilding industry constructed new shipping at a consistent pace. Between 1816 and 1829, an average of ninety thousand tons of new ships was built each year.[58] With the increased attention to passenger travel, more of these new ships were designed to carry passengers. By 1830, in fact, vessels that carried passengers across the Atlantic Ocean had been differentiated from ordinary tramp freighters. The newer ships were also larger. The average size of a ship built during the last half of the 1810s was 366 tons, whereas those built in the last half of the 1820s averaged 561 tons. Each ship built during the latter period could therefore carry more passengers.[59] Thus, the period of the 1820s saw an increase in the volume of shipping available for passengers and an increased interest in carrying passengers on the part of many shippers.[60] Because these shippers were U.S.-run companies, the supply increase was particularly large on routes to the United States.

Other factors related to the expansion of shipping services were the establishment of ticket offices, company agents, and other aids to emigration. Offices that specialized in selling transatlantic passages were formed as early as 1817 in Ireland. These businesses quickly began advertising their rates, available ships, and dates of embarkation. Not surprisingly, most of the advertisements were in northern Irish newspapers, although some also appeared in newspapers in the south.[61] By the 1820s, the passenger broker business had been established. In Liverpool, the firm of Fitzhugh and Grimshaw began chartering vessels to carry passengers,

---

[57] Somewhat ironically, when steamships began regularly crossing the Atlantic during the 1840s and 1850s, the first types of business they took away from the packet companies were fine freight and cabin passengers, forcing them to turn to steerage passengers to stay in business.

[58] Calculated from information in Hutchins, *American Maritime Industries*, p. 189.

[59] Hutchins, *American Maritime Industries*, p. 215.

[60] See the discussion in Jones, "Background," pp. 12–13.

[61] Adams, *Ireland*, pp. 76–7.

advertising the ships in British and Irish newspapers, and sending agents throughout both countries to sell tickets and generally try to attract business. The practice of agents traveling the countryside to sell tickets was also apparent on the Continent. In both settings, the entry of competitors ensured that fares remained as low as feasible.[62] Thus, whereas in earlier times passengers wanting to cross the Atlantic Ocean usually had to find an available ship, the period of the 1820s saw, in many ways, the establishment (or reestablishment) of a shipping business that sought out passengers.

Declines in the Cost of Immigration

The increased supply of passenger shipping caused the fares for transatlantic travel to the United States to fall into the early 1830s. From the five-to seven-pound or higher rate that prevailed during the early 1820s, fares declined to four to five pounds during the last few years of the 1820s.[63] Passage costs to the United States remained above those to Canada, however, which in 1827 were two to three pounds. Fares to the United States finally fell close to those to Canada in 1831 and 1832. Adams describes an "extraordinary drop in fares to the United States which began about 1831" apparently caused by a falloff in the timber trade, which caused a surplus of shipping to develop.[64] One could now travel from Ireland through Liverpool to the United States for a fare of from three pounds to three pounds and ten shillings. Fares to the United States direct from Ireland may have been more expensive. Fitzpatrick cites a case where steerage passage from Ireland to New York cost four and a half pounds in 1832.[65] During most of the remainder of the antebellum period, fares from both the United Kingdom and the Continent stayed in the general

---

[62] Jones, "Background," pp. 16–17; Doerries, "German Transatlantic Migration," pp. 122–3.

[63] Jones, "Background," p. 16; Adams, *Ireland*, p. 161. Both authors obtain their data on fares from newspapers, although some of Jones's data are based on testimony in one of the British Parliamentary Papers. Actually, much work remains to be done on fares, especially in determining a consistent time series. In addition, a good deal of truth is contained in a statement made in Taylor's book: "The fare for emigrants using sailing ships 'necessarily varies,' as one commentator put it in 1856, 'more or less on each ship' depending on the time of year, competition, and masters and agents determinations of what the market would bear." See Taylor, *Distant Magnet*, p. 94.

[64] Adams, *Ireland*, p. 162.

[65] Fitzpatrick, "Emigration," p. 581.

range of three pounds and ten shillings to five pounds, except for a few specific years.[66]

The rates that began to prevail during the early 1830s were generally as low as or lower than those in the eighteenth century, although fare information for earlier periods is sparse. It is believed that fares during most of the colonial period averaged five to six pounds in peacetime.[67] More specifically, Grubb estimated the cost of shipping German indentured servants before 1773 was five to ten pounds in peacetime with no significant variation over time. Fares for this group then doubled between 1773 and 1815 before reaching the very high levels after 1815.[68] On the other hand, Kelly found a Belfast newspaper that listed a fare of three pounds and five shillings in 1773. A similar rate apparently prevailed in 1791, although it is not known how typical these were.[69] Whatever the specific numbers for the colonial period, by the early 1830s, fares were as low as they had ever been. In fact, the overall costs of immigrating for passengers fell even more than the fare decrease because of the greater certainty of leaving at a specific time.

However, the decline in fares is only part of the reason for the large fall in the cost of immigration that occurred. An equally important factor was the development of new mechanisms that allowed more individuals to be able to afford those fares. The most important change was the development of the remittance system. Here, previous immigrants would either send money back home or buy prepaid tickets for their friends or family from a shipping company or a shipmaster.[70] As early as 1816, two-thirds of the passengers on one ship from Belfast to Boston had prepaid tickets; such tickets were common on voyages to Canada in the early 1820s.[71] By the early 1830s, remittances and prepaid tickets for Irish passengers

---

[66] Gould, "European Inter-Continental Emigration," p. 612. Adams cites fares of two to two and a half pounds in 1834 and one to one and a half pounds in the early 1840s. See Adams, *Ireland*, pp. 162, 229. Wegge finds fares from Bremen to New York averaged about 4.3 pounds between 1832 and 1857, although the fare fell to 3 pounds in 1843 and rose to 7 pounds in 1854. See Wegge, "Chain Migration," p. 975. I converted her average fare of about 30 thaler into pounds using historical exchange rates. Also, see the description of fares in Taylor, *Distant Magnet*, p. 94. Keeling has suggested a slightly higher range of five to six pounds. Keeling, *Business*.

[67] Walton and Rockoff, *History*, p. 35.

[68] Grubb, "Long-Run Trend," p. 183.

[69] Kelly, "Resumption," p. 70.

[70] For a more complete discussion of how previous immigration lowers the cost for future immigrants, see Massey et al., "Theories," pp. 448–50.

[71] Adams, *Ireland*, pp. 96, 101–2, 149. Adams' source for the two-thirds figure is a Belfast newspaper.

had become widespread, both to the United States and Canada. Fitzhugh
and Grimshaw, the Liverpool shipping agents, sold prepaid tickets worth
more than $12,000 in 1830 and more than $19,000 in 1834, and also
received cash to be transferred to individuals in Ireland. Two Belfast
shipping agents claimed that one-third of their passenger tickets sold
in 1834 had been prepaid in the United States. Remittances paid for
more than one-half of the ten thousand Irish passengers in 1838.[72] By
1846, total remittances to Ireland amounted to more than $1 million.[73]
Less direct information is available on remittances to Great Britain and
Germany until the 1840s. Between 1840 and 1845, North estimated
that total immigrant remittances averaged $1.8 million per year. Of this
total, $0.5 million was to the Continent. No breakdown is provided for
the remainder that was from the United Kingdom.[74] Thus, although the
largest flow of remittances and prepaid tickets was apparently to Ireland,
they were a factor in assisting the immigration of individuals from all of
the source countries.[75]

A variety of other factors also reduced the cost of immigration. Many
times the remittance funds were included with a letter describing conditions and opportunities in the United States. Irish newspapers printed a
number of these letters as early as 1816.[76] Between 1833 and 1835, in
fact, more than 700,000 letters from New York to Ireland went through
the Liverpool post office.[77] Many other letters were sent to people in Great
Britain and Germany and some of these were also published in newspapers.[78] Besides money, the letters often contained information about jobs
and instructions of what to do upon arrival in New York City. Such letters
further reduced the costs to prospective immigrants. Also operating in the
same direction was the huge number of emigrant guides, manuals, and
travel accounts published throughout Europe. Between 1835 and 1860,
more than two hundred travel guides were published in Great Britain

[72] Adams, *Ireland*, pp. 180–1, 226.
[73] Fitzpatrick, "Emigration," p. 600.
[74] North, "United States Balance of Payments," pp. 614–15. In fact, North provides esti-
    mates for remittances back to 1820, but does so based on the volume of immigration
    three years earlier and a constant per-migrant remittance, so the accuracy of the earlier
    figures is not clear.
[75] Wegge, "Chain Migration," provides empirical evidence on the importance of "chain
    migration" in Hesse-Cassel in Germany between 1832 and 1857.
[76] Adams, *Ireland*, pp. 100–1, 180.
[77] Fitzpatrick, "Emigration," p. 584.
[78] Erickson, *Invisible Immigrants*; Kamphoefner et al., *News*; Jones, "Background,"
    pp. 19–20; Walker, *Germany*, pp. 62–3.

alone.[79] Finally, improvements in internal transportation within Europe reduced the immigrants' cost of getting to the port of embarkation. These changes are discussed in Chapter 5.[80]

Given that fares to Canada are thought to have been low by the early 1820s, one issue that needs to be addressed is why more people did not sail to Canada and then travel on to the United States. To a certain extent, immigrants did use this route but mainly those from Ireland. The timber ships from Canada usually did not go to the Continent, a fact that limited the passenger market to Canada. During the early 1820s, however, quite a few Irish immigrants sailed for Canada. It has been estimated that perhaps 90 percent of the Irish sailing to Canada during the 1820s went on to the United States. However, moving to the United States by traveling overland after arriving in Canada was not easy or cheap at the time. It was possible to move into the northeast United States by steamboat, because these began operating on Lake Ontario in 1817 and Lake Champlain in 1816.[81] Yet using these required an additional cost and they were limited as to destination. Reaching many parts of the United States would have required taking both a steamboat and then traveling overland. Thus, for the poorer passengers who sailed directly to Canada, getting to most destinations in the United States might not have been very much cheaper than sailing directly to the country.

A final issue to consider is how important the decline in the costs of immigration was to explaining the abrupt increase in the volume of immigration to the United States in 1831 and 1832. Although clearly of importance, other events also appear to have been important. In particular, by the early 1830s, the state of the U.S. economy had improved from the 1820s, an event that is discussed in greater detail in the next chapter. Furthermore, Europe experienced record cold in the winter of 1829–30. Bread prices increased to extremely high levels during the next winter. Unrest broke out in parts of Europe in 1830 and the situation continued to be unsettled through 1832.[82] Finally, cholera outbreaks occurred during 1832 and 1834 and some individuals may have immigrated to flee this disease.[83] The response of Europeans to these events was to emigrate.

---

[79] Jones, "Background," p. 19.

[80] For the 1900–14 period, Keeling, *Business*, has estimated the actual transatlantic fare paid by an immigrant accounted for only about one-half of the total costs of migrating. Arguably, the fare portion might have been even smaller during the antebellum years.

[81] Bukowczyk, "Migration," p. 30.

[82] Hansen, *Atlantic Migration*, pp. 120–7.

[83] Hansen, *Atlantic Migration*, p. 127.

Large numbers were able to do so because of the greater amount of shipping, the presence of remittances, the generally low fares, and improved prospects in the United States.

Summary

It is of interest to speculate about the course of average annual immigrant volume had the Napoleonic Wars not occurred. The argument in this chapter suggests the volume would not have jumped around 1830; instead, the increase would have been more gradual. Population in Europe began a sustained rise during the last half of the eighteenth century. Although farmers were able to increase food production, the larger population eventually put pressure on the standard of living, at least for parts of society. Thus, over time the demand for immigration services increased substantially, especially in Ulster and southwest Germany where population density was high and the possibilities of earning seasonal income off the farm were limited. Had the outbreak of the Napoleonic Wars not occurred – which led to a disruption of shipping and caused high transatlantic transportation costs into the 1820s – more individuals would have left Europe between 1790 and 1830. In reality, the jump in immigration around 1830 had to await a number of developments that reduced the costs of immigration and improved the ability of potential immigrants to pay those fares. The supply of ships designed to carry passengers increased, remittances in the form of prepaid tickets and cash sent home to friends and family became more important, the volume of letters sent back to Europe providing information about the United States increased, better information concerning the immigration process developed, and government restrictions on leaving Europe declined. The only factor that might have kept immigrant volume low before 1830 was slow growth in the United States, but that assumes U.S. growth would have been the same without the Napoleonic Wars.

After the early 1830s, shipping continued to increase by sizeable amounts, driven by the developing cotton trade as well as a rise in passenger travel. The growing demand for passenger service resulted from immigration spreading into new areas of Germany and Ireland as information became more widespread and protoindustry began to be pressured. The volume of shipping kept up with the higher demand so fares did not show any trend after the early 1830s. Much of the increase in shipping occurred among U.S. companies, which remained the major player on the transatlantic route until the late 1850s. The total tonnage of all U.S. shipping increased from 1.2 million gross tons in 1830 to 5.5 million gross tons in 1861.[84] The number of ships operated by the packet companies increased from thirty-six in 1830 to fifty-six in 1855. Many other ships carried on a regular trade of cotton to Europe and immigrants to the United States.[85] The ships continued to grow in size. The average tonnage rose from 561 tons in 1830 to 1,500 tons in 1850.[86] During the latter years of the antebellum period, shipping also increased from other sources. Beginning in the middle 1840s, as sources of timber near the East Coast became exhausted in the United States, Canadian-built ships became more competitive. British companies began to purchase and use these ships to carry both freight and passengers. In addition, British shipbuilding firms were able to access new European sources of ship timber, allowing them to remain in business even after the British Navigation Acts were repealed in 1849.[87] Therefore, when the potato famine drastically increased the demand for transatlantic transportation beginning in 1847, quite a bit of shipping was available to meet that demand.

[84] Hutchins, *American Maritime Industries*, p. 272.
[85] Albion, *Square-Riggers*, p. 274.
[86] Hutchins, *American Maritime Industries*, pp. 260–2.
[87] Hutchins, *American Maritime Industries*, pp. 301–9.

4

Push, Pull, and Other Factors in Antebellum Immigration

The last chapter examined the increasing desire to emigrate from Europe and the declining cost of immigration into the late 1820s as reasons for a jump in the volume of immigration. This chapter completes the story by including an examination of economic conditions in the United States. More generally, however, the chapter investigates whether antebellum immigration can be explained by using the concepts of push factors – events in Europe – and pull factors – events in the United States. In fact, it is argued that few changes in immigrant volume can be explained as being due solely to either push factors or pull factors. One possible exception concerns fluctuations in U.S. economic activity – a pull factor – that has often been found to cause a change in immigration. Sufficient data exist to allow an empirical examination of aspects of this relationship for the antebellum years. Even here, however, the connection is found to be far from exact. Thus, no simple or consistent factors explain the rising volume of immigration and the yearly fluctuations in the flow during the entire antebellum period. Overall, however, the analysis in this chapter results in a more comprehensive explanation for both the sharp increase in immigration around 1830 and the generally rising volume through 1860.

Push and Pull Factors: A Definition and Previous Work

The model of immigration presented in Chapter 3 suggests that immigration occurred when individuals expected their economic situation in the United States to exceed that in Europe, and the difference was sufficiently large to cover the monetary and psychic costs of migrating. The potential immigrant having sufficient knowledge of the various benefits and costs also influenced the decision. In a similar manner, the model can be used to explain changes in the volume of immigration over time. Presumably, if the economic gain from migrating increased (decreased), because of either a deterioration (an improvement) in conditions in Europe or an improvement (a deterioration) in conditions in the United States, then the volume of immigration would increase (decrease), other things remaining constant. The first of these – changes in conditions in Europe – are usually referred to as *push factors*, while the latter – changes in conditions in the United States – are called *pull factors*.[1] However, even the simple model of immigration discussed in Chapter 3 suggests that immigrant volume could increase because of changes in other factors, such as a decline in the monetary or psychic costs of immigrating. Thus, push and pull factors by themselves cannot provide a comprehensive method for examining changes in the volume of immigration.

It is useful at this point to recast the analysis in Chapter 3 – explaining the secular increase in the volume of immigration that occurred around 1830 – in terms of the various factors. The underlying cause of the increased desire to immigrate was a push factor, which was rapid population growth in Europe that caused a decline in the standard of living. However, one important event was neither a push nor a pull factor: improvements in the shipping market led to a decline in transportation costs. The argument in Chapter 3 also placed some importance on an increase in the volume of remittances from previous migrants (neither a push nor a pull factor by our definition), a decline in European government restrictions on leaving (again, neither push nor pull), and an increase in information about the United States among potential immigrants (a pull factor). Finally, the chapter also suggested that an improvement in economic conditions in the United States contributed to the increase (another pull factor).[2] Thus, the secular increase in immigrant volume occurring around 1830 resulted from a combination of push and pull factors, as well as factors that are properly classified as neither.

Early attempts at testing for the importance of push and pull factors were made by Harry Jerome, Brinley Thomas, and Dorothy Thomas.[3] These researchers related changes in immigration (either in total or from

---

[1] For a formal model that defines push and pull factors in this manner, see Wegge, "Push and Pull Migration." Her paper has clarified my thinking on these issues.

[2] This factor is discussed in greater detail in a subsequent section of this chapter.

[3] Jerome, *Migration*; Thomas, *Migration*; and Thomas, *Social and Economic Aspects*.

one country) to changes in the time series of U.S. economic variables and, if possible to changes in European economic variables. For example, although it greatly simplifies the complexity of his analysis, Brinley Thomas related immigration from England to U.S. railway building. For the period from 1831 until the late 1860s, he found that railroad building lagged immigration, while he found the opposite relationship for the period after 1870, although he replaced railroad building with overall investment.[4] On this basis, Brinley Thomas suggested that push factors were more important before the Civil War, especially during the late 1840s and early 1850s, and pull factors were more important after the Civil War.[5] The results of the other researchers for the period after the Civil War were similar. A criticism of this approach is that it is designed to determine whether push factors or pull factors were most important, that is, it does not allow both push and pull factors to be important at the same time, nor does it allow for the importance of factors that are neither push nor pull.[6]

In the 1960s and 1970s, an econometric literature developed that attempted to test for the importance of push and pull factors. Researchers used an empirical model where the annual volume of immigration was related to some combination of income or wage or population variables in both countries (or a variable measuring the differential between the countries), unemployment variables in both countries, and a variable or variables measuring previous immigration from a country.[7] Because of data constraints, most of this literature addressed immigration after the Civil War. A variety of different conclusions was reached. For example, Williamson concluded that positive pull factors and negative push factors operated in the period after 1870.[8]

Both at the time and subsequently, the econometric literature has been criticized.[9] One theoretical issue is that the volume of immigration is

---

[4] Thomas, *Migration*, pp. 92–4.

[5] Thomas, *Migration*, pp. 94–6.

[6] In particular, see the discussion in Wegge, "Push and Pull Migration."

[7] For examples of this literature relating to immigration to the United States, see Gallaway and Vedder, "Emigration"; Moe, *Demographic Developments*; Quigley, "Economic Model"; Tomaske, "Determinants"; Wilkinson, "European Migration"; Thomas, *Migration*, and Williamson, "Migration."

[8] Williamson, "Migration," p. 370.

[9] In particular, see Gould, "European Inter-Continental Emigration," pp. 622–70; Williamson, "Migration," pp. 363–9; and Neal, "Cross-Spectral Analysis." For a more recent critique, see Wegge, "Push and Pull Migration." The discussion in the next few paragraphs generally follows Gould and Wegge.

related to the *level* of explanatory variables. The definition of push and pull factors used here suggests the volume of immigration should be related to *changes* in the level of the explanatory variables, and not to the levels themselves. A second issue is that, given the difficulty of returning to Europe during the antebellum period, the immigration decision was based on the differential in expected lifetime incomes, and not based on differences in incomes over a short period. Therefore, the use of annual variables to measure expected lifetime incomes is inappropriate. For example, an increase (or a decrease) in incomes or wages during a particular year may have had little effect on lifetime incomes. Similarly, some researchers attempted to proxy the standard of living in the country of origin by using either the population growth rate or the birthrate, where each was lagged twenty years. Again, the theoretical connection of either variable to the *annual* volume of immigration is not clear.[10] Essentially, changes in an annual level of an income, wage, or population variable in a country or between countries may have had no effect on an existing differential in expected lifetime incomes, the factor that fundamentally drove immigration.

Of all the variables used in the econometric work, the most significant were those measuring previous immigration from a country, either as the total stock of migrants in the United States from that country or as the number who had arrived in the previous year or two. Sometimes both variables were used. The idea was that previous immigration from a country (the "friends and family effect") made it easier for others to follow, because the followers would have better information, might have prepaid tickets, and could get assistance in finding a job upon arrival. In analyzing the literature, Gould showed that relating current immigration to previous immigration provided excellent econometric results, even without any other variable being included. His conclusion was that the literature primarily showed "the rates of migration from various countries of origin to the U.S.A... were determined by much the same factors as in earlier decades – only we don't know what they were!"[11]

---

[10] In some parts of Germany, education ended at age 14, making this age a logical time at which to migrate to the United States. A lagged population growth variable might, therefore, reflect this event. Yet in many parts of Germany, as well as Ireland and Great Britain, education was far from universal, which would reduce this factor as a reason to use a lagged population variable.

[11] Gould, "European Inter-Continental Emigration," p. 660. Note the same criticism is made in Chapter 7 concerning studies of where the immigrants settled in the United States.

The variable that successfully explained some of the changes in annual immigrant volume, and that was a pull factor, was the unemployment rate in the United States.[12] Even after accounting for all the other factors affecting migration, an individual might be in a situation where they would benefit from immigration and still not move immediately. In particular, because the impetus for moving was to increase one's expected lifetime income, an individual would be less likely to make a current move if the odds were temporarily not favorable for finding a job in the United States relative to the home country. During the antebellum years, when the voyage by sail was quite long, an individual who moved at the "wrong" time could not easily go back to Europe. Thus, those immigrants who quickly needed to find a job in the United States had to be sure to migrate at a time when they would be able to find work. That was not likely to be the case when the United States was experiencing a high level of unemployment. Although potentially of importance, a change in the unemployment rate ignores many other influences on the immigration decision and thus, by itself, is most useful in explaining a change in immigrant volume at a certain time. Given its theoretical importance, later sections of this chapter specifically explore the empirical relationship between unemployment and immigrant volume for the antebellum period.

The Importance of Push, Pull, and Other Factors: 1832–1860

Because the empirical literature has not been very successful in explaining the reasons for the generally increasing volume of immigration between 1832 and 1860, this section takes a non-empirical approach. Doing so allows us to consider push, pull, and other factors at the same time, something the empirical literature does not do. The downside to a non-empirical approach, however, is that the relative contribution of the various factors can be determined only in very general terms.

Although showing a number of fluctuations, annual immigrant volume grew from more than fifty thousand in 1832 to more than one hundred thousand in 1845 (see Table 2.1 and Figure 2.1). A general explanation for this increase must again rely on a number of different factors. As shown later in this chapter and in Chapter 8, the U.S. economy continued to grow and real wages continued to increase. Thus, jobs were available

---

[12] For example, see Gallaway and Vedder, "Emigration," and Moe, *Demographic Developments*.

in most years for the arriving immigrants. Another pull factor was that information about opportunities in the United States spread to more parts of Europe, resulting in an increasing volume of immigration from these areas. On the push side, population growth continued in the European source countries, as did the disruptive effects of British industrialization. As described in Chapter 3, many European workers were forced to find other work opportunities. In short, both push and pull factors help to explain the continued increase in the volume of immigration. However, a factor that was neither push nor pull was also important. As the United States became home to a larger volume of immigrants, the funds sent back to Europe likely grew and made the transatlantic trip affordable for more individuals.[13] Thus, as in the explanation for the increase in immigration around 1830, push, pull, and other factors were all important in explaining the continued increase in the volume of immigration in subsequent years.

Beginning in 1846, immigrant volume rose by huge amounts, finally peaking at an antebellum record of over four hundred thousand in 1854. Virtually every economic historian would explain this increase as resulting from push factors, which were the outbreak of the potato famine in Ireland in 1846 and a variety of troubles on the Continent. Although these events were the precipitating causes of the increase in immigration, pull factors must have had some importance. After all, a larger percentage of the Irish (and the Germans) could have looked for work somewhere other than the United States. For example, many of the Irish went to Great Britain and a larger percentage would have done so had job opportunities not been available in the United States. Fortuitously for the starving masses, and as discussed later in this chapter, the U.S. economy grew rapidly during this time. In addition, given the horrific conditions in Ireland, previous immigrants to the United States probably provided a larger than normal amount of remittances (a factor that is neither push nor pull) in order to help relatives and friends emigrate. In this case, one might argue that pull and other factors increased in response to the huge push effect of the potato famine. Thus, from the perspective of immigration to the United States, push, pull, and other factors all explain

---

[13] For example, North, "United States Balance of Payments," pp. 614–15, assumes that the volume of remittances varied directly with the stock of previous immigrants. Another "other" factor, transatlantic fares, did not show any trend after 1830, but certainly fluctuations in fares from year to year could have also affected the volume of immigration in any specific year.

part of the increased volume. Although push factors probably accounted for most of the explanation, by themselves they do not provide a complete explanation.

Finally, immigrant volume underwent a sudden decline beginning in 1855, and the volume remained relatively low until after the Civil War. The causes of this event are discussed in more detail later in this chapter. For now, it is sufficient to say that both push factors and pull factors had some importance in explaining the large decline in volume.

Based on the discussion in this section, trying to determine whether push factors or pull factors were more important in explaining the trends in antebellum immigration is likely to be a fruitless exercise. Both types of factors were generally important, and it is apparent that the relative importance of the different types of factors varied at different times. In fact, factors that are not properly classified as either push or pull factors were sometimes critical to changing the volume of immigration. In addition, it appears that, during at least some periods, the operation of one factor may have caused some of the other factors to become more or less important. Thus, it is probably impossible to come to a firm conclusion as to the relative importance of the various factors.[14] As noted earlier, however, one circumstance when pull factors might have been of primary importance was when a downturn in the U.S. economy caused a downturn in immigration. It is to this relationship we now turn.

The Immigration–Economic Downturn Connection

The tendency for the volume of immigration to decline when there is an increase in unemployment in the United States – resulting from a downturn in the business cycle – is well supported.[15] Harry Jerome did the original work in this area in 1926.[16] He found a close relationship between the volume of immigration and economic activity for the period after the Civil War. The more recent econometric literature discussed

---

[14] The conclusion here is quite different from the impression given in Kenwood and Lougheed, *Growth*, pp. 47–8, who say: "During the first sixty years of the nineteenth century there is no doubt that the forces operating to generate intercontinental movements of labour were mainly of the 'push' type...." These authors, however, qualify this statement by discussing not only "the demographic and technological revolutions" in Europe but also the growth of financial assistance and transportation developments.

[15] For example, the authors of a leading textbook say "...the shorter-term fluctuations in emigrations seem to be systematically related to the business cycle (in) the United States." See Atack and Passell, *New Economic View*, pp. 233–4.

[16] Jerome, *Migration*.

earlier, which primarily uses the unemployment rate as a measure of economic activity, has found similar results. For the antebellum period, however, evidence on the relationship is more limited. Jerome's conclusion was: "(t)he evidence considered ... suggests that prior to the Civil War, although the relation between industrial conditions in (the United States) and the fluctuations in immigration is not obviously close, there is, nevertheless, some tendency for the effects of a depression to be evident in immigration after a period of time somewhat irregular in duration." [17] This statement is hardly a ringing endorsement of a close relationship between U.S. economic activity and immigration during the antebellum years. Given that Jerome's work was published in 1926, however, he had limited data available for the antebellum years – no direct measures of Gross Domestic Product, Industrial Production, or unemployment. Thus, it is not surprising that his conclusion was tentative. In fact, Jerome reached his conclusion based on a relationship between immigrant volume and the volume of U.S. imports, because the latter tends to be directly related to overall economic activity. Thus, the direct relationship between economic activity and immigrant volume is best supported for the post-bellum years. Given Jerome's results and the change in travel conditions brought on by the steamship, the relationship may have differed during the antebellum years.

Investigating the relationship for the antebellum years between economic activity and the volume of immigration is complicated by a number of issues, which are discussed in the appendix to this chapter. Although different measures of U.S. economic activity are available, a particularly appropriate measure for the antebellum period is Industrial Production because most immigrants found jobs in manufacturing or mining (see Chapter 7). Annual data on this variable are now available. [18] This section then examines the relationship between downturns in this variable and declines in the calendar year volume of immigration. [19] Given the existing data are yearly, a downturn in immigration could occur in either the same

---

[17] Jerome, *Migration*, p. 82. In his work, Jerome examines deviations from seven-year moving averages.

[18] Davis, "Annual Index." No annual index of output in agriculture, a sector attractive to some immigrants (see Chapter 7), is available. Annual GDP estimates are available in *Historical Statistics*, but these are quite conjectural for the antebellum period whereas Davis' index is based on the output of forty-three manufacturing and mining industries. See the discussions in Carter, *Historical Statistics*, pp. 3-27 to 3-28.

[19] Estimates of the volume of calendar-year immigration are developed in the appendix to this chapter. In particular, see Table A4.1. The appendix also discusses a variety of theoretical and data issues concerning the data used in this section.

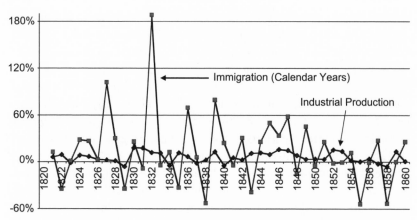

FIGURE 4.1. Fluctuations in Immigration and Industrial Production. *Sources:* Immigration percentage changes are calculated from Table A4.1. Industrial Production percentage changes are calculated from Davis, "Annual Index," Table III, p. 1189.

year as the decline in Industrial Production or the next year. The largest portion of immigration during a calendar year occurred during the spring and summer. Thus, if the downturn in Industrial Production began early in the calendar year, immigrant volume could have declined that same year. If the downturn began in the last half of the calendar year, then annual immigrant volume would probably not fall until the next calendar year.[20] In addition, not only should a decline in Industrial Production cause a downturn in immigration, but if the relationship is close between the variables, then all the downturns in immigration should be preceded by or contemporaneous with a decline in Industrial Production.

The annual percentage changes in both Industrial Production and the volume of calendar year immigration are presented in Figure 4.1. Ignoring the early 1820s when the volume of immigration was small and the immigration figures are most suspect, five periods exist when a decline in Industrial Production occurred: 1829, 1834, 1837, 1840, and 1857–8. In four of these periods – 1829, 1834, 1837, and 1857–8 – the volume of immigration underwent a substantial fall in either that year or the next.[21] The other year, 1840, is followed by a decline in immigrant volume in 1841,

---

[20] The analysis implies that potential immigrants in Europe received information concerning an economic downturn in a fairly short period. In fact, most economic historians believe that information did flow back to Europe very quickly. See the excellent discussion on this point in Gould, "European Inter-Continental Emigration," pp. 648–54.

[21] This finding also holds if the fiscal year values of immigration are used.

although the percentage decrease is much smaller than in the other ante-bellum years when Industrial Production declined. Finally, it is interesting to note that the largest decline in Industrial Production occurred during 1857–8, a well-known period of depression. During 1858, immigrant volume underwent one of its largest percentage declines, even though volume had already experienced a large decrease in 1855. Overall, this evidence is consistent with the belief that a decline in U.S. Industrial Pro-duction during the antebellum years caused a decline in the volume of immigration.[22]

Consider next the years when a decline in immigration is observed. Because of the uncertainty in the calendar year estimates of immigrant volume, the analysis ignores the years when the decline in this variable was small. Doing so leaves six years (ignoring 1822) when the estimated calendar year immigrant volume declined by at least 30 percent from the previous year – 1829, 1835, 1838, 1843, 1855, and 1858. As noted in the last paragraph, four of these years – 1829, 1835, 1838, and 1858 – are either contemporaneous with or immediately follow a year when Industrial Production declined. The declines in immigrant volume during the other two years – 1843 and 1855 – occurred even though Industrial Production did not decline. Thus, factors other than U.S. business condi-tions appear to have been important in explaining some of the downturns in the volume of immigration. In all, this discussion yields a list of seven periods when either Industrial Production or the volume of immigration or both declined.

If a downturn in U.S. business conditions was the primary cause of the decline in immigrant volume, then one other theoretical expectation can be pointed out. Other things being constant, immigration should have fallen by a relatively similar percentage from each of the source countries. Thus, further analysis can be done using the data for the individual coun-tries. For each of the seven periods, Table 4.1 presents evidence on the volume and the percentage change in the volume of immigration from the United Kingdom and Germany.[23] The number of immigrants for whom

---

[22] The correlation coefficient between calendar-year immigration and same-year industrial production is 0.79. The correlation coefficient between calendar-year immigration and previous-year industrial production is 0.76. The fact that immigration would change based on industrial production in either the current *or* the preceding year but not be generally related to industrial production in both years makes econometric analysis problematic, as does the fact that immigration also affected industrial production.

[23] Chapter 2 showed that the individual annual series on volume from Ireland and Great Britain cannot be used before 1847, so these two series are combined in Table 4.1.

TABLE 4.1. *U.S. Industrial Production and Immigration from the United Kingdom and Germany, Selected Years*

Year	Percent Change in U.S. Industrial Production	Immigration from the United Kingdom		Immigration from Germany		Immigration from Country Not Specified
		Volume	Percent Change	Volume	Percent Change	
1828	−6.0%	17,840		1,851		554
1829	(1828–9)	10,594	−40.6%	597	−67.8%	6,695
1834	−4.5%	34,964		17,686		5,069
1835	(1833–4)	29,897	−14.5%	8,311	−53.0%	44
1837	−1.4%	40,726		23,740		4,660
1838	(1836–7)	18,065	−55.6%	11,683	−50.8%	1,843
1840	−4.7%	42,043		29,704		118
1841	(1839–40)	53,960	+28.3%	15,291	−48.5%	627
1842	+2.8%	73,347		20,370		616
1843	(1841–2)	28,100	−61.7%	14,441	−29.1%	612
1854	+0.5%	160,253		215,009		658
1855	(1854–5)	97,199	−39.4%	71,918	−66.6%	334
1857	−5.9%	112,840		91,781		22,301
1858	(1857–8)	55,829	−50.5%	45,310	−50.6%	801

Sources: Percent Change in U.S. Industrial Production: Calculated from Davis, "Annual Index," Table III, p. 1189; Immigration: Carter et al., *Historical Statistics*, Series Ad107, Ad108, Ad111, and Ad97.

the country was "Not Specified" is also shown.[24] The remainder of this section separately investigates each of the seven periods. In each case, we first consider whether an economic downturn occurred and whether immigration declined by similar percentages from each of the two major source countries. The historical literature is also examined to see whether it indicates that an economic downturn took place at the time.

1828–9

Whether the economic downturn in 1829 caused a similar size decrease in immigration from both the United Kingdom and Germany is not clear because of the huge increase in the numbers with country "Not Specified" between 1828 and 1829. Depending on where the "Not Specified" individuals actually left from, the percentages could be similar or vastly different. Here, Davis' index – which shows a 6 percent decline

---

[24] Chapter 2 explained that virtually all of the individuals with country "Not Specified" were actually from a European country.

in 1829 – is in agreement with the limited historical information. Hansen addresses this period and reports that some immigrant returnees to Europe in the fall of 1828 "spread pessimistic reports regarding the opportunities for work" in the United States.[25] Curiously, Adams, the major historian of Irish immigration, does not consider these years even though the records show a 41 percent decline in immigrant volume between 1828 and 1829 from the United Kingdom. Overall, although it is by no means certain, the evidence indicates that a downturn in the U.S. economy was probably the primary cause of the decrease in immigrant volume in 1829.

1834–5

Davis' index shows a substantial decline in Industrial Production in 1834. Although volume declined from both major source countries, the size of the decreases was quite different, even if all the "Not Specified" were actually from the United Kingdom.[26] In most cases, previous historians have not recognized that an economic downturn occurred in 1834. Thus, Davis' index may be incorrect during this period. Instead, historians have resorted to other explanations to explain the decline in immigration during 1835. Adams discusses a variety of factors during 1834 that affected Irish immigration: cholera broke out in Quebec, several hundred emigrants were killed in shipwrecks, the cost of passage rose, a new passenger act took effect, and declines in canal projects and the wages paid to canal workers occurred during the winter of 1834.[27] The latter factor is the only suggestion found in the previous literature that problems in the U.S. economy were a factor in the decrease in immigration. Hansen also cites the shipwrecks and the outbreak of cholera that occurred during 1834. Although he does not directly discuss the state of the economy in 1834 and 1835, Hansen asserts that immigration picked up during 1836 because the "United States was experiencing another period of flush times."[28] None of these explanations, however, explains why immigration from the United Kingdom – from where most of the canal workers would have originated – fell less in percentage terms than that from Germany. Although the downturn in the U.S. economy in 1835 may have been a

---

[25] The information from Hansen in this paragraph is from Hansen, *Atlantic Migration*, pp. 121–2. The quote is on p. 121.
[26] If all 5,069 were from the United Kingdom in 1834, then the decline from here in 1835 would still have been only 25%, far below the 53% decline from Germany.
[27] Adams, *Ireland*, pp. 186–7, 229–30.
[28] Hansen, *Atlantic Migration*, pp. 127, 135. The quote is from p. 135.

factor in decreasing immigrant volume, a comprehensive explanation is missing for this period.

1837–8

The decline in volume in 1838 is virtually equal across the major source countries and thus is fully consistent with being caused by a downturn in U.S. business conditions. In fact, all of the previous research agrees with this assessment. For example, Hansen says that, because of economic problems in the United States, there was "(l)ittle wonder that the movement fell off in the year 1838."[29] Similarly, both Jones and Walker also discuss the U.S. commercial crisis that occurred in 1837.[30] On the other hand, Davis' index indicates that Industrial Production fell by a surprisingly small percentage in 1837, although the increase in 1838 was also small. Apparently, the economy virtually stagnated for about two years. Such a view would be consistent with the U.S. business cycle being the major cause of the decline in immigrant volume in 1838.

1840–1

The downturn in total immigrant volume that occurred between 1840 and 1841 is not consistent with the 4.7 percent observed decline in U.S. Industrial Production in 1840. The problem is that the volume of immigration from the United Kingdom actually increased between 1840 and 1841. Erickson explains that the early 1840s were years "of high food prices, poor harvests, falling real wages and high unemployment" in Great Britain.[31] Thus, even though U.S. conditions were not good, immigrants may have been leaving even worse conditions in Great Britain.[32] As to Germany, the sizeable decline in immigrant volume is what would be expected because of the downturn in the U.S. economy. Walker, although not directly referring to 1840 or 1841, suggests that immigration was directly related to grain prices from 1820 until the middle of the 1850s.[33] The graph he presents shows a fall in the price of grain in 1841, suggesting

[29] Hansen, *Atlantic Migration*, p. 136.
[30] Jones, *American Immigration*, p. 85. Walker, *Germany*, p. 45.
[31] Erickson, "Emigration in 1841: Part I," p. 348. Also, see Gayer et al., *Growth*, pp. 242–4.
[32] Davis' index may also be wrong at this time. For example, Adams suggests that U.S. business conditions improved in 1841 and the wages paid to laborers increased. See Adams, *Ireland*, p. 224.
[33] Walker, *Germany*, pp. 43–5. Walker's idea is that the food-consuming lower class made up most of the emigrants. When food prices were high, this group suffered deterioration in their standard of living and thus had greater incentive to emigrate.

the decline in German immigration came not only from the deteriorating U.S. economy but also from improved conditions at home. Thus, the differential changes in immigration from 1840 to 1841 can perhaps be explained by drastically different economic conditions in the European countries of origin, with these conditions being more important than the changes in the U.S. economy.

1842–3

The connection between U.S. economic activity and the volume of immigration is very uncertain for 1843. Industrial Production in the United States increased 2.8 percent in 1842 and 11.4 percent in 1843.[34] Yet immigrant volume fell from both the United Kingdom and Germany, with the decrease being substantially larger for the United Kingdom (62 percent vs. 29 percent).[35] Even more peculiar, most of the existing literature discusses a downturn in the U.S. economy, although other factors are sometimes added. For example, Adams cites a letter written in February 1843 indicating that public works in the United States had generally ceased in the two preceding years, causing more Irish to go to Canada.[36] In addition, Adams cites the effects of a new passenger act passed in 1842.[37] Hansen also suggests that business conditions in the United States deteriorated during 1842, and then notes the volume of immigration was lower beginning in the spring of 1843.[38] Besides U.S. conditions, evidence exists that economic conditions in Great Britain improved in 1843 from a trough reached in 1842, which reduced the pressure to leave.[39] In Germany, however, grain prices rose somewhat during 1843, which would increase the incentive to leave.[40] Although the events in the United Kingdom and Germany are consistent with the larger fall in immigration from the United Kingdom, they are not consistent with any decline in the volume from Germany given the growing U.S. economy.

It is interesting that the results for 1840–1 and 1842–3 are opposites. In the former case, Davis' index indicates a decline in business conditions

---

[34] Real GDP also increased 2.0% in 1842 and 4.5% in 1843. See Carter et al., *Historical Statistics*, Table Ca9, p. 3–24.

[35] Only a small number is in the "Country Not Specified" category each year, therefore this factor does not affect the percentages.

[36] Adams, *Ireland*, p. 225. Also, see Way, *Common Labour*, pp. 205–8.

[37] Adams, *Ireland*, p. 229–30.

[38] Hansen, *Atlantic Migration*, pp. 144–5.

[39] Gayer et al., *Growth*, pp. 304–6.

[40] Walker, *Germany*, p. 44.

but no across-the-board decline occurred in immigrant volume, and the historical literature proposes additional reasons for the decline that did occur. In the latter case, the historical literature suggests that U.S. business conditions deteriorated in 1842 – and the decline in immigration during 1843 is consistent with that view – whereas Davis' index shows no decline. One possibility is that the historical literature uses information that is not representative of overall U.S. business conditions. Of course, Davis' index could also be incorrect for the period of the early 1840s.[41] Finally, the early 1840s could have been a period when conditions in the source countries were a more important determinant of immigration than those in the United States. Overall, the causes of the fluctuations in immigrant volume during the period from 1840 through 1843 are not clear.

1854–5

Total immigration from Europe fell from 406,000 in 1854 to 188,000 in 1855, a decline of 54 percent. A similar number arrived in 1856 as in 1855. The existing literature provides four different explanations for the decline in immigrant volume, making the discussion of this period more extensive than the previous ones.[42] First is the U.S. business cycle. Although Fogel discusses problems resulting from a downturn in railroad construction in the Midwest and Hansen a Western drought, other researchers suggest that the entire economy went into a depression late in 1854.[43] Yet an economic downturn would be expected to decrease the volume of immigration by an approximately equal percentage from all of the major source countries. Table 4.1, however, shows the decline was much larger for Germany (67 percent) than for the United Kingdom (39 percent). In fact, Davis' index, which was developed after all the existing literature that has been cited, shows that a small *increase* in Industrial Production occurred in 1855.[44] Thus, all indications are that a general

---

[41] The period is particularly confusing, although a previous footnote indicated that real GDP also rose during this period. Smith and Cole, *Fluctuations*, pp. 73, 84, indicate that domestic trade was fairly level from 1840 through 1843, with the 1842–3 downturn being because of a large fall in foreign trade. Thorp, *Business Annals*, pp. 122–3, labels the entire period from 1840 through the first half of 1843 as a depression. Edward Phillips' nephew, in a letter written in December 1842 says that " . . . (t)imes are bad all over the United States owing to the scarcity of money, which causes all business to be dull." See Erickson, *Invisible Immigrants*, p. 273.

[42] See the more extensive discussion of each reason in Cohn, "Nativism."

[43] See Commons et al., *History*, pp. 613–14; Rezneck, *Business Depressions*, p. 103; Ross, *Workers*, p. 157; Fogel, *Without Consent*, p. 358; Fogel, *Slavery Debates*, pp. 57–9; Hansen, *Atlantic Migration*, p. 303; and Walker, *Germany*, p. 173.

[44] The annual real GDP figures show a rise of 3.9% in 1854 followed by a 1.0% rise in 1855. See Carter et al., *Historical Statistics*, Table Ca9, p. 3–24. Johann Bauer, one of

economic downturn did not occur. The state of the U.S. economy cannot then explain the huge decrease in immigrant volume that occurred between 1854 and 1855.

A second reason advanced in the existing literature is the Crimean War, which was hypothesized to lower immigration in several ways.[45] The increased demand for shipping to move troops to the Crimea led to an increase in shipping rates during 1854. The outbreak of war also led many European governments to try to curtail emigration in order to have more males available as soldiers. Finally, the war with Russia led to Russian wheat disappearing from the European market, with a consequent rise in farm prices reducing the pressure on farmers to leave. Yet the Crimean War as an explanation for the decrease in immigration in 1855 suffers from issues of timing. The British and French declared war in March 1854 and the main fighting took place in the fall of 1854. Beginning in early November, the fighting waned and remained sporadic throughout the remainder of the war. In addition, the existing evidence on shipping prices shows a rise in 1853 and 1854 and then a decline in 1855.[46] Finally, the participating countries should have mainly felt the effects of the Crimean War. As has been shown, however, immigration declined much more from Germany – a nonparticipant – than from Great Britain.[47]

The sudden and large decline in immigration in 1855 resulted from a combination of the other two factors.[48] The first of these was an improvement in European conditions from the potato famine, that is, a lessening push factor. The Irish economy had become prosperous by the early 1850s and German agricultural conditions improved after 1853. In fact, by 1855, grain prices were falling, although still at high levels.[49] Thus, the necessity for potential immigrants to leave Europe fell.[50] In fact, the volume of Irish immigration declined as early as 1852. The precipitating event for the large decline in immigration in 1855, however, was the final factor, which was an outbreak of nativism in the United States.

the immigrants introduced in Chapter 1, wrote a letter home in June 1855 from Illinois, where he said, "You can see how thriving the conditions are here." See Kamphoefner et al., *News*, p. 155.

[45] Hansen, *Atlantic Migration*, p. 304.

[46] See the evidence summarized in Cohn, "Nativism," Table 3, p. 372.

[47] The volume of immigration from Great Britain fell by only 19% between 1854 and 1855.

[48] For a more comprehensive analysis, see Cohn, "Nativism."

[49] Walker, *Germany*, p. 44.

[50] To some extent, the high volume of individuals who emigrated in previous years also meant that fewer people were left to leave. The smaller supply of labor in Europe would also have been a factor in improving the lot of the individuals remaining at home.

In June 1853, a papal envoy, Monsignor Bedini, arrived in the United States to try to resolve a number of disputes. His visit, which lasted throughout the remainder of 1853, precipitated widespread outbreaks of violence against Catholics for the first time since 1844. One effect of this negative pull factor was an immediate decline in immigrant volume from the main Catholic country, Ireland. German immigrants had traditionally emigrated from southwest Germany, an area that was almost entirely Protestant. Although a larger portion of the German immigrants was Catholic by the 1840s, Protestants still dominated the total flow. Thus, little of the violence was directed at Germans, therefore immigration from Germany continued at a high level throughout 1854. During the last half of the year, however, the Know-Nothing Party suddenly became very prominent.[51] Their nativist platform, which for the first time enjoyed widespread electoral success, along with continued outbreaks of violence, must have caused a large share of the potential immigrants to change their minds about moving to the United States, especially in light of the improved economic conditions at home.[52] This factor explains why the volume of British immigration, comprised of individuals who blended more easily into the U.S. landscape, fell only 19 percent during 1855, much less in percentage terms than the declines from Ireland and Germany. It also explains why a larger proportion of the Germans who did immigrate during 1855 went to Illinois, Wisconsin, and Iowa, states where the nativist movement was weak because of the large existing German influence.[53] Thus, the substantial decline in immigration to the United States during 1855 had little to do with the U.S. business cycle or the Crimean War. It is instead explained by a combination of a widespread outbreak of nativism in the United States in conjunction with improved economic conditions in Europe.[54]

Events during the next few years emphasize the importance of the nativist outbreak to immigrant flows at this time. The Know-Nothing movement continued to enjoy electoral success throughout 1855,

[51] More detailed discussion of the Know-Nothing Party is provided in Chapter 8.

[52] As discussed earlier, it is likely potential immigrants quickly found out about the changing environment in the United States and adjusted their plans. See Gould, "European Inter-Continental Emigration," p. 651, who forcibly argues that information about current conditions in the United States flowed quickly back to Europe.

[53] See the evidence presented in Cohn, "Nativism," Table 4, p. 378.

[54] Note also that these events, so different from the typical forces that affected the volume of immigration, may be the reason Brinley Thomas concluded that a "structural change" occurred in the U.S. economy in the late 1860s. Most of his data began in 1840, therefore the downturn in volume in 1855 dominates his antebellum data. See Thomas, *Migration*, pp. 93, 159–63.

although the party disintegrated in 1856. The first fissure occurred in February 1856, when the Know-Nothing Party met to choose their presidential candidate for the 1856 election. The choice was former President Millard Fillmore. His willingness to coexist with slavery caused many Northern delegates to bolt the party and hold a separate nominating convention in June 1856.[55] Besides the split on the issue of slavery, the sharp decline in the volume of immigration in 1855 lessened the economic pressure from immigration and reduced nativism as a political issue. Thus, by the middle of 1856, it became apparent that nativism was no longer an important political force. In fact, in the presidential election in November, Fillmore attracted just 22 percent of the popular vote and carried only the state of Maryland.

Immigrants responded almost immediately to the decline of nativism. From July 1855 through June 1856 – when nativism was still an important force – the volume of immigration from Great Britain, Ireland, and Germany totaled about 98,000. From July 1856 through June 1857 – after the obvious decline of the nativist movement – the total rose to 131,500. In particular, Irish immigration increased by 43 percent and German immigration by 60 percent. In contrast, British immigration fell slightly.[56] Although Davis' index shows that a 4 percent rise in Industrial Production occurred in 1856, the strong increases in Irish and German immigration along with the slight decline in British immigration suggests the immigrants were responding more to the improved political climate in the United States than to any improvement in economic conditions.

1857–8

The last downturn in the volume of immigration during the antebellum period occurred in 1858. In August 1857, the economy first began to exhibit signs of problems. In fact, the events heralded the beginning of the most severe depression of the antebellum period. The onset of the depression was quick, as Davis' index shows a 2.2 percent decline in 1857, and then a further decline of 5.9 percent in 1858. Little doubt exists that the economic depression caused the volume of European immigration to fall from 216,000 in 1857 to 111,000 in 1858. The volume also fell by virtually equal percentages from each of the major source countries – 50.5 percent from Great Britain, 50.6 percent from Ireland, and 50.6 percent from Germany. Little change occurred in immigrant volume during 1859, as

---

[55] Holt, "Antimasonic," pp. 605–14; Billington, *Protestant Crusade*, pp. 407–36; Baker, *Ambivalent Americans*, p. 3.
[56] Cohn, "Nativism," pp. 370, 379.

the economy was slow to recover. When the economy finally did begin to recover, volume from Europe rose to 141,000 in 1860, and then fell in 1861 with the outbreak of the Civil War. Regardless of what caused the fluctuations during other parts of the antebellum period, clearly the 1857–8 depression was the factor leading to the decline in immigration during 1858.

In conclusion, a relationship appears to exist during the antebellum years between downturns in Industrial Production and the volume of immigration. Beginning in 1829, during each of the five years in which Industrial Production declined, immigrant volume fell during either the same year or the next year. The connections during two periods – 1834–5 and 1840–1 – are, however, somewhat inconsistent. In addition, there were two years – 1843 and 1855 – when the volume of immigration underwent a substantial decline without a fall in Industrial Production. Overall, the findings of the empirical analysis are consistent with those of Jerome mentioned earlier. A connection between a decline in economic activity and a decline in the volume of immigration is apparent in much of the data, but the overall relationship is far from exact.

The Immigration–Economic Expansion Connection

If downturns in the U.S. economy caused declines, at least sometimes, in the volume of immigration, did U.S. expansions lead to increases in immigrant volume? An earlier section of this chapter provided an affirmative answer by suggesting that the growth of the U.S. economy was an important factor in causing the long-term increase in annual immigrant volume. This section provides additional evidence by examining two specific periods. One is the increase in immigrant volume in 1831 and 1832. The other is the period of the potato famine.

1831–2

The jump in immigrant volume in 1831 and 1832 followed a rapid increase in Industrial Production beginning in 1830, timing consistent with the former being caused by the latter. In fact, the two largest annual percentage increases in Davis' index during the entire 1820–60 period occurred in 1830 and 1831. Another sizeable increase occurred in 1832. These large increases were quite different from the slow growth of Industrial Production during the 1820s. In 1829, the index was only 36 percent greater than it had been in 1820. Then, during the next *two* years, the index of Industrial Production increased by 40 percent. Similarly, the

1820s saw only a slow increase in immigrant volume, with the total then undergoing a huge jump in 1831 and 1832.

The increase in Industrial Production in the early 1830s caused an increase in the demand for immigrant workers, and was the final factor in explaining the sudden rise in volume in 1831 and 1832. The rapid population growth after 1750 caused a large number of Europeans to be interested in immigrating to the United States. The other factors discussed in Chapter 3 – the fall in ocean transportation costs, the reduction in government restrictions, the improvement in shipping, and the rise in remittances and prepaid tickets – all increased the ability of individuals to immigrate by the end of the 1820s. When Industrial Production suddenly underwent a sizeable increase in a short period of time during the first few years of the 1830s, the large number of potential European immigrants became actual immigrants.

1845–54

This period includes the potato famine in Europe and the years immediately following. Whatever importance the state of the U.S. economy had in explaining fluctuations in immigration during the early 1840s, the onset of the potato famine caused a large increase in immigration during the last half of the 1840s. The story has been told in detail elsewhere, so it is only briefly summarized here.[57] The potato fungus damaged the crop in the United States in the early 1840s.[58] It worked its way to Europe, eventually arriving in the fall of 1845 in Ireland, a country that had become extremely dependent on the potato. The effects were evident by October, but less than one-half of the total potato crop failed, therefore the initial consequences were not overwhelming. At about the same time, the potato crop also began to fail in parts of Germany and Great Britain.[59] Immigration to the United States rose in 1846 by 34 percent from 1845, with more individuals arriving from all of the affected countries. Sporadic crop failures had occurred in other years and the fact that the current problems were caused by a recurring fungus was not understood. Thus, it was not clear to contemporaries that the crop would also fail in 1846. In fact, the potato crop experienced near total failure in Ireland in 1846. Yields

---

[57] For more complete versions, see Woodham-Smith, *Great Hunger*; Ó Gráda, *Black '47*; Mokyr, *Why Ireland Starved*; Ó Gráda, *Great Irish Famine*; and Hansen, *Atlantic Migration*, pp. 242–61. The potato famine is also the central issue in Guinnane, *Vanishing Irish*.

[58] Ó Gráda, *Great Irish Famine*, p. 40.

[59] Hansen, *Atlantic Migration*, pp. 245–6.

were higher in 1847 but less acreage had been planted in potatoes. The crop then failed again in 1848. British policy was not very forceful in combating the problem. The result was starvation beginning in the summer of 1846, with the worst effects being felt during 1847 and 1848. Although conditions improved after that, excess mortality continued to be experienced in certain areas into 1850 and 1851.[60]

One response to the horrible conditions in Ireland was to leave. In 1847 and 1848, approximately 110,000 Irish each year sailed directly to the United States. Many Irish also sailed to Canada – suffering frightful mortality on the voyage – and proceeded on to the United States.[61] Still others moved to Great Britain. The Irish flow to the United States increased to approximately 160,000 in 1849 and 1850 and then reached an all-time high of more than 220,000 in 1851.[62] With the return of prosperity by 1851, the immigration flow fell to approximately 160,000 in 1852 and 1853, and to slightly more than 100,000 in 1854. One reason the numbers remained high throughout the period is that previous immigrants were able to help their friends and family still in Ireland to leave. In total, about 1.5 million Irish left the country for good between 1845 and 1854.

Although the failures were less severe on the Continent, harvests were still smaller than normal in 1845 and 1846.[63] Thus, the prices of grains rose substantially throughout Europe beginning in late 1845 and remained high into 1847, a year with a relatively good harvest in Germany. Grain prices fell in 1848, but the year also saw the failures of revolutions in France and Germany. Although not many of the immigrants were actual revolutionaries, the event did cause many Germans to lose hope for change at home. All these events led to an increase in the numbers leaving Germany for the United States after 1845. An average of sixty-seven thousand Germans immigrated to the United States each year between 1846 and 1851. In 1850, German harvests were again lower than usual, and the yield continued to be small through 1853. Grain prices rose substantially from 1850 through 1854. The result was a large increase in immigration to the United States. More than 140,000 sailed to the United States in both 1852 and 1853, and the volume reached 215,000 in 1854. As with the Irish, many were probably helped by previous migrants.

---

[60] Ó Gráda, *Ireland*, p. 177.

[61] See Chapter 6 for a discussion of mortality on the transatlantic voyage.

[62] These numbers are the official figures. Although the breakdown between the British and the Irish is inaccurate for much of the antebellum period, the figures for the post-1846 period appear to be more accurate. See the discussion in Chapter 2.

[63] The material in this paragraph follows Walker, *Germany*, pp. 44, 134–74, and Hansen, *Atlantic Migration*, pp. 252–5.

The combination of outright starvation in Ireland, a reduced standard of living on the Continent, and the small harvests in Germany in the early 1850s caused the total volume of immigration to the United States to increase over the entire period from 1846 through 1854.[64] The increases from both Ireland and Germany in 1847 led to a 57 percent increase in total immigration from Europe compared to 1846. From 78,000 in 1844, the total arriving in the United States reached 248,000 in 1847 (Table A4.1). Volume fell somewhat in 1848, but the increase from Ireland in 1849 led to a jump in the total to about three hundred thousand in both 1849 and 1850. The further increase from Ireland in 1851 and then the large inflows from Germany between 1852 and 1854 pushed the total to more than 360,000 each year from 1851 through 1853. The antebellum peak occurred in 1854, when almost 406,000 individuals arrived in the United States from Europe. Overall, in the decade from 1845 through 1854, 2.8 million immigrants arrived directly from Europe.

However, push factors were not the only ones operating. The U.S. economy did not suffer through any downturns during the decade. Indeed, Davis' index of Industrial Production increases each year from 1840 through 1856.[65] In fact, some of the increases in Industrial Production after 1845 probably resulted from the increases in immigration, as the larger labor force increased production. In any case, it is fortunate that this decade of substantial misery in Europe did not see any major economic downturn in the United States. Thus, many of the Irish and Germans pushed out of their homelands were pulled to the United States by the prosperous conditions.[66]

Summary

The material in this chapter suggests the causes of antebellum immigration are complex, and cannot be easily summarized in terms of push, pull, and other factors. Indeed, the initial jump in volume around 1830 was due not

---

[64] British immigration reached record levels of more than 50,000 each year from 1849 through 1851. It fell somewhat in 1852 and 1853 but then reached a new peak in 1854.

[65] The traditional view of the 1840s is one of a number of small recessions. Davis, "Improved Annual Chronology," indicates that this view is incorrect. For the traditional view, see Thorp, *Business Annals*; Smith and Cole, *Fluctuations*; and Mitchell, *Business Cycles*.

[66] Some other years may have seen a similar effect of increases in Industrial Production leading to an increase in immigrant volume, although the two-way connection between the variables discussed at the end of the appendix to this chapter needs to be kept in mind. The large percentage increases in immigration in both 1836 and 1839 follow or occur during the same year as rapid increases in Industrial Production.

only to deteriorating conditions in Europe but also to a variety of nonpush factors, among them the decline in transatlantic transportation costs, the increase in remittances, and a large jump in industrial production in the United States in the early 1830s. Both push and pull factors – continued pressure on living standards in Europe along with a growing U.S. economy – contributed to the increasing annual volume after 1832. Even during the potato famine, the increased volume of immigration should not be solely attributed to a push factor because the U.S. economy did not experience any economic downturn.

The only circumstance when one effect seems to have clearly dominated is during some economic downturns in the U.S. economy. The two most prominent depressions during the antebellum period – those in 1837 and 1857–8 – caused a virtually equal decline in the volume of immigration from all of the major source countries. Although not as certain, the decrease in immigration in 1829 was probably also caused by a U.S. depression. However, according to Davis' index of Industrial Production, other large decreases occurred in 1834 and 1840, but the observed changes in immigrant volume are not consistent with the economic downturn. In each of these two cases, the differences may have been because of factors specific to each source country, but relatively little work along these lines has been done. However, not every antebellum decrease in immigrant volume was caused by an economic downturn. In particular, the reasons for the large decrease in volume in 1843 are unclear, although little evidence exists of general economic troubles in the United States. Similarly, the evidence is very weak for an economic downturn in 1855, a year that also saw a huge decrease in immigrant volume. Instead of economic problems, this fall in immigration was because of a combination of improved conditions in Europe and the outbreak of nativism in the United States. Overall, trying to explain changes in the volume of antebellum immigration as being caused exclusively by push factors or exclusively by pull factors, or even by a combination of both, appears to be an unproductive exercise.

Appendix 4.1
Theoretical and Data Issues in Relating Immigration to Unemployment

Determining a connection between the business cycle and the volume of immigration during the antebellum period is complicated by a number of theoretical issues. First, the economic theory of immigration directly examines the decision process for workers, who were primarily male during the antebellum period, except for the numerous Irish female servants. Dependent family members might still immigrate during a business downturn, as long as those already in the United States had sufficient savings to pay the passage costs. Thus, immigration would not decline to zero even in depressed economic conditions. Second, economic conditions in the home country must also be considered. If the home country's economy was booming at the same time the United States was experiencing unemployment – so immigration to the United States declined – then both push and pull factors reduced immigration. More generally, potential immigrants responded to both negative and positive conditions at home, potentially causing a large volume of immigration when conditions in the United States were not favorable or a small volume when conditions in the United States were favorable. The situation becomes even more complicated when the possibility of divergent conditions in the European countries of origin (or in the different parts of Germany) is considered in the analysis.

The third complicating factor is that the volume of immigration from different European countries could vary if the types of jobs their immigrants could obtain in the United States differed. In particular, the material in Chapter 7 indicates that the Irish and German employment patterns in the United States were quite different. The former group found jobs in factories, as laborers in building public works, and as servants, whereas the latter were employed more as merchants and artisans. Fourth, even if all other factors were favorable for immigration, individuals might delay their trip if conditions onboard the ships were temporarily deadly. Given the only method of reaching the United States was by a long sailing ship voyage, reports of shipwrecks or outbreaks of cholera or typhus on the journey (neither a push nor a pull factor) could result in a delay until the return of more favorable conditions.

Finally, the economic theory of immigration, as presented in this book, assumes the United States was the only possible destination country. In reality, a potential immigrant would compare his or her expected lifetime income in all possible destinations and make the best choice.[67] Thus, conditions in destination countries other than the United States could also influence immigration to the United States. During the antebellum years – with one exception – overseas immigration to countries other than the United States was small, and much of the immigration, such as that to Australia and Brazil, was subsidized and thus not available

[67] See the discussion in Wegge, "Push and Pull Migration."

to many potential immigrants. The one exception was Irish and British immigration to Canada. However, as discussed in Chapter 2, the final destination for many of these migrants was the United States. Thus, if an individual wished to leave Europe at this time and was not subsidized, the United States was the probable destination. The other possible move for an individual was within Europe. Yet the only sizeable permanent migrations within Europe consisted of some Irish who moved to Great Britain and a large number of Germans who settled in Russia and Poland in the 1820s.[68] Instead, most internal migration within Europe (and some of that from Ireland to Great Britain) was labor migration, where individuals moved temporarily to earn income with the objective of returning to their home.[69] Where both internal and external migrations were options, however, the external one was expected to be permanent during the antebellum years. Given this fundamental difference in the two types of migration, the possibility for intra-European labor migration would have had less influence on the immigration decision to the United States during the antebellum period than later.[70] Overall, it is clear that a wide variety of theoretical factors influenced the timing of the immigration decision and complicate any analysis. Many of these factors were particularly important during the antebellum period when the long sailing voyage usually meant the immigration was permanent.

Besides the theoretical factors, an analysis for the antebellum period is also complicated by a lack of data on the needed variables. For example, to explore the relationship between antebellum business cycles and immigration, we would like to relate – on a monthly or at least a quarterly basis – the volume of male immigrant workers from each European country to the levels of unemployment in the United States and the country of origin, although perhaps all adult workers should be used for Irish immigration. In fact, none of the needed data is available in the proper form, especially for any period less than annual.[71] Although annual estimates of immigrant volume are available for each of the major antebellum source

---

[68] Jones, *American Immigration*, p. 85. Walker, *Germany*, pp. 32–3, 37.

[69] See Moch, *Moving Europeans*, pp. 120–43. Recall that, in Chapter 3, it was argued that it was the lack of opportunities to earn income by internal migration that caused early immigration from northern Ireland and southwest Germany.

[70] See the more complete discussion on this point in Chapters 1 and 2.

[71] Quarterly figures for immigrant volume are available at least for the 1850s. See those reproduced in Cohn, "Nativism," Table 2, p. 370. The absence of any good measure for economic activity on less than an annual basis, however, means that most of the analysis must use annual data.

countries – Great Britain, Ireland, and Germany – these data cannot be directly used. In particular, the annual series on immigrant volume from Ireland and Great Britain are not accurate before 1847, given the artificial way in which they were derived. Even aggregating the two series to obtain one for the United Kingdom and using this series along with that for German immigration does not always provide accurate annual figures. For many years, a large number of individuals did not have their country of origin recorded, although most were certainly from Europe.[72] Therefore, no accurate annual series of the volume of immigration from specific European countries currently exist.

Even without a breakdown by country, it would be preferable to use total adult male immigrant workers, but accurate measures of these also do not exist. *Historical Statistics* provides data on total male immigrants, but these are calculated from percentages, so they are not the raw numbers. In addition, the male total includes children, U.S. citizens, and arrivals from places other than Europe.[73] Bromwell provides data that are broken down by gender and age and exclude U.S. citizens but they include arrivals from places other than Europe and are not broken down by country of origin.[74] Figures derived from his data would also include adult nonworkers. In addition, Bromwell's data end in 1855. Finally, as with the aggregate immigration figures, Bromwell's data are provided for the same fiscal years as the total immigration figures. Some of the years are from October to September, others cover January to December, two of the entries are for 15 months, and one entry is for 9 months.[75] Thus, the best measure that can be used for immigrant volume is the existing figures on total immigration, although I did adjust these to calendar year totals. The calendar year figures are presented in Table A 4.1, while the method used to carry out the adjustment is discussed in the notes to the table. Overall, the (admittedly crude) adjustment procedure does not result in large differences with the existing fiscal year estimates.

No annual estimates of unemployment are extant for the antebellum years for either the United States or the European countries of origin. Instead, I use the annual estimates of Industrial Production provided by Davis for the United States.[76] These should provide a particularly

---

[72] For additional discussion on the points in this paragraph and the next, see Chapter 2.

[73] Carter et al., *Historical Statistics*, Table Ad226–30, pp. 588–9.

[74] Bromwell, *History*, Table 2 for each year.

[75] See the discussion in Chapter 2.

[76] Davis, "Annual Index," Table III, p. 1189. This index has been used instead of the estimate of real GDP presented by Richard Sutch in Carter et al., *Historical Statistics*,

TABLE A4.1. *Immigration from Europe, Calendar Year Estimates, 1819–1860*

Year	Immigration	Year	Immigration	Year	Immigration
1819[a]	1,598	1833	55,354	1847	247,953
1820	7,993	1834	62,579	1848	211,162
1821	9,029	1835	42,031	1849	307,342
1822	5,908	1836	71,296	1850	293,498
1823	5,988	1837	75,699	1851	369,758
1824	7,693	1838	35,913	1852	363,904
1825	9,766	1839	64,442	1853	362,560
1826	10,065	1840	80,244	1854	406,200
1827	20,346	1841	76,843	1855	188,063
1828	26,517	1842	100,561	1856	186,625
1829	17,393	1843	62,031	1857	238,525
1830	21,932	1844	78,061	1858	112,155
1831	20,062	1845	117,142	1859	112,344
1832	57,862	1846	156,813	1860	141,695

[a] October–December only.

Sources: The fiscal year figures used are taken from Carter et al., *Historical Statistics.* For each year, I added the figures in series Ad91 ("Total for Europe") and those in Ad97 ("Other or unknown"). Based on data in Bromwell, *History,* for 1850, and data for 1832 adjusted for the missing ports, I estimated that immigration during the last quarter of each year comprised approximately 20% of total immigration for the calendar year. To begin the adjustment, I assumed that immigration during the last three months of 1819 was 20% of the fiscal year total for 1819–20. I subtracted this number from the fiscal year total for 1819–20, which provided an estimate for immigration from January through September 1820. I then adjusted this number to a calendar year estimate by assuming that immigration during the last quarter of 1820 was 20% of the calendar year total. I continued with this process working forward in time for all the fiscal year figures. The total for 1832 uses the estimated value for the last quarter of the year instead of the figure given in Bromwell, *History,* p. 73, because Bromwell's figure excludes arrivals at ports other than Boston and New York. The total for 1831 makes no adjustment for the three months where data are missing. See the discussion in Chapter 2.

accurate picture of the unemployment situation for immigrants. Industrial Production measures manufacturing and mining activity, which is where most of the immigrants got their jobs (see Chapter 7), especially after the increase in volume during the early 1830s. A decline in Industrial Production should therefore have raised unemployment in exactly the occupations most important to immigrants. One issue complicates the use

Table Ca9, p. 3–24. The discussion of the real GDP estimates (given on pp. 3–16 to 3–19) emphasizes how uncertain the annual estimates are. In addition, the Sutch series before 1840 interpolates between census years partly using the Davis index. See p. 3–27. Thus, footnotes in the text of this chapter do not cite Sutch's real GDP series for any of the pre-1840 discussion.

of this variable. Not only do changes in Industrial Production affect the volume of immigration, changes in the volume of immigration also affect Industrial Production. For example, a rapid rate of immigration increased the labor force available to work in manufacturing and mining and thus increased the level of Industrial Production. One needs to be careful, therefore, in interpreting the relationship between the two variables.

5

Who Were the Immigrants?

Although the number of people who left Europe for the United States increased over the antebellum years, who these individuals were has not yet been addressed. The popular view, summarized in the famous poem by Emma Lazarus, is that they were the "tired," the "poor," and the "huddled masses." Although the poem was written in 1883, well after our time period, it summarizes the view of many toward the immigrants who arrived before the 1920s.[1] This chapter uses data on the age, gender, and occupations of the immigrants to determine who the immigrants were relative to the European labor forces they left.[2] For the period before the large increase in volume around 1830, the Lazarus view is clearly incorrect – all immigrant groups were positively selected, that is, they were more skilled than the underlying labor forces they left. When immigrant volume increased, the skill levels fell and the situation becomes somewhat less clear. Over the entire antebellum period, however, a comparison of the arriving Germans, British, and Irish finds that the average skill level went from highest to lowest in the order listed. The data on who the immigrants were also adds to the discussions in Chapters 3 and 4 concerning the reasons they left Europe.

---

[1] The poem by Emma Lazarus containing these terms is called "The New Colossus" and is engraved on a plaque in the Statue of Liberty. See Jewish Women's Archive, "JWA."

[2] See Chapter 8 for a comparison of the arriving immigrants to the existing U.S. labor force.

TABLE 5.1. *Age and Gender of the Immigrants, 1820–1860*

Years	Percent Male	Percent Under Age 14	Percent Age 14–44	Percent Age 45 and Older
1820–1826	75	9	78	13
1827–1831	68	26	64	10
1832–1835	66	27	63	10
1836–1845	61	22	68	10
1846–1854	59	23	67	10
1855–1860	57	19	71	10

Source: Calculated from Carter et al., *Historical Statistics*, Series Ad222–Ad230.

Information on Age and Gender

Data on the gender and age of the total immigrant stream are available from the Passenger Lists for the 1820–60 period (Table 5.1). The male proportion always exceeded half. Because males were the primary workers, and immigration was designed to increase one's income, the large presence of males is not surprising. The percentage male, however, declined consistently, from 75 percent in the early 1820s to less than 60 percent after 1845. Presumably, this fall reflects an increasing family orientation to immigration over the antebellum period. More families were able to immigrate together because of the decline in fares, or in a chain-migration fashion as remittances became more important, factors previously discussed in Chapter 3. The change may also reflect in part the increasing presence of Irish immigrants in the total, as females were a more important component of Irish immigration than for other countries.

The data in Table 5.1 also show an interesting change in the age structure of the immigrant stream beginning in the mid-1820s. During the first part of the decade, few children immigrated. Given the high fares prevailing at the time, the lack of children in the immigrant stream is not surprising.[3] As fares declined, children generally constituted 20 to 25 percent of the immigrant stream. The rapid population growth occurring in Europe, however, meant that more than 25 percent of the population were less than fourteen years old. Thus, children were less likely to immigrate than adults, a result that again is a reasonable expectation of immigration

[3] The percentage under age fourteen is extremely small for the years 1821 through 1824 (1% or less of each year's total), so one has to wonder if another reason for the low percentage is sloppy recordkeeping.

being driven by economic factors: children would not immediately earn a higher income in the United States. During all periods, well over half of the immigrant stream was composed of adults between the ages of fourteen and forty-four.[4] These individuals were the ones most likely to benefit from immigrating, because their relative youth meant they had more years in which to earn higher wages in the United States. In turn, older workers were much less likely to leave Europe, because their potential gains were much smaller.

These data on gender and age indicate a change in the composition of the immigrant stream beginning in the latter part of the 1820s. During the first few years in which comprehensive records were kept, working-age males predominated. After 1826, although the male percentage continued to decline, little additional change occurred in the age structure of the immigrant stream. Overall, the changes that occurred are consistent with the discussion in Chapter 3: economic considerations were paramount in the immigration decision, fares declined throughout the 1820s, and remittances became a more important means of funding immigration.

Data on Occupations and Their Use

The data on the occupations of the arriving immigrants are more controversial and the remainder of this chapter is devoted to this discussion. Researchers have taken information on immigrant occupations from a variety of passenger manifests. During the colonial and early national periods, surviving manifests are not abundant. A sufficient number exist to provide estimates for Germany and Britain, but not for Ireland. After 1820, the Passenger Lists can be used because, as discussed in Chapter 2, these included a column to record the occupation of every immigrant. One immediate issue is what was done with women and children. If a woman listed an occupation, and it was not simply ditto marks referring to her husband's occupation, it was included in the summary figures from the Passenger Lists; otherwise, "no occupation" was recorded. Children under the age of fifteen also did not typically have an occupation recorded. The official statistics thus include a large number of individuals, almost always more than half, for whom no occupation was recorded.

---

[4] Although not apparent in the data in Table 5.1, most immigrants were between ages fifteen and thirty-five. The two immigrants introduced in Chapter 1, Edward Phillips and Johann Bauer, were forty-five and twenty-six, respectively, when they immigrated. See Erickson, *Invisible Immigrants*, p. 265, and Kamphoefner et al., *News*, p. 149.

In addition, the published information on occupations from the Passenger Lists for the antebellum years is not divided by country of origin; in fact, the official statistics even include the occupations of the U.S. passengers on the ships. To try to overcome these issues, a number of researchers have drawn samples from the Passenger Lists, centering mainly on the occupations of the males. In summary, a limited amount of evidence on the occupations of immigrants exists for the period before 1820. For the period after 1820, estimates are available based both on the entire set of Passenger Lists and on the samples that have been taken. A more general issue is whether the information contained on some or all of the passenger manifests was recorded accurately. This issue is addressed throughout the chapter and in Appendix 5.1.

Knowing the occupations of the immigrants is important because this information tells us about the relative skill level of an immigrant stream.[5] Determining this relationship is straightforward. The occupational composition of the immigrant stream is compared to that of the labor force the immigrants left. In economic terms, the question is whether the immigrants from each country were positively selected, that is, more skilled than the underlying labor force or negatively selected, that is, less skilled than the underlying labor force. In order to perform this test, occupations must be classified by skill level. The scheme used in this chapter, from least to most skilled, is as follows: unskilled workers (laborers and servants), farmers, artisans and other skilled workers, and white-collar workers.[6] In some cases, the "artisan" group is divided. Before discussing the reason for this division, one issue that needs to be addressed is whether this classification does in fact reflect relative skill levels. Although few would disagree with the placement of laborers and servants at the bottom of the skill scale and white-collar workers at the top, the relative position of the middle two categories is less certain. Farmers could have been fairly well off and simply looking for better prospects in the United States. On the

---

[5] Besides the author, the following also use occupations as a proxy for skills for European countries: Wegge, "Occupational Self-Selection"; Mokyr, *Why Ireland Starved*; Erickson, *Leaving England*; many of the articles in Canny, *Europeans*; and Carter and Sutch, "Historical Perspectives."

[6] The complete classification scheme is shown in Appendix 5.2, although only the most numerous occupations are listed in each category. In reality, a huge number of different occupations were listed on the Passenger Lists. As near as possible, I have attempted to classify these occupations to reproduce the categories used in the summary data from the Passenger Lists. Thus, the occupational categories used by other researchers were adjusted to those used in this chapter. Also, see the discussion in Carter and Sutch, "Historical Perspectives," pp. 19–23.

other hand, not all European farmers bought land in the United States. For these individuals, their lack of other skills may have left them in a worse position to find a good-paying job in the United States compared to workers in the artisan category. Such an assumption probably becomes more valid over the course of the antebellum period as a larger share of the immigrant stream began to work in manufacturing jobs in the United States. In any case, the uncertain relative classification of farmers and artisans should be kept in mind.

An issue connected to the occupational distribution of the immigrant stream is the reason that individuals immigrated. During the period of this book, Great Britain was going through the Industrial Revolution. As discussed in Chapter 3, the growth of low-cost British manufacturing in certain industries, especially textiles, pressured the jobs of workers in other countries. The basic question that arises is whether most of the immigrants were fleeing from the negative effects of the Industrial Revolution. In this context, researchers on English immigration have often divided the "artisan" group into "craftsmen" – those working in traditional industries not greatly affected by the Industrial Revolution – and "industrial workers" – those working (or losing jobs) in industries being affected by the Industrial Revolution, such as textiles and iron and steel. In Ireland, with the lack of an iron and steel industry, the "artisan" group is divided into "textile workers" and "other artisans." If changes brought about by the Industrial Revolution were "forcing" out immigrants, then "industrial workers" in England and "textile workers" in Ireland should show up in greater proportions among the immigrants than the underlying labor forces. Finally, as already discussed in Chapter 3, some researchers have advanced arguments that most German immigrants were fleeing economic distress because of the decline in protoindustry brought about by the Industrial Revolution.

More generally, the two uses of occupational data are related. If the immigrants were positively selected – especially if they consisted of white-collar workers, artisans in jobs not affected by the Industrial Revolution, and wealthy farmers – the implication is that they were seeking to better their lives and not fleeing from imminent economic distress. A finding of this type is reinforced if the immigrants carried quite a bit of cash with them and, given the costs of immigrating, were able to travel in large family groups. If the immigrants were negatively selected – especially if they consisted of poor unskilled workers and industrial workers who lost their jobs as the result of changes in the British economy – and traveled alone with little cash, they were more likely to have been "forced" out of Europe.

The Occupations of Pre-1820 Immigrants

Chapter 3 discussed the high costs of immigrating to the United States before the 1830s and the subsequent decline in these costs into the early 1830s. The fall in costs leads to an expectation that the skill levels of the immigrant stream also fell over the antebellum period. Before the early 1830s, the high costs would have made it difficult for low-income, low-skilled workers to immigrate. Thus, the early immigrant streams would have been comprised of individuals with higher skills, although the most highly skilled and wealthiest individuals had little reason to leave Europe. When the costs of immigrating declined, more low-skilled workers were able to immigrate. Thus, the skill levels of the immigrant streams in the 1840s and 1850s should have been lower than those before 1830. In addition, because the costs of immigrating fell in general, the decline in skill levels of the immigrant streams should have occurred from all of the major source countries. The material in this section and the next provides evidence in support of these theoretical expectations.

Because only a few years exist between 1815 and 1830 and, because the data from the Passenger Lists only begin in 1820, this section of Chapter 5 examines what is known concerning the skill levels of the immigrants before 1820. Although no data exist on the overall skill level of the immigrant stream for this period, partial data are available for Germany and Britain, and some qualitative information is available for Ireland. The data for the former countries are shown in Table 5.2.

During the colonial period and, indeed, into the early national period, the percentage of German immigrants with skills became larger. In particular, note the high skill level of those Germans who immigrated between 1815 and 1820. Almost three-quarters were white-collar workers or artisans. Given the very high transportation costs at this time, mainly the fairly skilled were able to afford the cost of the transatlantic voyage.[7] Yet it is also apparent that even the German immigrants arriving in 1709 were

---

[7] During these years, about 40% of the German immigrants to Pennsylvania came as indentured servants. See Grubb, "End," Figure 1, p. 799. These indentured servants had a high skill level. See Grubb, "German Immigration," pp. 431–4. One reason is that skilled workers earned more in the United States and could more quickly pay off the high transportation costs.

TABLE 5.2. *Male Immigrant Occupations, by Country of Origin,*
1709–1820 (percent of annual total in each group)

Country/Years	White Collar	Artisans & Skilled	Farmers	Unskilled
Germany				
1709	0.7	36.4	62.8	0.1
1733	3.9	49.0	47.1	0
1793–1807	6.2	59.1	30.4	4.3
1815–1820	9.8	63.8	22.6	3.8
England				
1774–1776	4.4	58.1	12.0	25.5

Sources: Calculated from Grubb, "German Immigration," Table 5, p. 432, and Grubb, *Immigration*, Table 21, pp. 107–9. Grubb's figures were reclassified to correspond to the categories in Appendix 5.2. The figures for England are originally from Bailyn, *Voyagers*.

highly skilled. Although few were in the white-collar group, more than one-third were artisans or other skilled labor, a fraction that was at least as large as the comparable percentage in either the U.S. or German labor forces.[8] In addition, almost no immigrants were unskilled workers. Then, over the period to 1820, the consistent trend was for the percentage of farmers to decline and the percentages of white-collar workers and artisans and other skilled workers to increase. These data are consistent with other work of a more qualitative nature. Wokeck found that single male colonial German immigrants came "from places that provided schooling and were young people with some skill."[9] Their literacy rate rose from 60 percent to 80 percent between the 1730s and the Revolutionary War. Grubb indicates the literacy level of German colonial immigrants was higher than among the entire German population.[10] Similarly, Fertig finds that literate German males were more likely to migrate.[11]

The only comprehensive empirical estimate of the occupational structure of the entire English colonial immigrant stream is for the end of the colonial period and is also shown in Table 5.2. Bailyn estimated that more than 60 percent of all English immigrants during the 1774–6 period

[8] Grubb, "German Immigration," p. 434, also makes this argument with respect to the U.S. labor force. The earliest estimate of the skill level of the German labor force is for 1849 (see Table 5.5), which shows that about one-third of the male labor force was white-collar or skilled. Presumably, this percentage was much smaller in the eighteenth century.

[9] Wokeck, *Trade*, p. 50.

[10] Grubb, "Colonial Immigrant Literacy," p. 65.

[11] Fertig, "Transatlantic Migration," p. 234.

were artisans or white-collar workers.[12] Again, this percentage must have been much more than the comparable one for either the English or the U.S. labor forces. Thus, the late colonial English immigrant stream was also highly skilled.

Both English and German immigration was composed partly of indentured servants and partly of immigrants who paid their own way. More specific information exists on the different groups of English immigrants over the colonial period. Bailyn found that indentured servants who arrived during the late colonial period fell into two categories. They were either young, single, skilled artisan adults, or young agricultural workers. Because about 40 percent of the latter group was female, the overall skill level of male indentures at the end of the colonial period was quite high. Much of the information available on the skill levels of the English indentured servants who arrived earlier in the colonial period is summarized in Canny.[13] He concludes that early in the eighteenth century English indentured servants were "young, of relatively low social status, with but modest skills." However, based partly on Galenson's work, Canny also finds that the skills of the indentured servants rose over the century and suggests that Bailyn's dual immigrant streams "has been a constant since the outset of the seventeenth century."[14] Finally, data on the approximately 20 percent of colonial English immigrants to the Chesapeake area who paid their own way are provided by Horn.[15] He finds their skill levels were much higher than those of the indentured servants. In fact, only about 4 percent of the free immigrants in his sample were from agricultural backgrounds or were unskilled.

No empirical estimates of the occupational structure of the Irish immigrant stream are available for the colonial period. Part of the reason may be that the volume of immigration from Ireland was relatively small until the 1760s and 1770s.[16] Qualitative information, however, indicates

[12] Bailyn, *Voyagers*.

[13] Canny, "English Migration," p. 44.

[14] Canny, "English Migration," p. 44; Galenson, *White Servitude*. This conclusion is reinforced by information on English immigrants during the seventeenth century provided by Menard, who finds that more than half of both free immigrants and servants were yeomen and artisans. Although Menard finds the percentage of immigrants with "low position increased" near the end of the seventeenth century, even at this time they were not leaving England in "hopeless desperation." See Menard, "British Migration," pp. 120–31.

[15] Horn, "To Parts."

[16] The one exception was during 1728 and 1729 when a total of 5,500 to 6,500 Irish immigrants arrived because of famine conditions at home. Otherwise, Irish immigration

that the skill level of the Irish immigrants was already fairly high in the
1760s and then rose during the 1770s.[17] The increase in skill levels was
caused by a decrease in the immigration of religious sects coupled with
more individual immigration. Miller agrees that Irish immigration grew
more secular during the immediate prerevolutionary period and describes
these immigrants as "mostly skilled artisans and indentured servants."[18]
Similarly, Wokeck comments that skilled men and boys were the most
sought-after Irish immigrants.[19] Overall, the sparse information available
on the Irish suggests their skill levels were also fairly high at the end of
the colonial period.

In summary, all the existing data on European immigration from the
three major source countries before 1820 suggest the immigrants were
very skilled at the end of the colonial period and were positively selected
from their underlying labor forces. During the earlier years of the eighteenth century, when religious motives for immigration may have been
of greater importance, European immigrants were probably less skilled
overall. Even at this time, however, it is likely that at least a substantial
minority of the migrants possessed a fairly high level of skill. Given the
relatively high cost of the voyage across the Atlantic Ocean before the
1830s, it is not surprising that higher skilled – and presumably higher
income – individuals comprised most of the immigrant stream.

The Occupations of Immigrants to 1860

Beginning in 1820, data on the occupations of the immigrants are available from the Passenger Lists. These are shown in Table 5.3 and Figure 5.1. They indicate the overall immigrant stream continued to be
highly skilled during the 1820s, with 55 to 70 percent being composed of
white-collar workers and artisans.[20] Between the 1820s and the 1840s,
the number of immigrants in all four groups increased, but the relative
importance of the occupational groups changed. By the last half of the

---

was small until the 1760s. Between 1730 and 1775, almost 48% of the Irish who arrived
did so in the last fifteen years of the period. Irish arrivals during the 1730s and 1740s
averaged 750 per year, while German arrivals averaged 2,000 per year. Between 1760
and 1775, an average of 1,650 Irish and 950 Germans arrived in the United States each
year. Calculated from Wokeck, *Trade*, Tables 2 and 4, pp. 45–6, 169–73.

[17] Cullen, "Irish Diaspora," p. 144.
[18] Miller, *Emigrants*, p. 162.
[19] Wokeck, *Trade*, p. 211.
[20] Edward Phillips, one of the immigrants introduced in Chapter 1, was an artisan. He had
been a handloom weaver of cotton cloths in England before he immigrated in 1817. See
Erickson, *Invisible Immigrants*, p. 265.

TABLE 5.3. *Immigrant Occupations, 1820–1860 (percent of total for each period)*

Time Period	White Collar	Artisans/Other Skilled	Farmers	Unskilled	Ave. Annual Total Listed with Occupations
1820–1826	36%	30%	23%	11%	4,805
1827–1831	27%	31%	22%	20%	8,919
1832–1835	19%	37%	29%	15%	24,704
1836–1845	14%	26%	32%	28%	37,087
1846–1854	6%	18%	33%	43%	150,415
1855–1860	14%	22%	27%	37%	93,562

Source: Calculated from U.S. Department of Commerce, *Historical Statistics*, Series C131–136. A more detailed breakdown appears in Carter et al., *Historical Statistics*, series Ad231–Ad245.

1830s, the white-collar percentage was usually the smallest of the four groups. The percentage of skilled immigrants remained fairly constant into the middle 1830s but then underwent a decline. The percentage of farmers fluctuated quite a bit from year to year but generally trended

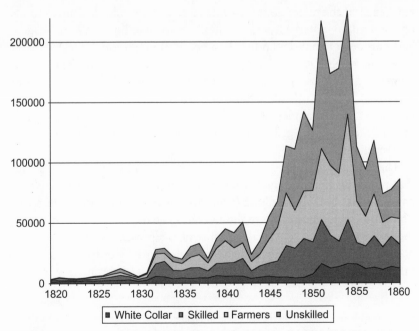

FIGURE 5.1. U.S. Immigrant Occupations, 1820–1860. *Source:* U.S. Department of Commerce, *Historical Statistics*, Series C131–136.

slowly upward. Lastly, the least skilled group, laborers and servants, experienced the steepest rise in percentage. The overall result was an increasing importance of immigrants with less skill. In 1834, for the first time but thereafter for every year except 1835, the farmer and unskilled groups together comprised at least 50 percent of the immigrant stream. Notice this change began well before the outbreak of the potato famine in 1846. The combined percentage rose to almost 60 percent in 1840 and to more than 70 percent in every year from 1845 through 1855.[21] Thus, according to the official figures, the sizeable increase in the volume of immigration experienced by the United States beginning in the early 1830s was not mainly because of more of the same immigrants arriving in larger numbers. Instead, the higher volume resulted from a much larger increase in the number of low-skilled immigrants who arrived, whereas a much smaller numerical change occurred in the volume of high-skilled immigrants. This general result is what would be expected given the decline in the costs of moving from Europe to the United States.

Although the numbers shown in Table 5.3 and Figure 5.1 are the most comprehensive available, they may be misleading for many reasons. First, the data are available only in aggregated form. Thus, it is not clear whether the change in skill levels occurred for immigrants arriving from each of the major source countries or was specific to a single country. Second, as noted earlier, the numbers include both U.S. passengers and European females who listed an occupation, although most females appear in a "No Occupation" column in the original source. Third, on a number of the Passenger Lists, the words "Laborers" or "Farmers" are entered at the top of each page and ditto marks are used for the occupations of the remainder of the passengers. Fourth, questions have been raised concerning the general accuracy of the occupational entries on the Passenger Lists.

The first two problems can be overcome by using a body of research that primarily examines male immigrants from specific countries. Occupational distributions resulting from this research appear in Table 5.4.[22] The third issue requires more discussion. Probably about one-fourth of the lists have entries where all or most of the passengers have the same occupation recorded, many of them through the use of ditto marks.[23] The official estimates shown in Table 5.3 and Figure 5.1 presumably include

---

[21] This calculation is based on the data behind Figure 5.1.

[22] The data for Germany for 1815–20 are repeated from Table 5.2.

[23] Glazier et al., "Socio-Demographic Characteristics," p. 245, estimate that about 30% of the lists for the Irish immigrants are "questionable."

TABLE 5.4. *Male Immigrant Occupations, by Country of Origin,
1815–1860 (percent of annual total in each group)*

Country/Years	White Collar	Artisans & Craftsmen	Industrial Workers[a]	Farmers	Unskilled
Germany					
1815–1820	9.8	63.8		22.6	3.8
1836–1845	4.6	38.4	4.6	46.7	5.7
1846–1853	4.7	32.9	5.5	49.3	7.6
England					
1831	12.4	33.1	16.5	24.6	13.4
1841	9.7	30.8	25.3	19.1	15.0
1846–1854	5.6	36.7	17.3	14.7	25.7
1851	7.2	31.1	9.3	23.0	29.5
1836–1845	5.0	31.5	4.9	18.4	40.2
1846–1853	3.6	25.5	5.1	22.1	43.7
Ireland					
1820	21	21		37	21
1851	2	11		8	79
1820–1834[b]	4.7	16.9	13.5	16.9	48.0
1835–1846[b]	3.2	13.0	10.8	12.5	60.4
1847–1848[b]	2.7	12.8	13.1	11.2	60.2
1846–1851	5.1	5.7	4.2	10.5	74.3
1836–1845	1.1	9.7	2.0	10.3	76.9
1846–1853	1.7	13.8	1.3	8.4	74.8

[a] Includes textile workers, iron and steel workers, and engineers for England and Germany. Includes textile workers for Ireland.

[b] Includes females.

Sources: Germany: row 1: calculated from Grubb, "German Immigration," Table 5, p. 432, and Grubb, *Immigration*, Table 21, pp. 107–9. England: rows 1 and 3: Erickson, *Leaving England*, Tables 3.6, 4.13, pp. 106–7, 150; row 2: Erickson, "Emigration in 1841: Part II," Table 4, p. 25 (these are slightly different from those given by Erickson – her percentages do not add to 100%, so I adjusted based on other information in the article); row 4: Van Vugt, "Prosperity," Table 2, p. 342. Ireland: rows 1–2: Blessing, "Irish Emigration," Table 2.3, p. 20. Blessing's figures in row 1 have been adjusted slightly to account for 5% of the labor force whose occupation was unknown; rows 3–5: Ó Gráda: "Across the Briny Ocean," p. 88; row 6: Glazier et al., "Socio-Demographic Characteristics," p. 268. All rows labeled "1836–1845" and "1846–1853": Cohn, "Occupational Evidence," Figures 1–3, pp. 394–5.

these questionable lists as written. Erickson, Van Vugt, Glazier, and most other researchers who took samples from the Passenger Lists for Great Britain and Ireland, simply did not include any of these questionable lists in their samples.[24] I have previously questioned the practice of excluding

[24] Erickson, "Uses," p. 322; Van Vugt, "Prosperity"; and Glazier et al., "Socio-Demographic Characteristics." The practice of most researchers has been to follow

these lists from samples of immigrants.[25] In comparing characteristics
by occupation, I found that age, size of traveling group, and number of
children were statistically different for laborers relative to other immigrants.[26] When the demographic information on the questionable lists
with "laborers" at the top is examined, the results indicate that a large
percentage of these passengers, much larger than on the good lists, actually were unskilled workers. Similarly, ships with "farmers" at the top
were more likely to sail from certain ports, and these ports recorded
many more farmers on the good lists than did those from the other
ports.[27] Thus, I determined that the occupational distributions acquired
from the good lists needed to be adjusted in order to obtain a more accurate (and different) sample. The adjusted distributions – shown in the
bottom two rows for each country in Table 5.4 – include a larger percentage of farmers in the German occupational distribution and a larger
percentage of unskilled workers in the Irish and British distributions.
The remainder of the entries in Table 5.4 are based solely on the good
lists.[28]

According to the data in Table 5.4, the average skill level of the
immigrant stream over the antebellum period definitely declined for Germany and Ireland and probably declined for England. In the large-scale
movement of German immigrants between 1815 and 1820, almost three-
fourths of the males were in the skilled or white-collar groups and only
about one-fifth were farmers. By the end of the 1830s, however, the
percentage in the farmer group more than doubled, while that in the
unskilled group was larger than ever before. In contrast, the artisan percentage fell below one-half of all immigrants. My estimates (rows 2 and 3)

Erickson, who describes the "questionable lists" as "worthless." Her sampling technique
substituted other lists for these, and says doing so involved no change in the average number of passengers carried, the ports of embarkation, or the dates of arrival in her samples
of UK emigrants. See the discussion in Erickson, "Emigration in 1841: Part I," p. 350.

[25] Cohn, "Occupations"; and Cohn, "Occupational Evidence."

[26] Laborers were younger, more likely to travel alone and, if they had children, traveled
with fewer children. All of the lists in my sample with "Laborers" at the top and ditto
marks were from the United Kingdom.

[27] All of these ships in my sample were from the Continent.

[28] Comparing the "1846–1854" row with the "1846–1853" row for England shows the
sizeable difference the approach can make. I have not included the samples used in Ferrie,
Yankeys. He does not report his complete samples from the Passenger Lists, but uses
only those individuals that he could also find in U.S. Census material. Not surprisingly,
Ferrie's samples thus contain a larger percentage of White-Collar workers compared to
the work by all other researchers. His final sample, however, does include individuals
from the "questionable" lists, with the occupations recorded taken at face value.

show the White-Collar category declining to under the percentage of Unskilled workers.[29] Thus, it is evident that the average skill level of the immigrant stream from Germany fell as the total volume of German immigration increased during the antebellum period.[30]

Empirical estimates of the occupational distribution of Irish immigration also indicate a decline in skill levels. The data in the first two rows from Blessing show a dramatic increase in the percentage of unskilled workers between 1820 and 1850.[31] The changes here were somewhat different from the changes that occurred for Germany. The immigration of (male) laborers and servants came to dominate the Irish flow to such an extent that the percentages in each of the other Irish occupational groups declined. The figures provided by Ó Gráda include both males and females (rows 3–5 for Ireland) and show the same basic, although not quite as dramatic, change. The estimates provided by Glazier (row 6) and the author (rows 7–8) are very similar to those given by Blessing and thus reinforce the fact that the skill level of the male Irish immigrant stream had fallen by the late 1830s. Overall, Blessing's comment that "(i)n the early decades of the century skilled artisans were more numerous; by the late 1830s the majority were unskilled rural laborers from the 'peasant' sectors of the society" seems very accurate.[32] Thus, the average

---

[29] One complicating factor is that the data provided by Grubb, "German Immigration," for 1815–20 are for German arrivals in Philadelphia, while the data for 1836–53 and 1840–50 are for arrivals in New York. However, because most Germans arrived in Philadelphia during 1815–20 and in New York during 1836–53 (see Chapter 7), the discussion in the text is accurate for the major part of German immigration. Grabbe, "European Immigration," Tables 1, 2, pp. 192, 194, estimates that about three-fourths of the "Germans and Swiss" immigrants arrived in Philadelphia between 1810 and 1820.

[30] Wegge, "Hesse-Cassel Emigrants," pp. 377–8, finds that the laborer percentage from Hesse-Cassel increased dramatically from 1841–51 to 1852–7, although the increase at least partly reflects better coverage of "illegal" emigrants beginning in 1852. Johann Bauer, one of the immigrants introduced in Chapter 1, was different from many of the Germans arriving in the early 1850s, because Bauer had apparently worked for a merchant in Germany. See Kamphoefner et al., *News*, p. 149.

[31] Blessing, "Irish Emigration."

[32] Blessing, "Irish Emigration," p. 19. Mokyr found a similar decline in the skill levels of the Irish immigrants in his data that cover 1820 to 1848 – the percentage of laborers increased from 26% in 1820–4 to 46% in 1840–4. The percentage of total Irish immigration in all of Mokyr's skilled groups fell over the same period. See Mokyr, *Why Ireland Starved*, p. 249. Mokyr's figures include both males and females. It is unclear from Blessing's discussion whether his figures include both males and females or only males. Miller, *Emigrants*, p. 267, also discusses "the growing number of Irish emigrants without skills or education" before the famine.

skill level of the Irish immigrant stream shows the same decline over the antebellum period that was found for German immigration.

The numerical estimates reported for nineteenth-century English immigrants in Table 5.4 indicate their skills also probably fell over the antebellum period, although this conclusion is not as certain. To some extent, what happened to the skill level of the English immigrant stream depends on what is done with the questionable lists. In addition, the estimates in rows 1 through 4 for England are for males age twenty and older, whereas the data in the last two rows are for males age fifteen and older. Some of the difference in estimates may therefore be because of the teenage males being less skilled than those age twenty and older. In addition, a small portion of those classified as "farmers" were actually "farm laborers," so the unskilled worker percentage should be slightly larger. Keeping these points in mind, the data for the English immigrants indicate the major changes occurred in the unskilled percentage, which exhibited a distinct rise after 1831, and the white-collar percentage, which declined from its 1831 figure in all the samples. Adjusting for the questionable lists reinforces these trends by increasing the percentage of unskilled workers in the total. In contrast, the percentages of both craftsmen and farmers remained relatively constant over the antebellum period. Finally, the percentage of Industrial Workers fluctuated, although generally declined after 1841. Thus, although the evidence is not as definitive as for the Germans or the Irish, it suggests the average skill level of the English immigrant stream also declined after 1831.

Overall, the major conclusion of the last two sections is that the skill level of the immigrant stream was relatively high throughout the Colonial period and into the 1820s, and then underwent a substantial decline in a fairly short period of time beginning around the early 1830s.[33] Adjusting for the questionable lists reinforces this basic finding. The change in immigrant skills is fully consistent with the argument in Chapter 3 that the costs of immigrating across the Atlantic Ocean fell into the early 1830s. The lower costs, because of the reduced fares, increased remittances, better information, and so on, meant that a much greater percentage of Europeans had the option of moving to the United States. The larger volume of immigration beginning in the early 1830s was then associated

---

[33] This trend is also apparent in a measure of the rate of entrepreneurship among the immigrants. See Ferrie and Mokyr, "Immigration," Figure 1, p. 130. The rate fell from about 30% in the 1820s to about 10% after 1840. Discussion of the effects of immigrant entrepreneurship on the U.S. economy is provided in Chapter 8.

TABLE 5.5. *Male Labor Force Distributions, by Country and Occupation*
(percent of annual total)

Country/Years	White Collar	Artisans & Craftsmen	Industrial Workers	Farmers	Unskilled
Germany					
1849	8.8	16.8	7.4	57.3^a	9.7^b
England					
1831	10.7	21.6	13.2	33.8	20.7
1841	9.7	29.7	15.3	28.0	17.3
1851	10.7	30.2	15.7	27.3	16.2
Ireland					
1841	5.0	10.5	7.1	21.1	56.2
1851^c	5.1	5.8	20.4	16.8	51.7

^{a} Includes laborers.
^{b} Servants only.
^{c} Entire labor force.

Sources: Germany: Calculated from Hoffmann, *Das Wachstum*, Tables 15 and 20, pp. 196–7, 204. England: 1831 and 1851: Erickson, *Leaving England*, Tables 3.6, 4.13, pp. 106–7, 150; 1841: Erickson, "Emigration in 1841: Part II," Table 4, p. 25. Ireland: 1841: Ó Gráda, "Across the Briny Ocean," Table 4.5, p. 86; 1851: Glazier et al., "Socio-Demographic Characteristics," Table 11, p. 268.

with a much greater increase in the numbers of individuals with low skills than high skills.[34]

Comparisons to European Labor Forces

The estimates just discussed of the occupational distribution of the immigrant stream of each country can be compared with that country's entire labor force to determine whether the immigrants were positively selected or negatively selected. The labor force distributions for males are shown in Table 5.5 for each of the three major source countries, except for the 1851 figure for Ireland, which includes females. Those individuals with occupations that comprise a larger percentage of the immigrant stream

---

[34] The decline in the skill level of the immigrant stream during the antebellum years has also occurred during more recent years, although for a different reason. Immigrants admitted to the United States after 1965 have been found to be much less skilled than those admitted before 1965. This decline is because of the changes in the national origins of the immigrant stream resulting from a change in U.S. immigration policy in 1965. See the discussion in Borjas, "National Origin."

than the labor force were more likely to leave from Europe. This comparison has been done by a number of researchers for Ireland and England.[35] A discussion of how the entire German immigrant stream compared with the German labor force is provided here for the first time. The results of these exercises are somewhat influenced by what a researcher chooses to do with the "questionable" lists, because the previous section indicated that the occupational distributions of the immigrant streams differed between the questionable and good lists.

The comparison for Germany is complicated by the fact that labor force figures do not exist before 1849 and the 1849 figures do not distinguish between farmers and laborers. A comparison of Tables 5.4 and 5.5, however, indicates that the German immigrant stream was positively selected during colonial times and remained so throughout the antebellum period. Between 1836 and 1853, German artisans and craftsmen were most likely to immigrate to the United States. All other groups were less likely to be found among the immigrants.[36] A similar result would hold for the 1815–20 immigration, because the artisan component of the immigrant stream was even larger at that time.[37] Although not shown here, a finer breakdown for the 1836–53 period indicates those most overrepresented among the immigrants were artisans and small shopkeepers who were involved in construction, food preparation and selling, and the clothing and woodworking trades. Farmers were found among the immigrants in about the same proportion as in the entire labor force.[38] On the other hand, textile workers were among the most underrepresented groups of immigrants, as were servants and white-collar workers. These results are consistent with more qualitative descriptions of the German immigrants. In a number of places, Walker describes the immigrants as mainly from the lower middle class. He sees them as being composed of small farmers, village shopkeepers and artisans, with few coming from large towns. In Walker's view, the immigrants were those who had property that could be

---

[35] Cohn, "Occupational Evidence"; Glazier et al., "Socio-Demographic Characteristics"; Erickson, *Leaving England*; Van Vugt, "Prosperity"; Mokyr, *Why Ireland Starved*; and Ó Gráda, "Across the Briny Ocean."

[36] Wegge, "Occupational Self-Selection," finds the same result for her sample of emigrants who left Hesse-Cassel between 1852 and 1857. She also provides a discussion of why artisans were the most likely group to emigrate from Germany during these years.

[37] The white-collar group may have also been overrepresented among the immigrants in 1815–20.

[38] To see this result, compare the sum of "Farmers" and "Unskilled" in Table 5.4 to the "Farmers" entry in Table 5.5. Note that the latter entry includes unskilled workers. Very few German immigrants are listed as Servants on the Passenger Lists.

turned into cash to fund the trip. They were individuals not yet in distress but they were under pressure and had something to lose.[39] Thus, both the empirical and the qualitative evidence indicate most German immigrants were not fleeing direct economic distress caused by the Industrial Revolution.[40]

An examination of English immigration yields somewhat different results. Over time, the English labor force changed to having more artisans and industrial workers and fewer farmers and unskilled workers. As noted previously, the immigrant stream changed to include more unskilled workers, but fewer white-collar workers. In 1831, the immigrant stream was somewhat more skilled than the English labor force, with white-collar workers, artisans and craftsmen, and industrial workers being overrepresented and the other two groups underrepresented. In later years, the most overrepresented group was unskilled workers, particularly if the estimates that include the questionable Passenger Lists are used. Artisans and craftsmen became about equally represented in the immigrant stream. Yet the general view of British immigration researchers is that most of the immigrants, including the unskilled workers, were not among the poorest in England. Jones says the British immigrants into the 1830s were small farmers, the "better" class of laborers, and skilled workers rather than poor laborers and craftsmen. For later years, Jones finds more farm laborers but his conclusion is the same as that given by Walker for German immigrants. The English immigrants were not the poorest citizens but those with something to lose.[41] Although disagreeing with Jones on the occupational distribution of English immigrants, Erickson and Van Vugt also view many of the British immigrants as being relatively well off. In particular, they find that wealthy farmers were very overrepresented among those classified as farmers.[42] On the other hand, their estimates indicate that, at least in 1831 and 1841, Industrial Workers were overrepresented among the immigrants. The opposite conclusion is reached for this group if the questionable lists are taken into account. In summary,

---

[39] Walker, *Germany*, pp. 47, 110, 130, 157. On page 7, Walker describes the 1816 emigrants as being driven by despair to leave Germany. Recall, however, that most of those who left Germany became stranded in the Netherlands because they were not able to afford the voyage to the United States and eventually returned to Germany.

[40] These data provide little support for the more recent view advanced by Kamphoefner that the decline of protoindustry was the major factor in causing most Germans to immigrate (see the discussion in Chapter 3).

[41] Jones, "Background," pp. 38–9, 43–5, 90.

[42] Erickson, *Leaving England*, pp.148–9; Erickson, "Emigration in 1841: Part II," pp. 26–30. Van Vugt, "Prosperity," pp. 341–2; Van Vugt, "Running," p. 417.

an argument can be made for the English immigrant stream being either positively or negatively selected by the 1840s and 1850s. Controversy also exists concerning whether a sizeable proportion of the immigrants were fleeing the immediate effects of the Industrial Revolution.

For Ireland, the immigrant stream changes from being positively selected to negatively selected over the course of the antebellum period. Although the occupational distribution of the Irish labor force is not available before 1841, the early immigrant occupational distributions strongly imply that unskilled workers were the only group significantly underrepresented in the immigrant stream. In fact, Adams describes the early Irish immigrants as being skilled artisans, shopkeepers, and professional men. Even in the 1830s, he sees the "better" class as going to America. Only after 1835 does Adams view laborers as forming the bulk of the immigrants.[43] Adams' view is very consistent with the information in Table 5.4. After the early or middle 1830s, most researchers find that unskilled workers become the only group significantly overrepresented among the Irish immigrants. The findings on artisans range from slightly underrepresented to slightly overrepresented among the immigrants. White-collar workers, industrial workers, and farmers are all underrepresented in the immigrant stream. Although the outbreak of the potato famine does not appear to drastically change the occupational composition of the Irish immigrant stream, recall from Chapter 2 that a larger portion of the immigrant stream began leaving from the poorer southern and western areas of the island. Thus, not surprisingly, evidence of fleeing distress is more apparent for Ireland than Germany or England. Yet the distress appears to have been the generally difficult conditions in Ireland, especially after the onset of the potato famine, and not the effects of the Industrial Revolution. In addition, even during the potato famine, the poorest of the poor were not the ones fleeing, probably because they could not afford the cost of the passage. In fact, Ó Gráda and O'Rourke emphasize that the poorest of the poor typically remained in Ireland (and many became casualties of the famine).[44]

Evidence on the size of traveling groups supports the previous arguments. For immigrants arriving from the three major source countries between 1836 and 1853, the author found adult German immigrants were older and traveled in the largest groups. The English immigrants

[43] Adams, *Ireland*, pp. 63, 106–9, 177, 214.
[44] For example, see Ó Gráda and O'Rourke, "Migration," p. 16.

were in the middle on both counts and the Irish were the youngest and most likely to travel alone.[45] Similarly, Erickson finds for her 1831 and 1841 samples that 26 percent of the British but 40 percent of the Irish traveled alone. Just for 1841, 24 percent of the British traveled with children, while only 14 percent of the Irish did.[46] For the Irish, Ó Gráda's samples for 1820–48 show 53 percent of the males and 38 percent of the females traveled alone.[47] During the famine years, Glazier finds that 43 percent traveled alone.[48] These results are primarily driven by the difference in the occupational distributions of the immigrants from the various countries because laborers and servants were generally younger and poorer. Both factors would make them more likely to travel alone or, if married, to have fewer children. Overall, this evidence is consistent with the German immigrants being the most skilled (and wealthy), the English in the middle, and the Irish the poorest.[49]

The very limited data available on the amount of cash carried by the immigrants also supports the general argument advanced in this section. The only overall figure is provided by the Commissioners of Emigration of the State of New York. They surveyed all arriving passengers in 1856 and found the average amount of cash held by each person was $68.08.[50] As to the individual countries, Wegge has provided the best data from

45 Cohn, "Comparative Analysis," Table 3, p. 70. Adult German passengers averaged slightly more than twenty-nine years of age, adult English slightly more than twenty-seven years, and adult Irish under twenty-six years. "Adult" passengers were those fifteen and older. Only one-third of the Germans traveled alone, while more than 35% of the English and more than 42% of the Irish did. For couples traveling with children, German and English immigrants sailed with an average of more than two and a half children, while Irish couples sailed with just more than two children. It is, of course, impossible to determine with complete accuracy if someone was traveling alone. Most of the Passenger Lists group the passengers by family and often use ditto marks for the last name. Someone listed by themselves without any apparent family is assumed to have been traveling alone, although he or she may have been traveling with friends. The reason for this convention is that, even if this person was traveling with friends, each person was probably paying only one fare.
46 Erickson, "Emigration in 1841: Part I," Tables 13 and 15, pp. 362–3.
47 Ó Gráda, "Across the Briny Ocean," Table 4.7, p. 88.
48 Glazier et al., "Socio-Demographic Characteristics," Table 9, p. 267.
49 Grubb, "German Immigration," pp. 433–4, similarly argues that the German immigrants were older and more skilled than the English immigrants during the late colonial period. Wegge, "Occupational Self-Selection," makes the point that the wealthiest Germans did not emigrate. Yet the Germans who did emigrate were clearly well off, especially compared to the Irish.
50 Kapp, *Immigration*, p. 142. This figure is, however, suspect. See the discussion in Kapp.

her sample of more than fifty thousand German immigrants who left Hesse-Cassel between 1832 and 1857. For all immigrants where an entry concerning cash is included, the average carried was the equivalent of $125 (176 thaler, about £25 in 1845, or about £1300 in 2004). Even deleting those individuals who carried more than $700 (1000 thaler), the remainder left with about $76 (107 thaler).[51] The British farmers who left apparently had financial capital equal to £50 to £200, although it should be recalled that these individuals were among the wealthiest of the British immigrants.[52] These limited data support the argument that the German immigrants were positively selected and neither they nor the British farmers were fleeing from imminent economic distress.

In conclusion, before the 1830s, the immigrant stream of each of the three major source countries was much more skilled than the labor force they left. Although skill levels fell beginning in the early 1830s, the German immigrant stream remained more skilled than the underlying labor force, although the differential was not as large. The English immigrant stream, overall, may have become similar to that of the English labor force over the antebellum period. In particular, German and English immigrants were most likely to be artisans or other skilled workers, although each country also sent a sizeable number of farmers. These groups were more likely to travel with their family and many carried a fair amount of cash. The English immigrant stream also contained a large portion of unskilled workers, although probably not the poorest. Few unskilled workers came from Germany. The situation for Ireland after the early 1830s is different. Unskilled workers were the only occupational group that was significantly overrepresented in the immigrant stream. Yet quite a bit of work indicates the immigrating unskilled workers were not the poorest ones in Ireland. Even though the cost of immigrating to the United States had fallen, it was still too high for the poorest Irish. They remained in Ireland and disproportionately became casualties of the famine. Of the three major source countries, only England may have had many Industrial Workers among their immigrants, although this conclusion is controversial. Thus, the immigrants traveling to the United States during the antebellum period were generally not fleeing the effects of the Industrial Revolution, although as discussed in Chapter 3, all were facing a deteriorating economic future had they remained in Europe.

[51] Wegge, "Hesse-Cassel Emigrants," Table 5B, p. 380.
[52] Van Vugt, "Running," p. 417.

Comparison Among Countries of Origin

The analysis in the previous sections suggests that, after the first half of the 1830s, the German immigrants were generally more skilled and wealthier than those from England. The Irish immigrants trailed on both counts. Unskilled workers comprised a much larger portion of the Irish immigrant stream than of the British, and few unskilled workers appeared in the German stream. Four factors explain these differences among the immigrant streams. First, both the Irish and the English populations spoke the English language, therefore poor laborers from these countries could adjust more easily to the U.S. labor market.[53] In contrast, few Germans spoke English, a factor that reduced the gain that could be obtained from a move to the United States, especially for the poorer individuals. To counteract this disadvantage, more-skilled individuals, who could expect a larger gain from moving, formed the bulk of the German immigrant stream to the United States. Second, German laborers in Hesse-Cassel were so poor that their transportation to the United States cost a minimum of a full year's wages.[54] Although unskilled workers in other parts of Germany may have earned somewhat higher wages, the transportation costs relative to wages must have still been very large. In contrast, for Irish unskilled workers, and presumably also for the British, the transportation cost was only about half of a year's wages.[55]

Third, as discussed in Chapter 3, about 50 percent of all remittance dollars from the United States were sent to Ireland. The greater access to these funds allowed many more Irish, especially poorer individuals, to be able to afford the passage costs relative to the English or the Germans. Fourth, the German immigrants lived further from an embarkation port, a factor that led to a longer overall trip, at least until the late 1840s or the 1850s. The longer travel time, which is detailed in Chapter 6, led to a larger period of foregone income for Germans immigrating to the United States. To achieve a net gain, German immigrants therefore had to earn a higher wage in the United States. Obviously, more skilled individuals would be more likely to do so. The four factors combined after the early 1830s to make the Irish immigrant stream the poorest and

---

[53] Public schools established in Ireland during the 1820s led to an increase in literacy in the English language. See Blessing, "Irish Emigration," p. 16.

[54] Wegge, "Occupational Self-Selection," p. 386.

[55] Ó Gráda, "Across the Briny Ocean," p. 87. In addition, Hansen, *Atlantic Migration*, p. 197, says the Irish could often get last-minute bargain rates in Liverpool (sometimes 50% off) whereas emigrating Germans more often paid full fare.

least skilled, and the German stream the wealthiest and most skilled. Even so, the transportation costs were still sufficiently large that the poorest Europeans were unable to immigrate to the United States.

Summary

Relative to the labor forces they left, the European immigrants arriving in the antebellum United States before 1830 were highly skilled. Thus, rather than receiving poor individuals forced out of their European homes, the United States welcomed (and Europe lost) high-quality individuals. Given the high costs of transatlantic travel before 1830, this finding is not surprising. The fall in the overall cost of immigrating during the 1820s thus did more than simply increase the volume of immigration. It made a permanent move an option for individuals with lower incomes. One effect was an increase in the number of females and children who immigrated. A second effect was a decline in the average skill levels of the immigrant streams from all three major source countries. A third effect was the disappearance of the indentured servant system, because more individuals could afford to pay their own way to the United States.[56] Thus, because of the greater ease of reaching the United States by the 1830s, the immigrant stream entering the country after the early 1830s differed in important ways from that entering before the 1830s.

The lower cost of immigration, due particularly to the large amount of remittances received, affected Ireland the most. After the early 1830s, unskilled workers so dominated the Irish immigrant stream that it became less skilled than the Irish labor force. Furthermore, it is likely that many of the Irish were fleeing economic distress, even before the onset of the potato famine, although not many were fleeing the distress caused by the onset of the Industrial Revolution. Even so, the poorest of the Irish unskilled workers could not afford the cost of immigrating and remained in Ireland, many to become casualties of the potato famine. Even with the decline in skill levels, the German immigrant stream remained more skilled than the German labor force, probably because almost all German immigrants faced a language barrier and laborers in particular found it difficult to afford the costs of immigrating. Although, as always, the information is less certain, it appears the English immigrant stream was in the middle. With the available data, it is impossible to tell whether

---

[56] Grubb, "End." Also, see Steinfeld, *Invention*, pp. 164–9, for discussion of other factors important to the decline of the indentured servant system.

the English immigrants were, on average, more or less skilled than the underlying labor force, or whether many English were fleeing the effects of the Industrial Revolution. However, the evidence indicates that not many of the Irish or the Germans were fleeing the economic distress caused by the Industrial Revolution. The picture presented in many textbooks – that European immigrants of the period were mainly pushed out of Europe – thus needs to be revised.

Appendix 5.1
The Believability of the Occupational Information on the Passenger Lists

The chapter discussed the so-called questionable Passenger Lists, those where all, or almost all, of the pages had "laborers" or "farmers" at the top and used ditto marks for the remainder of the page. Obviously, these lists were filled out quickly and the occupational information on them is not totally accurate. The issue examined in this appendix is whether the occupational information on the good lists can be assumed to be reasonably accurate.

A number of grounds exist for questioning the accuracy of the occupational information on the Passenger Lists. Because many of the lists from the same port are in the same handwriting, they appear to have been completed by professional clerks at the port of embarkation.[57] The clerks likely had no expertise in accurately recording immigrant occupations or other information, and probably had little incentive to be completely accurate. For example, one study found that 79 percent of the passengers leaving from Bremen between 1847 and 1854 were listed as being from "Germany" rather than a specific Germanic country.[58] The questionable lists from all of the major source countries are evidence of sloppy work on the occupational entries. In addition, even if the clerks wanted to be accurate, the occupational information they recorded would have been what they were told by the immigrant, which may have been true or may have been the occupation they desired to obtain in the United States. In at least one instance, in fact, new (and inaccurate) lists were prepared on the ship before arrival in the United States.[59] Departure lists still exist

[57] Mageean, "Nineteenth-Century Irish Emigration"; Swierenga, *Faith*.
[58] Zimmerman and Wolfert, *German Immigrants*, p. xi.
[59] See the story discussed in Wegge, "Hesse-Cassel Emigrants," p. 363. For a discussion of the advantages of data collected regionally in Germany, see pp. 367–70 in the same source.

for Hamburg. A comparison of these with the U.S. Passenger Lists found that, although many of the lists were identical or nearly so, others were very different.[60] On the other hand, Swierenga has found few differences between the lists for the Dutch records.[61] Overall, therefore, uncertainty exists concerning the accuracy of the occupational information on the Passenger Lists.

However, for most of the immigrant flow no alternative to using the U.S. Passenger Lists is available to determine occupations during the antebellum period. As discussed in Chapter 2, virtually no comprehensive data exist from European sources before the 1850s. The issues and problems with the Irish and British data were also discussed in Chapter 2. For Germany, work has been done or is currently in process on emigration from a number of German states.[62] This work has already added and promises to add substantially more to our knowledge of German immigration from a number of regions. From the perspective of the United States, however, it is not clear whether this work will ever provide a comprehensive picture of the *entire* German immigrant stream. Furthermore, as has been discussed about some of Kamphoefner's work, drawing conclusions concerning the entirety of immigration based on the study of one region can lead to inaccurate inferences.

As a final comment on the accuracy of the information on the Passenger Lists, note that many of the conclusions discussed in this chapter were based on an analysis of these data, and these conclusions broadly agree with existing views in the literature. One additional piece of evidence is shown in Table A5.1, where data, taken from the good lists, on the occupational distributions of German immigrants by port of embarkation are presented. These data are broadly consistent with existing views of immigration. Le Havre drew immigrants almost totally from southwest Germany, the area of partible inheritance, small farm size, and extreme land pressure. It is not surprising that ships leaving from Le Havre contained the largest percentages of farmers in the sample. Bremen and Antwerp drew immigrants from wider areas of Germany and their occupational distributions are more balanced. The ports of Hamburg, London, and Liverpool all sent immigrants who traveled through Hamburg. The occupational distributions of Germans leaving from these ports

---

[60] Günther, *Auswandererlisten*. Hamburg was, however, the least important of the embarkation ports for the Germans. See Table 6.2.

[61] Swierenga, *Faith*.

[62] See the discussion in Wegge, "Hesse-Cassel Emigrants," p. 361. One example of such work is the study by Kamphoefner, *Westfalians*.

TABLE A5.1. *Occupational Distribution of Male German Immigrants, by Port, 1836–1853 (percent of column total)*

Occupation	Le Havre	Antwerp	Bremen	Hamburg and British Ports
Farmers	69%	50%	52%	32%
Unskilled	7%	13%	3%	14%
Artisans and Skilled	22%	35%	40%	47%
White Collar	2%	2%	5%	7%

Source: Data underlying the results reported in Cohn, "Occupational Evidence."

were virtually identical – another indicator of the accuracy of the information on the good Passenger Lists – and thus they are combined in Table A5.1. Hamburg and the British ports drew many immigrants from north and east Germany, the areas of large-scale farming. As a result, ships leaving from these ports contained the smallest percentage of farmers. In summary, the data in Table A5.1 indicate the occupational information available from the good Passenger Lists is reasonably accurate, given what we know about how German immigrants left their country. Unfortunately, as discussed in detail earlier, the good lists may not be an accurate indicator of the occupational distribution of the entire immigrant stream.

Appendix 5.2
Classification of Occupations

Major occupations included in each class are listed.

    I. Unskilled Workers
        Laborers – laborers
        Servants – domestic servants
        Other Unskilled – carriers, packers, porters, soldiers, seamen, fishermen, barbers.
    II. Farmers – farmer, cultivator, peasant, farm laborer (explicitly listed as such).
    IIIa. Artisans and Other Skilled Workers (Craftsmen)
        Building trades – carpenters, bricklayers, masons, plasterers, painters, plumbers, brickmakers.
        Mining – miners; stonecutters, quarrymen.
        Food trades – brewers, bakers, confectioners, butchers, millers, malsters.

Metal trades – blacksmiths, locksmiths, goldsmiths, jewelers, tinsmiths, silversmiths.

Clothing trades – tailors, milliners, shoemakers, hatters, glovers, clothiers.

Woodworking trades – coopers, joiners, carvers, wheelwrights.

Leather – saddlers, tanners, curriers.

Mechanics – all mechanics, not otherwise designated.

Miscellaneous other – bookbinders, printers; glassmakers; papermakers; oil and colormen; chemical workers.

IIIb. Industrial Workers

Textiles – clothmakers, spinners, weavers, stockingmakers.

Iron and Steel – engineers, gunmakers, cutlers, lockmakers; coachmakers, wagonmakers; founders, smelters; machinists.

IV. White-Collar Workers

Clerical – clerks.

Commercial – merchants, shopkeepers; innkeeper; dealers.

Professional, Technical, and Managerial – accountants, doctors, teachers, lawyers, preachers, writers, other learned professions; manufacturers.

6

The Trip from Europe to the United States

By the end of the nineteenth century, a journey from almost anywhere in Europe to the United States took about ten days – a few days by rail to an embarkation port and about a week on a steamship. A sizeable portion of the immigration that occurred was thus temporary, as many individuals found it easy to come to the United States to work for a season or a few years and then return home. During the antebellum years, however, few actual immigrants – as opposed to merchants or soldiers – anticipated returning to Europe, and the evidence shows that few did.[1] Moving between Europe and the United States at this time involved a much longer trip. The immigrants first had to get from their farm or village to a port from which they could leave, arrange for and wait for passage on a sailing ship, and then endure the long voyage across the Atlantic Ocean. These aspects of the immigrant's trip are examined in this chapter. Included is information on internal transportation within Europe, data on which cities served as major embarkation ports and why they did, and the regulations imposed on the process by the various governments. The immigrants' experience onboard the ship is examined, especially with respect to the mortality suffered, along with the mortality they experienced immediately after arrival. The entire discussion explains why few immigrants wished to repeat the trip to return to Europe.

---

[1] See Chapter 1 for a discussion of the evidence on the size of return migration.

The Ports of Embarkation

The port of embarkation played a central role in the immigrant's trip. The immigrant had to plan how to get from his or her home to the port, and, in order to reduce the overall costs of the trip, arrive at a time that would minimize his or her wait for a ship. A good deal of anecdotal evidence exists on which ports the immigrants left from, but comprehensive data are not available. Although the Passenger Lists recorded the port of embarkation for each ship, summary data were never published. Therefore, these data can only be estimated from the various samples that have been taken.

The most complete set of samples from the Passenger Lists have been drawn to analyze mortality. The samples cover the entire 1820–60 period for 2,643 ships arriving in one of the five major arrival ports in the United States: New York, New Orleans, Philadelphia, Baltimore, and Boston.[2] Information on the breakdown by port of embarkation for the number of ships and the number of passengers arriving at each port is shown in Tables 6.1 and 6.2. The purpose of the samples was to analyze mortality and not the port of embarkation, therefore only ships that provided some evidence concerning mortality were included in the samples.[3] Thus, these samples would not provide an accurate representation of the relative importance of the ports of embarkation if the tendency to record mortality differed by port of embarkation. On the other hand, the samples are large. Together, the five samples include almost 600,000 passengers, more than 12 percent of the 4.84 million estimated in Chapter 2 as having arrived directly from Europe between 1820 and 1860. Thus, any bias resulting from the methods used to collect the samples probably has only a small effect on the figures shown in Tables 6.1 and 6.2.

The data in Table 6.1 indicate that ships carrying passengers bound for the United States left from a large number of ports in both the United Kingdom and the Continent. Exactly where the ships left from depended on the port of arrival. Ships sailing to New York City left from the largest

---

[2] Cohn, "Passenger Mortality." The samples drawn for Baltimore and Boston discussed here had little useable data on mortality and so were not included in the paper cited. The total number of ships arriving from Europe with passengers is not known. The Passenger Lists include arrivals from foreign ports other than Europe and ships arriving from Europe with, for example, one cabin passenger.

[3] A complete discussion of the procedure used to choose the ships in the samples is discussed in the mortality section of this chapter. Generally, the estimates of ships and immigrants from the more minor ports can be considered to be the least accurate.

TABLE 6.1. *Number of Ships, by Ports of Embarkation and Arrival, 1820–1860 (percentage of column total)*

Port of Embarkation	Arrivals at					All 5 Ports
	New York	New Orleans	Philadelphia	Baltimore	Boston	
Great Britain						
Liverpool	44.3%	41.8%	69.4%	27.9%	78.2%	47.2%
London	7.5	0.8	2.3	–	0.8	5.3
Bristol	1.9	–	1.4	–	–	1.4
Glasgow	2.7	–	–	–	0.8	1.8
Other Britain	0.8	–	3.2	–	1.5	0.8
Ireland						
Belfast	0.8	1.0	0.9	–	–	0.8
Cork	0.6	0.2	–	–	7.5	0.8
Limerick	0.7	–	0.9	–	–	0.5
Dublin	0.8	1.2	0.5	–	–	0.8
Galway	0.5	–	–	–	1.5	0.4
Londonderry	0.2	–	10.0	–	–	1.0
Other Ireland	1.0	–	1.4	–	–	0.6
Continent						
Le Havre	13.6	22.1	3.2	5.9	–	13.4
Bordeaux	–	5.9	0.5	–	–	1.1
Bremen	9.1	21.8	5.0	48.5	–	11.7
Hamburg	7.5	1.6	0.5	–	–	5.3
Antwerp	3.8	2.1	–	1.5	–	2.9
Rotterdam	2.1	0.2	0.9	14.7	1.5	2.0
Amsterdam	0.8	0.8	–	1.5	–	0.7
Gothenburg	0.8	–	–	–	7.5	0.9
Other Scandinavia	0.5	–	–	–	0.8	0.5
Other Continent	0.3	0.4	–	–	–	0.2
TOTAL SHIPS	1,733	490	219	68	133	2,643

Sources: New York, New Orleans, and Philadelphia: Data underlying Cohn, "Passenger Mortality," Table 2, p. 7. Baltimore and Boston: New samples from the Passenger Lists for each city.

number of ports. More than 60 percent left from a United Kingdom port and, of these, 72 percent left from Liverpool. A sizeable number also left from London, with a smattering from a large number of other ports in both Great Britain and Ireland. Turning to the Continent, Le Havre, Bremen, and Hamburg (in that order) were the most important embarkation ports for ships sailing to New York, although a number of other ports also appear on the list. The passenger trade to Philadelphia

TABLE 6.2. *Number of Passengers, by Ports of Embarkation and Arrival,* *1820–1860 (percentage of column total)*

Port of Embarkation	Arrivals at					
	New York	New Orleans	Philadelphia	Baltimore	Boston	All 5 Ports
Great Britain						
Liverpool	57.1	41.5	74.7	21.6	88.9	56.8
London	5.3	0.3	1.1	–	0.1	4.1
Bristol	1.0	–	1.3	–	–	0.8
Glasgow	1.8	–	–	–	0.2	1.4
Other Britain	0.3	–	0.8	–	0.3	0.3
Ireland						
Belfast	0.4	0.2	0.5	–	–	0.4
Cork	0.3	0.1	–	–	4.0	0.5
Limerick	0.5	–	0.2	–	–	0.4
Dublin	0.5	1.4	0.1	–	–	0.6
Galway	0.3	–	–	–	0.7	0.2
Londonderry	0.1	–	13.2	–	–	0.7
Other Ireland	0.4	–	0.4	–	–	0.4
Continent						
Le Havre	13.9	20.8	2.7	4.5	–	13.3
Bordeaux	–	1.6	0.1	–	–	0.2
Bremen	7.4	29.5	4.2	57.7	–	10.9
Hamburg	5.5	1.3	0.1	–	–	4.2
Antwerp	2.9	2.4	–	1.0	–	2.5
Rotterdam	1.2	0.3	0.6	13.8	0.6	1.3
Amsterdam	0.3	0.4	–	1.4	–	0.3
Gothenburg	0.3	–	–	–	4.9	0.5
Other Scandinavia	0.2	–	–	–	0.3	0.2
Other Continent	0.2	0.1	–	–	–	0.1
TOTAL PASSENGERS	437,583	77,119	28,598	12,986	31,349	587,635

Sources: New York, New Orleans, and Philadelphia: Data underlying Cohn, "Passenger Mortality," Table 2, p. 7. Baltimore and Boston: New samples from the Passenger Lists for each city.

was even more concentrated on Liverpool, with a sizeable contingent also arriving from Londonderry. Ninety percent of the ships arriving at Philadelphia left from somewhere in the United Kingdom. Of those ships leaving from the Continent, almost all sailed from Bremen or Le Havre. The immigrant trade to Boston was the most concentrated on Liverpool, which was the embarkation port for almost 80 percent of the arriving ships. With a sizeable number arriving from Cork, ships leaving from a United Kingdom port accounted for slightly more than 90 percent of all arrivals. Very few ships arrived from the Continent, but Boston was the only city where more than a tiny percentage of ships arrived from Scandinavia.

Immigrant traffic to the southern ports of New Orleans and Baltimore had a different pattern. In both cases, more ships left from the Continent than from the United Kingdom. For New Orleans, although Liverpool was the single most important embarkation port, almost 55 percent of the ships left from a port on the Continent because many German immigrants desired to travel to western areas of the United States, and access was easy through New Orleans. Of the continental ports, Le Havre and Bremen were of almost equal importance. Interestingly, Hamburg barely appears on the list, whereas Bordeaux, which sent few ships to any other U.S. port, had an active passenger trade with New Orleans, perhaps reflecting business connections between French merchants and those of French descent in New Orleans. Ships arriving at the port of Baltimore were most likely to have left from the Continent. Almost three-quarters of the ships sailed from a continental port, with Bremen and Rotterdam being the most important. Overall, the data in Table 6.1 indicate that a good deal of geographic specialization prevailed in the Atlantic immigrant trade.

With only a few differences, the data in Table 6.2 on total passengers present the same general picture of the immigrant trade. The most important difference is that for the three northern arrival ports, Liverpool accounted for a larger share of passengers than ships. This difference occurs because ships leaving from Liverpool, on average, carried more passengers than those leaving from the other European ports. The same general point holds for ships leaving from Bremen for the southern ports of Baltimore and New Orleans, but not to New York. Ships leaving from Le Havre carried an average or slightly smaller number of passengers, whereas those leaving from Hamburg and London carried fewer passengers than average. Overall, 89 percent of the passenger traffic leaving for the United States left from these five European ports. Of these, Liverpool single-handedly accounted for more than 47 percent of all ships and almost 57 percent of the passengers. For the three major ports on the Continent, Le Havre accounted for 13 percent of both the ships and U.S.-bound passengers, while 11 percent of the passengers and 12 percent of the ships left from Bremen. The two remaining important ports, London and Hamburg, each sent 4 percent of the departing passengers on their way and each accounted for 5 percent of the departing ships.

Except for Liverpool and Le Havre, some changes occurred in the importance of the other ports over the antebellum period. Liverpool accounted for 51 percent of all ships to New York City in the 1820s,

37 percent in the 1830s, 49 percent in the 1840s, and 43 percent in the 1850s. Similarly, Le Havre's importance as a port did not change much over time. In contrast, both Bremen and Hamburg became more important embarkation ports for arrivals in New York City. Neither Bremen nor Hamburg had any of the ships in the sample arriving in New York in the 1820s. Bremen accounted for only 6 percent of the ships arriving during the 1830s, but comprised more than 12 percent of the ships arriving during the 1850s. Similarly, Hamburg had 5 percent of the ships arriving in the 1830s and 9 percent of those arriving in the 1850s. London declined as a port of importance, especially after 1840. Of the ships arriving in New York, 16 percent left from London before 1840, whereas only 6 percent did between 1840 and 1860.

As discussed in previous chapters, most studies using the Passenger Lists have centered on immigrants from one country. Thus, other researchers have provided only a limited amount of data that can be used to check the accuracy of the estimates in Tables 6.1 and 6.2. Erickson has presented some useful information on departures of the Irish and British immigrants from the British Isles. In 1841, she finds that 83 percent of the British and Irish passengers arriving at five U.S. ports came from Liverpool, 8 percent came from London, 4 percent from Scottish ports, 2 percent from Belfast, and the remainder from other ports.[4] These figures are generally comparable to those that can be calculated from Table 6.2 if only the British and Irish ports are considered. Similarly, Ferenczi provides figures for Germans leaving from Bremen, Hamburg, and "foreign ports" between 1844 and 1854. He finds that 47 percent of the German emigrants left from the two German ports. In Table 6.2, if the "foreign ports" are considered to be Le Havre, Antwerp, Rotterdam, and Amsterdam, the author's calculations indicate that 46 percent of the Germans left from the two German ports.[5] Thus, to the extent the figures in Tables 6.1 and 6.2 can be checked with other data, they appear to be quite accurate, at least for the major ports.

Traveling to the Port of Embarkation

The data in Tables 6.1 and 6.2 show that five ports – London, Liverpool, Le Havre, Bremen, and Hamburg – were the most important embarkation

---

[4] Calculated from Erickson, "Emigration in 1841: Part II," Table 3, p. 353.
[5] Ferenczi, *International Migrations*, Table IV, p. 696. It is not clear if Ferenczi included the British ports among the foreign ones. I have not done so in making the comparison. On the other hand, not all of the passengers from Le Havre, Antwerp, Rotterdam, and Amsterdam would have been Germans.

ports for European immigrants, with each accounting for at least 4 percent of the total passenger arrivals. Why London was among these five is clear, because the city has always been the major port for Great Britain. The reasons for the other four ports being on the list are less clear. This section explains the dominance of these ports by examining the immigrant's journey in Europe from his or her farm or village. The discussion also explains the changes that occurred over time in the relative importance of the ports.

The length of the trip to an embarkation port during the first half of the nineteenth century could vary considerably, depending on the immigrant's country of origin.[6] Irish roads were fairly good, having improved by a substantial amount after 1750. By 1825, coach service between Belfast and Dublin took only about half a day and it took less than a full day to travel from Dublin to Cork.[7] Although many Irish immigrants would have walked to the embarkation port or used a wagon to haul their belongings, the rapid coach speeds emphasize the generally good quality of the Irish roads.[8] Thus, the trip to an embarkation port did not take very many days, especially given the island's small size.[9] On arriving at the port, the individual or family often had to arrange passage. Because the timber trade occurred between numerous Irish ports and Canada, passengers could usually locate a ship leaving for the latter country. Finding transportation to the United States from Ireland, except from Belfast, was more difficult, because little trade occurred between the two countries.[10] Some ships leaving Liverpool or other British ports tried stopping at Irish ports to pick up the available passengers. Getting into and out of port was difficult in the era of sailing ships and costly because of the time consumed. This factor helped reduce Irish immigration to the United States during the 1820s. Thus, many Irish immigrants began to travel across the Irish Sea to Great Britain on small vessels, but the fares were often high and the trip could be delayed if the wind was blowing the wrong direction.[11] Of those who undertook the journey, some found work and stayed in Great Britain while others boarded a ship to the United States.

[6] For a discussion of the trip undertaken by Irish (and German) immigrants in the eighteenth century, see Wokeck, *Trade*.

[7] Ó Gráda, *Ireland*, p. 132.

[8] Adams, *Ireland*, p. 119, says that most Irish emigrants walked to the embarkation ports.

[9] Neither canals nor railroads were used very much in Ireland during the antebellum period. See Ó Gráda, *Ireland*, pp. 135–7.

[10] Earlier in the nineteenth century, flax and other products were exported from the United States to Ireland, but this trade was never large and it died out in the 1820s. See Hansen, *Atlantic Migration*, pp. 179–80, and Page, "Transportation," p. 734.

[11] Adams, *Ireland*, p. 33.

The situation changed for the Irish once steamboats began to cross the Irish Sea in 1824.[12] The overall costs fell drastically and often the trip to Great Britain was included as part of a transatlantic fare.[13]

For the Irish taking the new steamboats, the port of arrival in Great Britain was usually Liverpool. Even with the voyage from Ireland, a typical Irish immigrant could reach Liverpool within a week, more or less, of leaving home. Liverpool was the major port at which U.S. raw cotton was imported into Great Britain, so the city had a sizeable volume of trade with the United States. This factor caused the early packet lines to choose Liverpool as their British destination, as discussed in Chapter 3. Although the cotton ships returned to the northern United States with British manufactured products, these goods accounted for only a small amount of the space the raw cotton had used. The ships thus had available space for passengers and a financial incentive to carry them. Liverpool was also geographically close to Ireland, so all factors worked to cause the city to become the primary embarkation port for Irish immigrants to the United States.[14] Adams estimates that 50 percent of the Irish left through Liverpool as early as 1827, with the percentage rising to more than 80 percent after 1834.[15] Glazier finds that 77 percent of the Irish left through Liverpool between 1846 and 1851.[16] Thus, only a minority of the Irish continued to leave directly from Ireland. Except for the Irish traveling from Londonderry to Philadelphia, however, no Irish port was very important (Table 6.2). In fact, although it was estimated in Chapter 2 that Irish immigration accounted for 42 percent of total European immigration to the antebellum United States, only 5 percent of the ships bound for the United States left directly from an Irish port.

The concentration of shipping at Liverpool attracted most of the English immigrants, although Table 6.1 shows that London was also a popular port. Getting to Liverpool was fairly easy for the British, and especially the English, immigrants by the early part of the nineteenth century. The eighteenth century saw a drastic improvement in internal transportation in England as the result of road improvements and canal

---

[12] Ó Gráda, *Ireland*, pp. 137–8.

[13] Hansen, *Atlantic Migration*, p. 183.

[14] Adams, *Ireland*, pp. 230–2. After transatlantic steamships began operating, the companies began stopping at Irish ports after leaving Liverpool or Glasgow. The first occurrence was in May 1859. See Flayhart, *American Line*, p. 116, and Bonsor, *North Atlantic Seaway*, p. 504.

[15] Adams, *Ireland*, p. 204.

[16] Glazier et al., "Socio-Demographic Characteristics," Table 7, p. 265.

building. On roads, the average travel speed for passengers increased from 2.6 miles per hour in 1750 to 6.2 miles per hour in 1800 and 8.0 miles per hour in 1820. Part of the reason for the increase was the development of fly-machines – coach services that maintained a high speed by frequently changing horses – which by 1770 were traveling to all major cities.[17] Because of the improvements, the travel time from London to Manchester by coach, for example, fell from ninety hours in 1700 to twenty-four hours in 1787.[18] From London to Liverpool took only two days in 1781 and must have been faster by the 1820s and 1830s.[19] Although the per-mile fare did not change much in real terms, potential immigrants benefited from the faster trips because of reduced foregone income. Of course, as the railroad network was built throughout Great Britain, travel times fell again by a substantial amount. By 1840, Britain had about fifteen hundred miles of railroads, and the mileage increased to about six thousand in 1850.[20]

The analysis in Chapter 2 made clear that the early German immigrants came from south and southwest Germany. The trip to the coastal cities was a distance of 250 to 400 miles. The easiest ports to reach were those on the Dutch coast. In theory, immigrants could travel down the Rhine River, which flowed from the relevant areas of Germany to Amsterdam or Rotterdam in Holland or Antwerp in northern Belgium. In fact, this path had been followed by German emigrants during the eighteenth century.[21] During the 1820s, however, the ports in the Low Countries did not attract many immigrants for two reasons. First, Holland experienced unsettled times as Belgium won its independence in the early 1830s. Second, ships from the United States did not often arrive at ports in the Low Countries because little trade occurred.[22] Eventually, the Dutch and Belgium ports experienced an increase in immigrant traffic as political conditions calmed and a railroad connecting Cologne and Antwerp was finished in 1842. Even then, however, the data in Tables 6.1 and 6.2 indicate that not many passengers traveled directly from Antwerp or the Dutch cities. Even many individuals who initially traveled to the ports in the Low Countries went by coastal steamer to Le Havre in order to board a transatlantic ship.

[17] Bogart, "Turnpike Trusts," p. 484.
[18] Pawson, *Transport*.
[19] Szostak, *Role*, p. 70.
[20] Mitchell, *European Historical Statistics*, Table F1, p. 315.
[21] Wokeck, *Trade*.
[22] Page, "Transportation," p. 732.

Most German immigrants in the first half of the nineteenth century left from either Le Havre in France, or Bremen on the northwestern German coast. Both cities had a direct trade with the United States that was growing in volume during this time.[23] Le Havre had the same trade with the United States as Liverpool, although smaller in volume. U.S. ships arrived at Le Havre carrying cotton that was used in the cotton industry in Alsace. Of course, both the cultivation of cotton and its export (to both Le Havre and Liverpool) grew tremendously in the United States during the early part of the nineteenth century. Thus, as was discussed in Chapter 3, this port was also one to which the early packet companies sailed. Bremen's trade with the United States was based on another important U.S. export: tobacco. Bremen became a major center for manufactured tobacco in Europe. The empty ships at both ports were quite willing to carry a return cargo in the form of (mainly) German immigrants. The trade of these ports led to many ships going from Le Havre to New Orleans, where more cotton was loaded, and from Bremen to Baltimore, where more tobacco was obtained (Table 6.1).

Le Havre was an attractive port for the delivery of cotton because it is situated at the mouth of the Seine River. The arriving cotton was transported upriver on barges and overland by freight wagons to Alsace, in eastern France, which had a cotton manufacturing industry.[24] German immigrants from south and southwest Germany, located just across the border from Alsace, would either take the same transportation modes back to Le Havre or travel by covered wagon or, if sufficiently wealthy, stage lines. French rivers were often not navigable and the roads, even in northeastern France, were probably worse than in England. By coach in 1785, it took four to five days from Strasbourg to Paris, and then another day or two to Le Havre.[25] For immigrants who moved their possessions in covered wagons, the journey to Le Havre took several weeks. Then, upon reaching the coast, the immigrants often had to wait anywhere between one and six weeks for an available ship, certainly longer than immigrants had to wait in Liverpool.[26] Over time, however, the wait was reduced as agents from the ships or boarding houses began to meet immigrants on the road.

---

[23] Much of the discussion concerning the cities on the Continent in the next few paragraphs follows Hansen, *Atlantic Migration*, pp. 185–95.

[24] Transportation on the river was not easy. As with many French rivers, the Seine had "shoals, rapids, weirs, islands, and sandbars." See Szostak, *Role*, p. 57.

[25] Szostak, *Role*, p. 71. Szostak explicitly compares English and French internal water and road travel and finds the English system was better on all counts.

[26] Hansen, *Atlantic Migration*, pp. 187–8.

Bremen was a latecomer to immigrant traffic because of two problems. First, the city was well north of the early emigrant areas. Bremen is located at the mouth of the Weser River, which flows south into the northern areas of the early emigrant territory. The river was navigable, but because of the many German states through which it flowed, travel was subject to frequent tolls and other man-made restrictions. Not until 1832, when the existing twenty-two tolls on the river were reduced to nine, did the Weser River began to be used as a regular emigration route. The formation in 1834 of the Zollverein, the tariff union pushed by Prussia that unified most German states into one market, assisted the process of reducing tolls. Yet it was only in the early 1840s when all the restrictions were removed and emigrants could easily take a steamboat down the Weser to Bremen.[27] The restrictions on water travel led many immigrants to move by wagon service, which took two weeks from Stuttgart.[28] German roads were not very good because the numerous German states built only for their own needs and not for through transportation.[29] Second, on the ocean side, the channel to Bremen became so silted that transatlantic ships had difficulty reaching the harbor. Bremen solved this problem by building a new port called Bremerhaven, which opened in 1830, twenty miles downriver. Thus, few immigrants left from Bremen before the 1830s. Over time, the spread of German emigration into northern areas of Germany, which were closer to Bremen, also helped to make Bremen a more important embarkation port in the 1840s and 1850s than it had been earlier.

Hamburg, being further east than Bremen, was at an even greater disadvantage. Hamburg is located at the mouth of the Elbe River, which flows southeast into the eastern section of Prussia, an area from which few individuals left until after 1840. The city also had very limited trade with the United States, therefore available shipping for the transatlantic crossing was sparse, although connections with Great Britain were good.[30] Thus, numerous Germans who wanted to leave from Hamburg instead spent three days on a small steamship crossing the North Sea to Hull, a city on the east coast of England. From there, they traveled across the country to either Liverpool, primarily, or London and sailed for the United States (and appear on the Passenger Lists as Germans arriving on a ship from a British port). In later years, when the volume of German immigrants who

---

[27] The steamboats were introduced on the Weser in 1843. See Walker, *Germany*, p. 88.
[28] Hansen, *Atlantic Migration*, p. 191–2.
[29] Szostak, *Role*, p. 54.
[30] Hansen, *Atlantic Migration*, p. 194, says in 1840, only 85 of 2,482 ships entering Hamburg came "from scattered ports of North America." Almost half arrived from Great Britain.

wanted to leave from northern and eastern Germany increased, making the passenger business sufficiently large on its own, Hamburg became a more important embarkation port. Overall, Germans left the country through a large number of embarkation ports.[31]

Substantial building of railroads in Germany did not occur until the latter part of the 1840s. Thus, water and road transportation remained much more important in Germany than England for a number of years. The decision to construct a railroad was originally in the hands of the separate state governments.[32] Thus, any lengthy line would encounter problems in coordinating among the states. In addition, the Prussian government was not interested in railroad construction and only in 1838 allowed private construction, subject to heavy oversight. Thus, by 1840, only about three hundred miles of railroads had been built. Continued Prussian opposition led to a collapse of building in the middle part of the 1840s. By 1850, only some thirty-five hundred miles had been built, a much smaller amount than in Great Britain, especially given the difference in the geographic size of the two countries.[33] Until the late 1840s or the 1850s, therefore, German immigrants had a much longer trip to reach a port of embarkation than did the Irish or English immigrants.

The basic conclusion from this discussion is that the European cities most important as embarkation ports for immigrants sailing to the United States were mainly those also important in the trade of freight. The reason is that few ships specialized in carrying passengers, at least before the advent of the major steamship companies. As detailed in Chapter 3, most immigrants traveled across the Atlantic Ocean, not on the packet ships, but on ships that had lost some freight traffic due to the competition of the packets. Because the packet lines specialized in carrying freight and the nonpacket ships still carried some freight to Europe, however, the immigrants who wished to sail to the United States found it easiest to arrange passage in the ports where these ships arrived. Given that the United States shipped cotton to Liverpool and Le Havre and tobacco to Bremen, these three ports became the major embarkation ports for the United States.

---

[31] Between 1836 and 1853 in my samples of Germans immigrating to the United States, 30% left from Le Havre, 21% from Bremen, 10% direct from Hamburg, 10% from Liverpool, 5% from London, and the remainder from a Dutch or Belgium port. Many Scandinavians also crossed the North Sea to England and left from Liverpool.

[32] The information in the remainder of this paragraph is from Tipton, "Government," pp. 118–22.

[33] Mitchell, *European Historical Statistics*, Table 5.1, p. 316.

From the perspective of an emigrant, the trip to the embarkation port was shortest for the British and longest for the Germans. In the former case, individuals might travel only a day or two to reach Liverpool, whereas Germans in the 1830s had a trip of at least two weeks, and often much longer, to a coastal port. The Irish trip was seldom longer than one week. Thus, as discussed in Chapter 5, German immigrants had larger forgone income that had to be overcome, a factor that contributed to the higher skill level of the German immigrant stream.[34] Over time, the German trip became shorter as internal transportation improved due to the introduction of steamships on the rivers, road improvements in Germany and France, and the building of the railroads. Waits at the embarkation ports also lessened for the Germans in the 1830s when ships began announcing their departure date.[35] By the end of the antebellum period, therefore, the difference in travel times to the embarkation ports had become smaller for immigrants from the different countries.

Estimates of Mortality on the Ships and After Arrival

The immigrant faced a long journey once aboard the sailing ship. The average length of the voyage was about forty-four days to New York, although some ships sailing from Liverpool arrived in thirty-five days.[36] The occasional ship could arrive even quicker, or the voyage could run into calm wind conditions and be delayed for a number of weeks. During the typical month and a half voyage, of course, some individuals would die. The general belief, which is supported by the analysis presented here, is that the mortality suffered during the voyage exceeded what would have been experienced had the individuals not taken the trip. This section examines the entire issue of mortality on immigrant ships, discussing how many people died, how that number compared to the death rate among nontravelers, which immigrants were most likely to die, and why the deaths occurred.

---

[34] A formal discussion of this point is presented in Chiswick, "Are Immigrants," p. 65, who concludes that the "larger are the out-of-pocket costs of migration . . . the greater is the propensity for favorable selectivity in migration." Chiswick's conclusion is based on the typical human-capital model used in this book, where individuals migrate because of income differentials.

[35] Moltmann, "Pattern," p. 19.

[36] Page, "Transportation," p. 737, gives an average of 44.25 days for sailing ships arriving in 1867. An average of 44.3 days can be calculated from data on ships arriving at Quebec between 1841 and 1855. See Eltis, "Free and Coerced Transatlantic Migrations," Table 2, p. 271. Also, see the discussion in Cohn, "Mortality," p. 294.

The literature on immigrant mortality provides a wide range of estimates about its size. In many cases, the impression is that the conditions faced by immigrants waiting for the ships and then onboard were terrible and resulted in very high mortality. For example, Wittke says that mortality on the immigrant ships was "comparable to . . . the middle passage during the African slave trade."[37] Wabeke, Davie, Page, and the textbook by Lebergott each present a similar view.[38] However, this view is in contrast to figures on immigrant mortality provided at the time by government officials. Beginning in 1853, U.S. authorities provided estimates for ships landing in New York.[39] British authorities also provided this information for ships sailing to Canada.[40] The government estimates are generally much smaller than those suggested earlier. More recent empirical work, which is reviewed next, provides estimates of immigrant mortality similar to the contemporary views.[41] Thus, the current view is that immigrants died at rates higher than nontravelers but lower than other groups of ocean travelers.

Only limited data are available from official sources before the late 1840s and, even then, it is not clear the government figures are correct. For those ships that arrived in the United States, the government estimates are presumably obtained from mortality information in the Passenger Lists. Because a column was included where the captain could record deaths on the voyage (see Chapter 2), officials simply summarized this information. Yet three concerns have been raised about these estimates. The first is whether all the deaths that occurred were actually recorded on the Passenger Lists. Even at the time, at least one informed individual doubted that all the deaths had been recorded.[42] The second is that some passengers died soon after arrival from diseases caught onboard the ships, deaths that would not have been recorded in the Passenger Lists. The third is that a few ships never made it to the United States, either because of shipwreck on the way or a return to Europe after the outbreak of an epidemic. The

---

[37] Wittke, *We*, p. 111.
[38] Wabeke, *Dutch Emigration*, pp. 108–9; Davie, *World Immigration*, pp. 92–4; Page, "Transportation," pp. 738–40; Lebergott, *Americans*, pp. 182–4.
[39] See U.S. Congress, *Report*. An excerpt from this report is provided in Abbott, *Immigration*, pp. 40–1.
[40] Much of these data are provided in MacDonagh, *Pattern*.
[41] See Jones, "Transatlantic Steerage Conditions," pp. 59–61, for a particularly good discussion of the issue.
[42] U.S. Congress, *Report*. This individual was involved in the collection of the Passenger Lists. He claimed that he had been told by boarding officers that ship captains often reported a higher number of deaths to doctors than were recorded on the Passenger Lists. See the discussion and quote from the *Report* in Cohn, "Mortality," p. 293.

analysis in this section first considers the data obtained from the Passenger Lists and then adjusts the resulting estimates using the available information on deaths after arrival and on shipwrecks and returned ships.

The best data on mortality from the Passenger Lists is for the port of New Orleans. Besides the basic Passenger List for each ship – which listed information concerning every passenger – each captain arriving in New Orleans was also required to complete a separate form concerning mortality. On this form, the captain was required to record the total number of deaths that occurred on the voyage.[43] On the microfilmed Passenger Lists for New Orleans, this document appears immediately after the basic Passenger List. Such a supplemental document does not appear for any of the other major ports of arrival.[44] Thus, one approach to estimating mortality would be to base it only on the Passenger Lists for New Orleans. The problem is that the voyage to this city was much longer than that to the East Coast ports. As noted earlier, given the variety of European ports from which ships left with passengers, the voyage to New York (and presumably the other East Coast ports) probably averaged about forty-four days. The voyages of both Edward Phillips and Johann Bauer, the two immigrants discussed at the beginning of this book, were about this length. Little comprehensive data exist on the length of the voyage to New Orleans, although a previous estimate provided an average of fifty-seven days.[45] Because the ships sailing to New Orleans took longer than those going to the other ports, a larger number of deaths would occur on the former ships. The accepted method of taking the differential voyage lengths into account is to compute the monthly mortality rate – the number of deaths per thousand boarded per thirty days – in addition to determining the percentage loss rate – the simple percentage of the embarking passengers who died on the voyage. The mortality rate figures can then be compared both among ports and to the population who did not migrate. Yet this solution is not perfect because it assumes that deaths occurred at a consistent rate during the voyage, something that probably was not true.

Thus, the New Orleans data need to be supplemented with samples taken from the Passenger Lists for the remaining major arrival ports.

[43] This form is reproduced in Cohn, "Passenger Mortality," p. 6.

[44] It is not clear whether the "mortality" form was specific to the port of New Orleans or if the forms for the other ports have been lost. Nothing in the original Passenger Act in 1819 required an explicit statement of mortality.

[45] Cohn, "Passenger Mortality," pp. 8–9. This average may be too small. Page, "Transportation," p. 736, says the voyage to New Orleans was "two or three weeks longer than to New York."

Here, an estimate of mortality has to be determined from entries in the column "Died on the Voyage" on the Passenger List. The Passenger Lists for Boston and Baltimore contain the least information on mortality as none or almost none of the lists have any entries in this column. The Passenger Lists for New York and Philadelphia are better in that many contain notations of deaths or, in a number of cases, the word "None" is entered in the column for deaths. For both of these ports, however, whether all captains recorded information on deaths is not clear. On some of the lists, the "Died" column is completely blank and on other lists, the amount of each immigrant's *luggage* is listed in the column for deaths, although one occasionally encounters a latter list where deaths are recorded over the luggage information. Thus, one must be suspicious of the official government figures that are a direct summary of the data on the lists. To account for this problem and to supplement the New Orleans data, samples that have been taken from the New York and Philadelphia Passenger Lists to investigate mortality have included only those ships that listed deaths or explicitly recorded that no deaths occurred. Thus, a large number of the lists not providing any indication concerning mortality have been ignored in drawing the samples from the Passenger Lists for New York and Philadelphia.[46]

This procedure provides the following onboard percentage loss rates and monthly mortality rates for immigrants. All of the samples underlying these findings include ships arriving over the entire 1820–60 period. Ships arriving in New Orleans lost 1.06 percent of the passengers who embarked, with a monthly mortality rate of 5.6 per thousand boarded.[47] Ships arriving in New York had a loss rate of 1.20 percent with a monthly mortality rate of 8.2 per thousand boarded. Ships arriving in Philadelphia lost 0.94 percent of the passengers embarking with a monthly mortality rate of 6.4 per thousand boarded.[48] The lower monthly mortality rate for New Orleans may be partly caused by there being too few ships with no deaths in the samples for the other ports, given the manner in which the samples were constructed. On the other hand, ships to New York were

---

[46] Cohn, "Mortality"; Cohn, "Passenger Mortality."

[47] Taking the 1.06% loss rate (10.6 per thousand boarded) and dividing it by 1.9 months (= 57 days) yields the monthly mortality rate of 5.6 per thousand boarded.

[48] Cohn, "Passenger Mortality," Table 3, p. 9. The ships in the three samples used in the cited paper account for 11% of all passengers listed as arriving between 1820 and 1860. The figures in the text differ from those given for New York in Cohn, "Mortality." The New York sample used in the latter cited paper was smaller than that used in the other paper.

more crowded and included a larger proportion of children. As discussed later, both factors would raise the expected mortality rate on voyages to New York. All of these factors can be taken into account in order to provide a more accurate estimate of passenger mortality. When this procedure is done, the resulting estimate of the monthly mortality rate on the voyage from Europe to the United States is 6.1 deaths per thousand boarded.[49] This figure is equivalent to 0.93 percent of all the immigrants who left Europe between 1820 and 1860 on ships that sailed for and arrived in the United States.

The mortality rates for immigrants on sailing voyages were typically higher than those for people who stayed home, ignoring the famine years in Ireland. At this period of time, annual mortality rates were in the range of 20 to 25 per thousand for England and Wales and 25 to 30 per thousand for Germany.[50] On a monthly basis, then, nontravelers died at a rate of 1.7 to 2.5 per thousand, a rate about two-thirds lower than the 6.1 per thousand rate estimated for immigrants on the ships. As is discussed in more detail later, this differential is too small because a larger percentage of the immigrants were between fifteen and forty-five, ages when mortality is low. Even so, European immigrants to the United States in the antebellum years had mortality rates comparable to or lower than many other groups of passengers on sailing voyages.[51] Mortality rates on immigrant voyages to Australia were somewhat lower, but these passengers were subsidized and selected by the British government. Indian and Chinese workers experienced monthly mortality rates of 10–20 per thousand boarded, and sometimes higher, on their voyages during the nineteenth century. The largest rates occurred on slave voyages, where monthly mortality rates usually averaged 45–70 per thousand boarded. Thus, although the voyage to the United States caused more Europeans to die than had they not undertaken the journey, the numbers of dead were not nearly as large as the losses suffered on slave voyages.

The loss rate figures on voyages to Canada were not very different from those on ships to the United States, except for 1847 and perhaps the years before 1840. Buchanan, the British agent at Quebec, estimated a loss rate on the vessels of 4.1 percent in 1832, although it is unclear

---

[49] See the discussion in Cohn, "Passenger Mortality," p. 15.
[50] Mitchell, *European Historical Statistics*, Table A.3, pp. 18–25. No precise data are available concerning the size of Irish mortality until the 1860s.
[51] The figures in the remainder of this paragraph are from Cohn, "Maritime Mortality," which includes references to the original articles that provided the estimates.

how representative this figure is for the years before 1840.[52] Figures that
are more exact are available for ships arriving in Canada beginning in
1840. Except for 1847 and the last quarter of 1853, the loss rate varied
from a high of 2 percent in 1846 to a low of 0.2 percent in 1858. In
most years, the loss rates were between 0.3 percent and 0.9 percent.[53]
During 1847, when the effects of the famine weakened the emigrants and
infectious diseases were rampant, the loss rate was truly horrendous on
ships carrying Irish immigrants bound for Canada. The currently accepted
estimates are that at least 16,000 died out of the 110,000 who sailed for
Canada that year, a loss rate of almost 15 percent.[54] Ships arriving in
the United States during 1847 did not experience such losses, although
the major reason appears to be that ships with disease onboard were
turned away from U.S. ports and had to continue on to Canada.[55] The
last quarter of 1853 also saw high loss rates, with about 10 percent of
the passengers bound for Canada dying before arrival.[56]

Annual loss rates for ships arriving in New York are shown in Figure 6.1. Loss rates were generally low, although variable, before the
increase in volume that began during the early 1830s. From the last part
of the 1830s until the late 1850s, years of growing and high immigrant
volume (see Figure 2.1), loss rates were usually between 1 percent and 1.5
percent, although again, these rates may be somewhat too large because
of how the ships in the New York sample were selected. The latter part
of the 1850s, years when immigrant volume was smaller relative to the
1846–54 period, again saw lower loss rates. Thus, some connection is
apparent between the overall volume of immigration and mortality on a
ship. During years of high volume, ships were more crowded, a factor
that will be seen to have increased mortality. Besides this relationship, no
secular trend is evident in the figures; loss rates were not much different
on ships arriving at the end of the antebellum period from what they had
been in the late 1830s.[57] Nor did the country of origin affect the ship's loss

---

[52] Calculated from information provided in MacDonagh, *Pattern*, p. 81.

[53] MacDonagh, *Pattern*, pp. 162, 170, 213, 219, 304.

[54] McInnis, "Population," Table 9.2, pp. 380–2. Many more died after arrival in Canada.
For all Irish emigrants to North America that year, MacDonagh estimates that 25,000
to 30,000 died out of the 215,000 who left. For a description of the situation in 1847
written in 1868, see the discussion in Abbott, *Immigration*, pp. 29–33.

[55] MacDonagh, *Pattern*, p. 184.

[56] MacDonagh, *Pattern*, p. 267. The causes of death in each year are discussed later in the
chapter.

[57] A regression of the average annual loss rate on the year of arrival yields a positive (0.17)
and significant coefficient ($t = 3.70$) for the year of arrival. If only the period from 1836

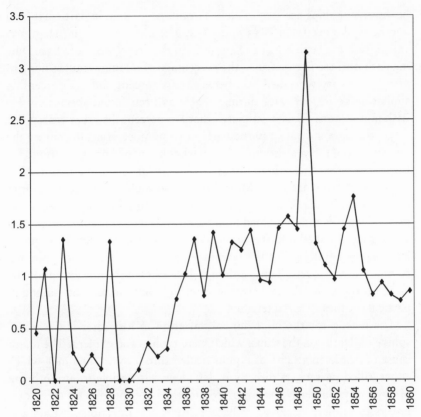

FIGURE 6.1. Percentage Loss Rates on Ships Arriving in New York, 1820–1860.
Source: Data underlying Cohn, "Passenger Mortality."

rate. However, research has found evidence that loss rates were higher
on ships arriving during the winter months, presumably because sailing
conditions were worse at that time of year.[58]

The mortality situation was particularly acute in certain years,
although not during 1847 because, as noted earlier, the United States
did not allow the disease-filled ships to land. High rates are apparent,

through 1860 is used, however, the value of the coefficient becomes negative (−0.05) and
insignificant ($t = -0.81$). More complex econometric analysis – for example, including
variables on crowding and length of voyage – encounters data issues. Crowding can only
be measured imperfectly because the tonnage (the only measure available) of the ship is
an imperfect (and perhaps inaccurate) measure of space. The length of the voyage is not
known because the Passenger Lists record only the arrival date, not the departure date.
See the further discussion in Cohn, "Mortality."

[58] Cohn, "Mortality."

however, for ships arriving in New York during 1849, in particular, and another spike occurs in 1853 and 1854. The high rate during 1849 prevailed from the beginning of 1849 through the first quarter of 1850. During each of these five quarters, the percentage of all immigrants sailing to New York City who died was between 2.9 percent and 3.2 percent. A similar spike in loss rates during 1849 has been found specifically for Irish immigrants. Glazier estimated that 8.9 percent died that year.[59] For 1853, the data indicate a particularly large number of deaths during the last quarter of the year, comparable to what happened on ships bound for Canada. During these three months, 3.5 percent of those going to New York died before arrival.[60] Mortality was so high that it led to a series of editorials in the *New York Tribune* expressing outrage at the situation.[61] The loss rate remained high, at 2.0 percent, in the first quarter of 1854, then declined into the summer, but then rose to 2.6 percent in the last quarter of 1854. For the remainder of the decade, the loss rate fell to much lower levels. Thus, although loss rates were not exceptionally large on the transatlantic crossing in most years, immigrants sailing at particular times suffered terribly.

The reason for the huge annual variation in loss rates is the major source of deaths on the ships, which were typhus and cholera. The major cause of deaths in 1847 was typhus (called ship fever at the time), which either killed passengers directly or left them susceptible to an outbreak of dysentery. Similarly, during 1849 and the latter portion of 1853, outbreaks of cholera occurred.[62] Both diseases are infectious.[63] Rats and mice, which were occupants of any ship, were carriers of typhus. The disease can be spread to humans through bites from fleas that have previously been infected by biting a rodent carrying the disease. Symptoms of the disease typically do not appear until a week or more after the

---

[59] Glazier et al., "Socio-Demographic Characteristics," pp. 255, 269. They find loss rates between 2.3% and 4.8% for the Irish for other years between 1846 and 1851. Even so, Glazier shows that mortality rates for the Irish on the ships bound for the United States were much smaller than death rates for those remaining in Ireland during the Famine.

[60] This figure is calculated from the data underlying the analysis in Cohn, "Mortality," Table 3, p. 297. During the third quarter of 1853, the loss rate on ships arriving in New York was only 1.1%.

[61] *New York Tribune*, November 19, 22, 26, and December 3, 1853, issues.

[62] Rosenberg, *Cholera Years*. Smallpox was also prevalent. See Commissioners of Emigration, *Annual Reports*. For a discussion of the cholera epidemics resulting from immigration written in 1873, see Abbott, *Immigration*, pp. 47–8.

[63] The information in the remainder of this paragraph is taken from the online encyclopedia, *Wikipedia*, entries on cholera and typhus. Although the contents of this encyclopedia change over time, the material presented in this paragraph has been confirmed through other sources.

fleabite. Fleas or lice then spread the disease from human to human either directly or in feces. Similarly, cholera can appear in water when it is contaminated by untreated sewage. Once someone is infected, the disease can be spread to others through the contamination of the food or water supply by the infected person's feces. Conditions on an immigrant ship enhanced the likelihood of an epidemic. Four adults often slept on a six-foot-by-six-foot berth, that is, when the berths did not collapse, or the ship was not overloaded. Virtually no space was available between berths. Toilets were not kept very clean. Food often spoiled.[64] Many of these problems reflected a lack of knowledge concerning the control of diseases. Thus, the presence of a person on the voyage infected with either disease could cause an epidemic to break out in mid-ocean. In the confined space of the ship on a long sailing voyage and with many passengers already weakened by seasickness, the spread of the infection could not be stopped easily. In this situation, a large number of passengers could die before the ship reached an American or Canadian port. On the other hand, if an epidemic did not break out on a ship, few deaths typically occurred. Erickson, for example, estimates a loss rate of only 1 in 220 (a loss rate of 0.45 percent) on ships leaving during 1841, a year with little disease.[65]

Thus, not only were loss rates small in most years, they were also small on most voyages. This analysis explains the pattern in Table 6.3, which shows the distribution of deaths on ships arriving in New York, New Orleans, and Philadelphia. For all three ports, at least 50 percent of the ships arrived with one or no deaths and at least 85 percent of the ships had four or fewer deaths. In fact, the percentages of ships with no deaths in the New York and Philadelphia samples may be too small, because the selection of ships in these cases ignored all of the lists that had no information about deaths. In reality, many of the ships not in the samples may have arrived without experiencing any deaths. Of the 2,442 total ships in the three samples, only 90 (less than 4 percent) had 11 or more deaths. Presumably, severe epidemics broke out on these ships during the crossing. These ninety voyages, however, accounted for 33 percent of all the deaths recorded in the three samples. The calculation emphasizes that most ships arrived in the United States without substantial loss of life.

---

[64] See Jones, "Transatlantic Steerage Conditions," pp. 61–71, for a comprehensive discussion of shipboard conditions.

[65] Erickson, "Emigration in 1841: Part I," p. 356. Her rate may be slightly too small as she apparently took the death information on the Passenger Lists – or the lack of it – at face value.

TABLE 6.3. *Distribution of Deaths by Voyage, 1820–1860 (number of ships in each category)*

Number of Deaths	New York	New Orleans	Philadelphia
0	225 (13.0)	229 (46.7)	98 (44.7)
1	689 (39.8)	99 (20.2)	68 (31.1)
2–4	578 (33.4)	92 (18.8)	42 (19.2)
5–10	170 (9.8)	53 (10.8)	9 (4.1)
11–20	36 (2.1)	11 (2.3)	1 (0.5)
21–30	21 (1.2)	4 (0.8)	0
31–40	8 (0.5)	0	1 (0.5)
41–50	2 (0.1)	0	0
51+	4 (0.2)	2 (0.4)	0
TOTAL	1,733	490	219

Note: The figures in parentheses are the percentage in each category of the total number of ships arriving at that port.
Source: Cohn, "Passenger Mortality," Table 5, p. 14.

The fact that a large percentage of the deaths resulted from outbreaks of epidemic diseases also implies that the probability of dying on the voyage was not the same for all ages. In particular, it would be expected that the very young and the elderly, individuals who were more susceptible to disease, would die at higher rates. In fact, exactly this sort of pattern has been found, not only for immigrants arriving from Europe but also for other groups of passengers.[66] Loss rates were four to six times higher for passengers between fifteen and forty-four years of age relative to those of the same age who did not migrate. On the other hand, children under five years of age and those older than forty-five died at rates ten times higher than nontravelers of the same ages.[67] Researchers examining other groups traveling on sailing ships have found a similar pattern. For example, infants and children experienced much higher mortality rates on immigrant voyages to Australia than did adults. Monthly mortality rates for infants averaged between 40 and 66 per thousand and those for children between 8 and 18 per thousand. For adults traveling to Australia, the monthly mortality rate was between 1 and 2.5 per thousand.[68] Thus, although all passengers died at higher rates on the ships relative to nontravelers, the greatest effects were on those least able to combat an infectious disease.

[66] Cohn, "Determinants."
[67] Cohn, "Corrigendum," Table 2, p. 338.
[68] Shlomowitz and McDonald, "Babies," Table 1, p. 87.

Besides the deaths on the ships that arrived in the United States, some ships never arrived. Given the difficulty in navigating due to sail propulsion, ships were often blown upon rocks, usually a fatal proposition for the ship because of the wooden hulls. Other ships simply never arrived in a North American port, presumably having gone down in the open ocean. Still other ships began the voyage, had an epidemic breakout, and returned to their home port or a port in Ireland, the westernmost portion of Europe. Although the literature is filled with numerous examples of each type of event, very limited hard evidence is available, especially pertaining to shipwrecks. British records, cited in the book by Guillet, indicate that "forty-four passenger vessels, out of 7,129 from the British Isles, suffered shipwreck, and 1,043 lives were lost" between 1847 and 1851.[69] These figures translate to 0.6 percent of all ships leaving from the British Isles and an average of twenty-four deaths per shipwreck. The low average number of deaths resulted because numerous wrecks were near or on the coast, allowing many passengers to reach shore on their own or to be rescued. In other cases, passengers were rescued by passing vessels.[70] To account for the deaths from shipwrecks, the number of deaths per arriving ship should increase by 0.15, a number that would increase the overall loss rate on the ships by 0.06 percent, that is, from 0.93 percent to 0.99 percent.[71] As to the voyages that turned back to a European port, the author is unaware of any systematic data concerning the number of ships involved or the number of deaths that occurred on these ships. In addition, many of the stories of returned ships occurred on ships sailing during the typhus-filled year of 1847.[72]

A final factor that needs to be taken into account is deaths occurring after the ships docked in the United States. In many cases, immigrants arrived at a U.S. port not yet dead but very sick. Beginning in 1847,

---

69 Guillet, *Great Migration*, p. 128. Similarly, Coleman, *Going*, p. 120, says that fifty-nine ships were wrecked between 1847 and 1853. See a more extensive analysis using these data in Cohn, "Passenger Mortality," pp. 16–17. In 1834, MacDonagh, *Pattern*, p. 84, indicates that 731 lives were lost on 17 vessels that foundered, an average of 43 lives lost per wreck, but these data were for ships sailing to Canada. In general, shipwrecks may have been more prominent on ships going to Canada. See Hansen, *Atlantic Migration*, p. 184.

70 Stories of individual shipwrecks and rescues are found in Coleman, *Going*, Ch. 8; Guillet, *Great Migration*, p. 13; and Laxton, *Famine Ships*.

71 The 1,043 deaths would be spread over 7,085 (= 7,129 − 44) arriving ships, a rate of 0.15 additional deaths per arriving ship. Because this figure is about 6% of the average number of deaths per ship, then the overall loss rate should increase by 0.06 percentage points. See the analysis in Cohn, "Passenger Mortality," pp. 16–17.

72 MacDonagh, *Pattern*, p. 176.

the newly formed Commissioners of Emigration of the State of New York sent the passengers who arrived with a contagious disease to the Marine Hospital on Staten Island, and those with other diseases and needs to a refuge and hospital on Ward's Island.[73] The Commissioners filed annual reports of their activities. A combined volume issued in 1861 provides each report and includes summary information, including deaths at both the Marine Hospital and Ward's Island.[74] Between 1847 and 1858, 8,294 immigrants died at the Marine Hospital and 11,953 died at Ward's Island.[75] Given that 2,487,335 immigrants arrived in New York during those years, the deaths at Marine Hospital equal 0.33 percent of arrivals, and those at Ward's 0.48 percent of arrivals.[76] The larger number of deaths at Ward's Island was due entirely to a much larger number of immigrants being sent there than to the Marine Hospital. The actual death rate per admission was much lower at Ward's Island than the Marine Hospital. Whether to include all of the Ward's Island deaths in determining the total that died because of the voyage is not clear, because some of these individuals would have died from diseases caught after arrival or as a result of other situations. For example, 2,092 of the deaths, 17.5 percent of the total, occurred in the refuge on Ward's Island, not in the island's hospital. Presumably, diseases or other factors associated with the voyage did not cause these deaths. In addition, pregnant women were sent to Ward's Island, and some of them would have died in childbirth, as would some of their newly born children (who had not been counted as a passenger on the ship). Of all the deaths at Ward's Island, in fact,

[73] Ward's Island is located in the East River in New York City.
[74] Commissioners of Emigration, *Annual Reports*. The complete workings of this organization are discussed in Chapter 7. MacDonagh, *Pattern*, p. 81, says that 5% of the immigrants to Canada in 1832 died after arrival but provides no information for other years.
[75] Commissioners of Emigration, *Annual Reports*, Table B (Marine) and Table C (Ward's), pp. 290, 302.
[76] Commissioners of Emigration, *Annual Reports*, Tables A and B. The figures for both the total arrivals and the total number of deaths include passengers from places other than Europe, such as the West Indies. The figure for deaths likely also includes a few U.S. passengers who died in the Marine Hospital. These are not separated in the *Annual Reports*. In July 1859, the Marine Hospital was replaced by a floating hospital operated by the Quarantine Commissioners. Settlement on Staten Island was nearing the grounds of the hospital and residents feared being infected. The Marine Hospital was burned down in September 1858, apparently by Staten Island residents, and then temporarily rebuilt until replaced by a floating hospital. See Commissioners of Emigration, *Annual Reports*, pp. 236–8, 257–8.

2,355 individuals, 20 percent of the total, were infants younger than one year of age.[77] Thus, although it seems likely that almost all of the deaths at the Marine Hospital were due to diseases caught on the voyage, it is less certain how many of the deaths at Ward's Island were a result of the voyage.[78]

A total of 4.84 million European immigrants arrived at a U.S. port between 1820 and 1860 (see Chapter 2). Assuming all the estimates provided in this section are correct and held over the entire period, then the total number of deaths can be determined. On the ships that arrived, 0.93 percent, or approximately forty-five thousand individuals, died before arrival. Between 0.33 percent and 0.81 percent, or between sixteen and thirty-nine thousand, died soon after arrival from diseases caught on the ships. Another 0.06 percent, or about three thousand individuals, would have died in shipwrecks. Using a middle estimate of the mortality figures for Ward's Island, the total deaths due to the voyage would be about 1.56 percent of those who sailed and did not return to a European port, or approximately 75,500 individuals.[79] This number does not include any deaths that occurred on the journey to the embarkation port or while waiting in the port to board the ship.

Thus, more than 98 percent of the immigrants who sailed for the United States arrived safely. The 1.56 percent death rate was higher than that experienced by nontravelers, with the major exception being the Irish immigrants during the potato famine. On average, deaths among immigrants were probably about five times higher than among those who stayed home. Most of the excess deaths occurred on voyages with epidemics of typhus or cholera, which were more likely in some years than

---

[77] A total of 5,703 births occurred at Ward's Island from 1847 to 1860. See Commissioners of Emigration, *Annual Reports*, Table C, p. 302. Some of these infants would have died shortly after birth and account for part of the total infant deaths provided in the text.

[78] Some individuals were sent to the Marine Hospital not directly from their arriving ship but after spending a period of time in New York City. Apparently, most, but not all, of these individuals spent only a few days in the city, becoming sick because of a disease caught on the voyage. Thus, diseases that were not caught on the voyage may have caused a few of the deaths at the Marine Hospital.

[79] Total deaths could have been as large as 2.13%, or 103,000, if all the deaths at Ward's are included and if the number of deaths on the ships that returned to Europe were as large as those at the Marine Hospital, although the latter assumption likely overestimates the deaths on the returned ships. In addition, the entire procedure overestimates total deaths to the extent that deaths after arrival may have been smaller on ships arriving in other ports and in New York in the less crowded years before 1847.

others. Thus, in most years and on most voyages, the extra probability of dying by sailing to the United States was small.

Reasons for the Higher Mortality

Even though epidemics were the major cause of high death rates on the voyage, three features of the transatlantic passenger market compounded the situation. One was a fundamental lack of information on the part of the immigrant. Each customer bought the product – the transatlantic voyage – once. Because multiple purchases were not made, a passenger could not learn over time, keeping his business away from suppliers who did not follow safe practices in favor of those who did. In fact, many of the unsafe conditions were not apparent to the immigrant until the ship was in the middle of the ocean. In turn, because of the lack of repeat business, shipowners and captains had little incentive to provide safe onboard conditions. In many cases, the ship's main business was hauling freight, a factor that contributed to the captain and owner's lack of interest in passenger safety. Although many immigrants received letters from previous migrants concerning what to do and not do and information was available from migrant newspapers and aid societies, the advice was not always helpful. One might be told to avoid a particular ship or captain, but doing so would not guarantee a safe voyage due to the large number of ships and captains. In addition, immigrants sometimes arrived at their port only to discover that the ship for which they had purchased a ticket had already sailed. With limited financial resources, the individual usually had to take what he or she could get.

The second feature was a fundamental lack of knowledge concerning the causes of disease. As discussed earlier, most of the deaths occurred on voyages that had an outbreak of typhus or cholera. Both diseases were more likely to be caught in the crowded conditions a passenger had to endure in the embarkation port while waiting to board his or her ship. Once aboard the ship, the continued crowded conditions contributed to the spread of disease, resulting in an epidemic on some occasions. If one broke out before the ship had gone very far, the ship might return to a European port. If the epidemic broke out in the middle of the ocean, however, little could be done. Yet the understanding of the causes of disease at the time – and what could be done to prevent them – was completely wrong. Contemporaries usually assumed that diseases were caused by "miasma," vapors that escaped from various items. Even so, some of the mortality could have been reduced by effective government regulations that kept obviously sick people from boarding the ships, a factor that Shlomowitz has argued lowered death rates on voyages to Australia.[80]

Thus, the third feature of the passenger market is that government regulation of the transatlantic passenger market was not very effective. The trade was regulated by both the United States and Great Britain.[81] U.S. regulations began with the Passenger Act of 1819, which also led to the collection of the Passenger Lists. This law set space requirements, limiting ships to carrying two passengers for every five tons of measurement. Additional laws were not passed until the late 1840s and continued to regulate the number and available space for passengers, while also adding regulations referring to ventilation, water, and food.[82] The enforcement of the law, however, was left to U.S. customs officials, at least until the establishment of the Board of Commissioners of Emigration of the State of New York in May 1847.[83] As noted earlier, this organization began handling immigrant arrivals in New York City. Yet, because they could only indirectly control the ships before departure, U.S. authorities could do relatively little to reduce mortality.

The British attempted to provide more comprehensive regulation at their ports of embarkation.[84] Numerous issues, however, prevented most of the regulation from being effective. A basic theoretical issue was the extent to which the government should intervene in a private market transaction between freely consenting parties. During the early years, the problems arising because of the one-time nature of the transaction were not appreciated. Then, once government did decide to intervene, they ran into myriad difficulties in trying to enforce the new laws. Initially, customs officials were supposed to enforce the law but they had little expertise in the area of passenger travel. Even after separate emigration officials were appointed, problems continued due to the volume of emigration, the lack of knowledge on the part of the officials, the "ingenuity" of shippers in getting around the laws, the lack of knowledge concerning what would

---

[80] Shlomowitz, *Mortality*. Also, see Haines and Shlomowitz, "Explaining," and Jones, "Transatlantic Steerage Conditions."

[81] Other European countries also had passenger acts. MacDonagh, *Pattern*, p. 307, claims their requirements were much less comprehensive than either U.S. or British law. On the other hand, Page, "Transportation," pp. 734–5, says that ships from Hamburg and Bremen had "a higher standard of sanitation" because of government regulations.

[82] A short summary of the laws, along with the actual laws, is provided in Bromwell, *History*, pp. 206–25. A discussion of the legislation is provided in Jones, "Aspects."

[83] Kapp, *Immigration*, p. 86.

[84] The discussion in this paragraph follows MacDonagh, *Pattern*.

work, and the uncertainly over what the officers could legally do.[85] In fact, in many cases, it was not clear that shippers could be prosecuted for disobeying the law, especially if problems occurred in the middle of the ocean. Overall, it was the end of the 1840s before the British regulation had much effect on the trade and, even then, the regulation was not as effective as it was designed to be.[86] Another issue is that, for a long period of time, the British laws did not apply to U.S. ships, which carried the majority of the passengers going to the United States. A final important factor is that the government was loathe to push enforcement too far because doing so might raise transatlantic fares and cause emigration to decline, potentially leaving the individual in a worse situation. Eventually, the introduction of the steamship either changed all three factors or, because of the speedier crossing, made each less important.

Other Aspects of the Immigrants' Trip

For many individuals, the entire trip from their home to the United States was not very pleasant, and often proved more expensive than it needed to be.[87] Not only did it take awhile to get to the embarkation port but once there, the potential immigrants had to deal with "runners," individuals who would meet the arriving groups and try to steer them to particular boardinghouses. At times, the runners would simply grab a person's luggage and take it to a boardinghouse, regardless of the individual's desires. Then, the rates actually charged at the boardinghouses were often higher than the runners had promised. If not paid, the immigrant's luggage would not be returned. Sometimes, prepaid tickets were not honored, or the immigrants were told they needed to pay more on fully paid tickets. Onboard the ships from the United Kingdom, at least until the 1850s, the immigrants were only provided with water and "bread, salt meat, and a few other supplies."[88] They had to bring the remainder of their food, and try to cook it at a crowded grate on deck, assuming the weather

---

[85] See the discussion in Scally, "Liverpool Ships."

[86] One historian has argued, probably correctly, that deaths might have been reduced more if each immigrant had been given their own chamber pot instead of the authorities trying to regulate the number of passengers, amount of space, the extent of provisions and water, and so on. See Gallagher, *Paddy's Lament*, pp. 204–5.

[87] Numerous authors discuss in much more detail the material covered briefly in this section. For example, see Hansen, *Atlantic Migration*; MacDonagh, *Pattern*; Kapp, *Immigration*; Scally, "Liverpool Ships"; and Page, "Transportation," pp. 744–7.

[88] Albion, *Rise*, p. 343.

did not keep everyone below deck. If the immigrant ran out during the voyage, he or she might have to buy food from the captain at exorbitant rates. In fact, sometimes the immigrants were told to carry less than they needed, so that exactly this situation would result. Ships from Bremen and Hamburg, on the other hand, provided cooked food for their passengers beginning in the 1830s.[89] Upon arrival at a port in the United States, the immigrants encountered another set of runners, who also tried to steer the individuals to certain rooming houses.[90] Alternatively, if the immigrant had prepaid tickets for another destination in the United States, he or she might again be told his or her tickets were no good or not fully paid.

Besides its attempts to improve onboard conditions, government also sought to inhibit the practices of runners through regulation. MacDonagh describes in detail the battles fought by the early British officials – retired Navy officers – assigned as emigration agents at the various embarkation ports.[91] Their efforts to reduce the influence of runners and unscrupulous shipping agents and captains met with limited success. Their powers were not always clear and the courts would not always support their decisions. Even when they made a little progress, the shipping agents would devise a new method to try to exploit the immigrants. The U.S. authorities dealing with the immigrants after arrival encountered similar issues. The early Emigration Commission reports are filled with discussions of runners and others exploiting the immigrants. The solution eventually adopted in the United States was the opening of Castle Garden in August 1855. Castle Garden was the first immigrant-landing depot in the United States, serving as such until it was replaced by Ellis Island in 1892. Once Castle Garden was open, virtually all ships were required to disembark their passengers at this depot. Emigration Commission officials kept out the runners and assisted the immigrants in a variety of ways. The operation of the Emigration Commission and Castle Garden is considered in more detail in Chapter 7. Similarly, after 1850, city officials in Bremen began meeting the incoming trains in order to direct the emigrants to certain hotels, protect them against extortion, and provide advice about the voyage. The system was rapidly copied by Hamburg.[92] British emigration officials also recommended a controlled departure place in Liverpool, but the size of the port caused the suggestion to be viewed as impractical.

[89] Page, "Transportation of Immigrants," p. 734.
[90] For a contemporary discussion of the potential problems facing immigrants upon arrival in New York City, see Abbott, *Immigration*, pp. 130–4.
[91] MacDonagh, *Pattern*.
[92] Page, "Transportation," p. 742.

Summary

To someone living in the twenty-first century, it is hard to imagine going through what the immigrants did in order to reach the United States during the first half of the nineteenth century. They undertook a trip that, given the very best of luck, lasted a month and a half, and could have lasted three months or more. Before the immigrants even reached the embarkation port, they engaged in some combination of walking, taking a "short" steamboat trip, driving a wagon, and riding on carriages or early railroads. At the embarkation port, the immigrants were beset with runners and others eager to take their money. Aboard the ships, they encountered crowded conditions and the possible outbreak of disease, with no place to flee to and little idea of how to protect themselves. This factor increased the odds of dying on the trip relative to staying home by a not insubstantial amount. Even if the immigrant was sufficiently fortunate to avoid an onboard epidemic, and the vast majority did, they might run out of food or water and have to buy these items at exorbitant prices. On finally reaching the United States, the immigrants again encountered runners anxious to take their money, a situation that continued until they reached their final destination. It was not until the government reforms instituted on both sides of the Atlantic Ocean during the late 1840s and early 1850s, near the end of the antebellum period, that some of the problems facing the immigrants were addressed.

The litany of problems discussed in this chapter emphasizes an important point concerning the economics of immigration during the antebellum years. The cost of getting to the United States was not small. In addition to the money the immigrants paid for the trip and the increased possibility of death on the trip, their costs were further increased by the fact that they did not earn any income while in transit. Thus, for individuals to be willing to voluntarily undertake such a trip – and almost all did so voluntarily during the antebellum period – the expected benefits in terms of the additional lifetime income that could be earned in the United States must have been larger than the costs. The next chapter investigates whether the large percentage of immigrants who successfully completed their trip to the United States in fact achieved the higher expected lifetime income.

7

The Immigrants in the United States

Chapter 6 discussed the trip of the European immigrants up to their arrival in the United States. This chapter investigates what happened then. The immigrants arrived at a number of U.S. ports and the figures for arrivals at each port are presented. However, most of the immigrants did not stay in the arrival port. Therefore, this chapter examines their geographic location in 1850. Because of financial or health limitations, not all of the immigrants who wanted to leave the city at which they arrived found it easy to do so. The large volume of arrivals in New York City, in fact, led the state to create the Commissioners of Emigration of the State of New York in 1847, as noted in the last chapter. Their operations in assisting the arriving immigrants are discussed in detail in this chapter. The large majority of immigrants who left the port cities went to locations where jobs were available and the types of jobs the immigrants obtained are examined. These data are then used to determine whether the immigrants achieved economic success in the U.S. labor market. The facts that immigration continued and rose in volume and that many early immigrants were able to assist others to migrate implies that the immigrants were better off in the United States, a supposition reinforced by the findings in this chapter.

The Ports of Arrival in the United States

Although European immigrants arrived at numerous ports in the United States during the antebellum period, five ports were of greatest importance. The most important arrival port during the antebellum period was New York City. Yet the dominance of New York was not of long

TABLE 7.1. *Immigrant Volume by Port of Arrival, 1823–1860 (percentage of period total)*

Time Period	Boston	New York	Philadelphia	Baltimore	New Orleans	Other Ports
1823–1825	7.4	54.6	10.1	8.3	8.1	11.5
1826–1830	6.6	59.0	11.0	9.3	8.4	5.6
1831–1835	5.4	62.6	7.1	11.0	7.6	6.3
1836–1840	4.6	64.4	4.5	8.3	11.2	7.0
1841–1845	8.0	66.3	4.2	5.4	10.7	5.4
1846–1850	9.3	66.5	4.8	3.6	12.1	3.7
1851–1855	6.3	73.5	4.2	2.9	10.6	2.5
1856–1860	6.2	76.3	2.6	3.6	8.8	2.4
TOTAL	7.0	70.0	4.5	4.4	10.5	3.7

Notes: Includes all passengers from 1823 through 1855. Includes only immigrants from 1856 through 1860. The "Other Ports" column does not include arrivals in San Francisco or other ports on the West Coast.
Source: U.S. Treasury, *Arrivals*, Table 8, pp. 86–7.

duration. During the colonial period, most immigrants landed in Philadel-phia.[1] At this time, the Europeans settled east of the Appalachian Moun-tains, and Philadelphia, besides being the largest colonial city, was a more convenient entry point.[2] As late as 1783–9, Grabbe estimated that 47 per-cent of all immigrants arrived in Philadelphia. Even between 1810 and 1819, Philadelphia still received 25 percent of the total number of immi-grants.[3] Philadelphia's position continued to deteriorate into the 1820s, when only about 10 percent of arrivals landed in the city (Table 7.1 and Figure 7.1). After 1835, Philadelphia's share never exceeded 5 per-cent. Instead, by the early 1820s, more than half of the immigrants came ashore in New York City. The other three important ports of arrival, Boston, Baltimore, and New Orleans, each received 8–10 percent in the 1820s. By the last half of the 1830s, New York's share had increased to almost 65 percent, and the percentage increased even more in the 1850s. New Orleans became a distant second as an arrival port, but consistently accounted for 10–12 percent of arrivals. By the 1830s, Boston's share was usually 5–9 percent, while the trend for Baltimore was similar to that for Philadelphia. By the latter half of the 1840s, fewer than 5 percent of

[1] Wokeck, *Trade*, emphasizes the importance of Philadelphia as an arrival port during the eighteenth century.
[2] Page, "Transportation," p. 736.
[3] Calculated from information in Grabbe, "European Immigration," Tables 1 and 2, pp. 192, 194.

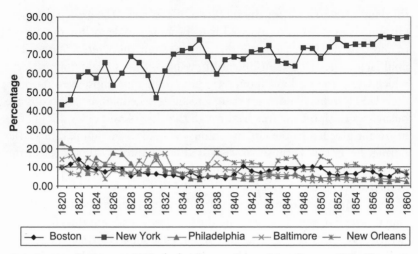

FIGURE 7.1. Passenger Arrivals by Port, 1820–1860. *Source:* U.S. Treasury, *Arrivals*, Table 8, pp. 86–7.

the total arrivals came ashore in Baltimore. Thus, the antebellum period was one where New York became the dominant arrival port and, over time, increased its dominance.

The success of New York City after 1810 was because of a number of factors.[4] The first was that New York City has a fine natural harbor. In particular, the presence of Long Island and Staten Island provide protection against the intensity of storms once ships reached the Upper Bay, where the major docking facilities were located.[5] Second, New York became the most important port for the freight trade. Although in fourth place in total tonnage in 1770, New York was able to capture much of the reexport trade during the 1790s. In 1797, for the first time, New York became the leader in total tonnage. Its leading position was reinforced because of events during and immediately after the War of 1812. The British had blockaded the city during the war, with the result that prices of manufacturing goods rose to high levels. After the war, the British decided to send most of their manufacturing goods to New York, attracted both by the high prices and by New York's central position along the coast, a

---

[4] The discussion in this paragraph follows Albion, *Rise*, pp. 8–16. For a discussion from the perspective of the decline of Philadelphia that emphasizes many of the same factors, see Lindstrom, *Economic Development*, pp. 32–40.

[5] In contrast, ships had to sail one hundred miles up the Delaware River to reach Philadelphia, and the river was often frozen in the winter. See Lindstrom, *Economic Development*, pp. 37–8.

third important factor for the success of New York. The growing importance of New York also allowed it to become the depot for the export
of most of the increasing cotton exports from the United States. The
final factor was the establishment of the packet lines beginning in 1817,
which were discussed in Chapter 3. These companies chose New York as
their U.S. terminus and, with their set sailing schedules, convinced more
businesses to ship their freight through the city. New York's dominance
in freight also led to the city assuming the lead in the immigrant traffic
during the 1810s, because, as discussed in Chapter 3, almost all of the
early immigrants sailed to the United States on ships primarily engaged
in the freight trade.

New York's position was reinforced by the construction of the Erie
Canal, which opened in 1825.[6] By the first few decades of the 1800s, settlement in the United States was occurring west of the Appalachian Moun-
tains and, as will be discussed later, a large percentage of the immigrants
went westward. The newer areas in the South were not attractive to
immigrants because the existence of slavery limited opportunities for free
whites. Any immigrant who did not wish to stay in the Eastern port cities,
therefore, would want to land at a port that gave them the easiest access
to the Old Northwest, the area from western Pennsylvania into Illinois.
Once the Erie Canal opened, New York became that port. Immigrants
arriving in New York could take a steamship up the Hudson River to
Albany, proceed across upper New York State on the Erie Canal, then
board another steamship in Buffalo and reach the Old Northwest.[7] Thus,
as is shown in Table 7.1, New York's share of the total arrivals rose
after 1825. The construction of the railroad network beginning in the
1830s simply intensified New York's advantage as the port with the best
connections to the western parts of the country.

None of the other ports were ever able to challenge New York's position of dominance. Both Philadelphia and Baltimore, ports that mainly
allowed immigrants to settle along the East Coast, attracted a diminishing
number of passengers. Boston continued to attract a somewhat larger
share of the passengers than Philadelphia and Baltimore because of the
large-scale presence of the Irish in Massachusetts. As shown in Chapter 6
(Table 6.2), almost all of the ships arriving in Boston left from the British
Isles, mainly the port of Liverpool, and thus primarily carried the Irish. In

---

[6] Much of the discussion in the next two paragraphs follows Page, "Transportation,"
pp. 736–7.
[7] Steamboats began operating on Lake Erie in 1822. See Bukowczyk, "Migration," p. 30.

particular, immigrant volume at Boston was comparatively large during the potato famine years between 1845 and 1849 (Figure 7.1). Limited economic opportunities in Boston, however, placed a ceiling on the total number of arrivals.[8] New Orleans was able to keep its share of the growing volume of immigration because it was an alternative way to reach the Old Northwest, in addition to being the easiest way to reach Texas. The Germans, who were most likely to go to the Old Northwest or to settle in Texas, comprised a large share of the arrivals in New Orleans. Passengers on ships from the European continent, who were mainly Germans, accounted for more than 56 percent of those arriving in New Orleans (Table 6.2).[9] Even so, the city never encroached on the supremacy of New York because the immigrants could encounter yellow fever in New Orleans. Even if they did not catch a disease upon arrival, the journey up the Mississippi River to St. Louis was dangerous and not much shorter than going through New York. Thus, the growing advantages of New York City and the disadvantages of the other ports combined to make New York City the most important arrival city throughout the antebellum period. The further increase in New York's importance during the 1850s is likely because of the workings of the Emigration Commission of the State of New York, as explained later.

Assistance on Arrival (Mainly in New York)

For many years, when an immigrant ship arrived in the United States, each individual simply disembarked and went on his or her way. Yet in all of the arrival cities, some assistance was available for the new arrivals. If they remained, the immigrants often became a burden on the city's current population and thus much, but not all, of the assistance had the objective of helping the immigrants move elsewhere. Not surprisingly, given the larger volume of arrivals, the most extensive assistance system developed in 1847 in New York City. Although that system is the main topic of this section, the assistance available before 1847 is discussed first.

Every major arrival port in the United States had immigrant aid societies, most of which were in existence by the early part of the nineteenth

---

[8] O'Connor, *Hub*, pp. 152–4.
[9] The Commissioners of Emigration provided annual totals by nationality for arrivals in New York City. See Commissioners of Emigration, *Annual Reports*. Attempts to use these in conjunction with the data in Table 7.1 in order to provide more exact estimates by nationality for arrivals at each port proved fruitless. This inconsistency is another reason for using all the volume data from the Passenger Lists carefully.

century. Given the early importance of the port of Philadelphia, a society for the relief of Irish immigrants was founded in 1792.[10] In New Orleans and other port cities, immigrant aid societies were founded no later than the 1830s.[11] Each society originally acquired much of its funds from the general public. With the increasing volume of immigrants arriving in New York, it became more difficult to assist the newly arrived individuals with funds from charitable contributions. In response, New York passed a law in 1824 requiring ship captains to post a $300 bond for each immigrant to indemnify the city in case the person became a public burden. The bond was seldom posted because captains could be released from paying it by instead paying a head tax of $1.50 for each immigrant.[12] In Baltimore, the immigrant aid societies for the British, Scots, Irish, and Germans all ran into financial problems in the late 1820s.[13] In response, Maryland also adopted the head tax and, in fact, its use spread to every important port city.[14] In each city, the money was used for relief activities, including finding jobs in other cities for many immigrants. In addition, in New York City, some immigrant agents established private almshouses and private hospitals for the care of immigrants, although the quality of the hospitals, in particular, varied widely.[15]

The system of assistance being provided by each city and the immigrant aid societies worked reasonably well when the volume of immigration was small and a large percentage of the arriving immigrants were fairly well off. During the decade of the 1830s, however, as discussed in Chapter 5, more low-skilled and poorer immigrants began arriving in the United States. Then, when the potato famine broke out in 1846, the total number of individuals leaving Europe increased dramatically. In 1845, immigration set a record at more than 114,000 immigrants. Two years later, the volume reached almost 235,000 and increased to about 300,000 in 1849. With New York being the port of entry for more than 65 percent of the European immigrants, the numbers arriving in New York similarly jumped. In 1845, 76,500 individuals arrived, and the total number of immigrants reached almost 130,000 in 1847. Many of the arrivals in the latter year, especially from Ireland, were not in very good

[10] Nash, *First City*, pp. 146–7.
[11] Searight, *New Orleans*, p. 95. Browne, *Baltimore*, p. 88. Albion, *Rise*, pp. 350–1.
[12] Page, "Transportation," pp. 746–7. Albion, *Rise*, p. 349.
[13] Browne, *Baltimore*, p. 88.
[14] Olson, *Baltimore*, pp. 91, 118. Page, "Transportation," p. 747.
[15] Albion, *Rise*, p. 350. Kapp, *Immigration*.

health. These individuals quickly became a burden on the city of New York, both in terms of their possible starvation and their potential to spread disease among the resident population. In anticipation of these problems, the state of New York set up the Emigration Commission of the State of New York, which began to operate in May 1847.[16]

The Emigration Commission assisted the arriving immigrants in a number of ways, as detailed by the data presented in Tables 7.2 and 7.3. As briefly discussed in the last chapter, the Commission provided medical care for large numbers of sick immigrants in two places. The Marine Hospital cared for immigrants with contagious diseases, mainly typhus, cholera, and smallpox.[17] All arriving ships had to pass quarantine at this time. Even so, the incubation period for some of the diseases was sufficiently long that a number of immigrants spent some days in New York City before being admitted to the Marine Hospital. Thus, as shown in Table 7.2, many of the individuals in this hospital were admitted from the city, whereas others were taken to the hospital directly from the ship. In total, almost 54,000 immigrants – 2.1 percent of all arrivals in New York City – were cared for at the Marine Hospital from 1847 through 1859, when the hospital was closed.[18] Beginning in 1849, the Commission reports also provide the total number of days that patients spent at the hospital, so the average stay can be calculated. Through 1853, the average stay was slightly less than a month, although in later years, the average stay fell to under three weeks. A logical inference is that immigrants arriving during the high-volume period from 1847 through 1854 were less healthy than those arriving during the period of smaller volume. This finding is consistent with the trend in loss rates discussed in Chapter 6.

[16] Knowledge concerning the potato famine in Ireland in 1846 and the expected increase in immigration was well known in New York and led to the founding of the Emigration Commission in the first half of 1847, just as the large increase in volume began. The Commission continued to operate until 1890 when the federal government assumed responsibility. See Page, "Transportation," p. 749. For a brief discussion of arrivals in Boston during this period, see O'Connor, *Bibles*, pp. 112–14. For a description of the workings of the Emigration Commission written in 1870, see Abbott, *Immigration*, pp. 172–6.

[17] During some years, those arriving with smallpox were sent to separate smallpox hospitals.

[18] As discussed in Chapter 5, the Marine Hospital recorded a total of 8,294 deaths. Thus, the deaths were a little more than 15% of those admitted. It is also noteworthy that the Commission made sure that at least one of the doctors spoke German. See Commissioners of Emigration, *Annual Reports*, pp. 138–9.

TABLE 7.2. *Data on Immigrant Assistance at Marine Hospital and Ward's Island, 1847–1860*

Year	Total Alien Arrivals	Admittances to the Marine Hospital			Average Stay at Marine Hospital[b] (days)	Admits to Ward's[c]	Average Stay at Ward's Island[b](days)
		From Vessels	From City[a]	Total			
1847	129,062	3,983	2,949	6,932	–	1,629	–
1848	189,176	3,587	4,524	8,111	–	3,491	–
1849	220,603	1,215	4,339	5,554	28.3	6,927	56.3
1850	212,796	622	2,446	3,068	30.2	8,098	63.6
1851	289,601	1,487	4,622	6,109	28.3	12,514	50.5
1852	300,992	1,240	7,130	8,370	23.5	12,553	50.5
1853	284,945	1,805	2,672	4,477	28.8	11,517	64.1
1854	319,223	1,861	2,577	4,438	18.5	12,487	73.4
1855	136,233	410	1,707	2,117	21.5	9,090	76.7
1856	142,342	578	978	1,556	19.8	5,339	68.9
1857	183,773	810	967	1,777	17.3	6,701	59.8
1858	78,589	595	572	1,167	17.7	4,625	63.5
1859	79,322	66[d]	177[d]	243[d]	19.7	3,048	56.6
1860	105,162	–	–	–	–	3,701	55.7
TOTAL	2,671,819	18,259	35,660	53,919	–	101,622	–

[a] Sum of the "Number received from City" and "Number received from other Sources." Most are in the former category.

[b] For Marine Hospital, calculated as "Number of Days Spent in Marine Hospital" divided by "Total Number Treated." For Ward's Island, calculated as "Number of Days on Ward's Island" divided by "Total Number Cared For and Treated."

[c] Only includes new admittances during the year, excluding births and those remaining from the previous year.

[d] Partial year data, because the Marine Hospital was closed on June 27, 1859.

Source: Commissioners of Emigration, *Annual Reports.* Column 1 data are from Table A, p. 288. Data in columns 2, 3, and 4 are from Table B, p. 291. Column 5 and column 7 data are calculated from each year's Annual Report. Column 6 data are from Table C, p. 302.

TABLE 7.3. *Data on Non-Medical Forms of Assistance by the Commissioners of Emigration, 1847–1860*

Year	Number Sent Back to Europe[a]	Number Forwarded Elsewhere in United States	Number Given Temporary Relief	Number Helped with Jobs	Number Given Relief in Another NY County	Number Given Other Help[b]	Number of Letters Written
1847	–	798	503	–	–	1,165	–
1848	–	2,102	6,640	–	5,369	645	–
1849	–	2,999	16,854	–	5,566	1,360	–
1850	53	2,248	27,314	8,000	5,937	320[c]	–
1851	311	7,080	23,941	18,204	12,550	1,583	–
1852	433	4,168	117,568	14,971	18,432	1,229	1,586
1853	271	2,991	44,514	14,334	9,351	1,035	1,668
1854	444	4,164	69,085	13,964	10,504	1,861	1,512
1855	570	4,426	93,925	15,151	12,175	695	1,301
1856	54	501	11,172	9,378	5,261	397	1,061
1857	64	361	5,411	10,933	4,253	812	2,007
1858	170	301	4,144	9,346	4,200	205	476
1859	68	77	4,582	7,150	2,407	440	–
1860	67	301	5,237	7,717	2,104	486	–
TOTAL	2,505	32,517	430,890	129,148	98,109	12,233	9,611

[a] Includes only those sent back to Europe at Commission expense. Beginning in 1856, others were sent back at the expense of the shipping companies.

[b] Includes those sent to city hospitals, private hospitals, various smallpox hospitals, new admittances to lunatic asylums, and those buried at Commission expense. The total does not include support of those admitted to lunatic asylums in previous years for which the Commission provided continuing support. Burials usually comprised the majority of the total.

[c] The number whose burials were paid for by the Commission was not listed this year.

Source: Yearly Reports for each year in Commissioners of Emigration, *Annual Reports.*

A large number of other immigrants were cared for at the Emigrants' Refuge and Hospital on Ward's Island.[19] The hospital cared for immigrants sick with a noncontagious disease, while the refuge admitted "the helpless and chronically infirm, pregnant women waiting childbirth, and others not requiring hospital treatment."[20] In total, slightly more than one hundred thousand immigrants were admitted to Ward's Island through 1860, 3.8 percent of the total.[21] On Ward's Island, the average stay was usually around two months, substantially longer than at the Marine Hospital. The Island saw a number of births, and there were apparently so many children that a school was opened in 1856.[22] During a number of years, the Commission's *Annual Reports* discuss improvements to Ward's Island and the help the Commission received from many of the immigrants in the refuge. Thus, many of the able-bodied immigrants provided at least some work in exchange for their care. Essentially, the Commission took the position of not aiding immigrants at their homes in the city if they were "unwilling to be sent to Ward's Island."[23] However, Ward's Island did not take those considered insane, although the Commissioners often requested money to open their own insane asylum. Instead, most of these immigrants were sent to the City Asylum in New York City, although the Emigration Commission paid for their support. In addition, a few immigrants each year were treated at city hospitals, and the Commission provided reimbursement for their care.

Besides caring for the sick, infirm, and mentally unbalanced, the Emigration Commission provided other assistance to the arriving immigrants, as shown in Table 7.3. A small number were sent back to Europe at Commission expense but "at their own request."[24] A somewhat larger number were "Forwarded Elsewhere in the United States." It is not completely clear from reading the reports, but this assistance was probably not of a monetary nature, at least until Castle Garden was founded. It probably consisted mainly of advice on how best to get to other destinations. By

[19] The name of the historical complex on Ward's Island in many current sources is given as the State Emigrant Refuge. The name used in the text is the name it was called in the *Annual Reports* of the Commissioners of Emigration. In any case, the entire refuge was "the biggest hospital complex in the world during the 1850s." See *Wikipedia*, entry on Ward's Island.

[20] Commissioners of Emigration, *Annual Reports*, p. 143.

[21] As noted in Chapter 6, total deaths at Ward's Island were 11,953, almost 12% of those admitted.

[22] Commissioners of Emigration, *Annual Reports*, p. 202.

[23] Commissioners of Emigration, *Annual Reports*, p. 115.

[24] Most of the annual reports use this phrase.

far the largest number of immigrants assisted, 16 percent of all arrivals, were provided with "temporary relief." This help usually consisted of dinner, a night's lodging, and breakfast. Presumably, the Commission was endeavoring to save many of the immigrants from the machinations of the runners. Beginning in 1850, a labor exchange was set up, where some of the arriving immigrants (about 6 percent of arrivals between 1850 and 1860) were matched with available jobs throughout the United States. The word on this feature spread quickly back to Europe, because the *Annual Report* for 1851 says some of the arrivals that year came with the idea of using the Commission's labor exchange.[25] The Commission also paid for burials for a number of the arriving immigrants, a category that comprised the majority of those in the "Number Given Other Help" column. For those immigrants who wished to go elsewhere but did not have the funds, the Commission also wrote letters to friends or relatives in the United States asking for money. The reports indicate that funds were frequently sent in response.

The law setting up the Emigration Commission specified that immigrants could receive aid for a period of five years after their arrival if they lived anywhere in New York State. Although the Commission did not directly assist individuals outside of the area of New York City, it did reimburse counties for their expenses in doing so. Over the period 1848 through 1860, the other counties in New York State helped almost one hundred thousand individuals for which they were reimbursed. This category was one example of the Commission's help for immigrants who may have arrived in an earlier year. Thus, simply summing all the totals in Tables 7.2 and 7.3 involves some double counting. Double counting could also occur if an individual died at the Marine Hospital or Ward's Island, and then was buried at Commission expense. A number of other possibilities exist, although the reports generally indicate that the vast majority of those helped had arrived that year, or in some cases, during the immediate preceding year. In addition, most of the categories are probably mutually exclusive. Thus, the sum of those listed in Tables 7.2 and 7.3 – 870,000 individuals or 32.6 percent of all arrivals between 1847 and 1860 – is an overstatement, but probably not a major one, of the actual number of arriving immigrants helped by the Commission.

The activities of the Emigration Commission were funded by the same $1.50 head tax that had been previously imposed. As the volume of immigration rose through 1854, and the activities of the Commission

[25] Commissioners of Emigration, *Annual Reports*, pp. 80–1.

expanded, the tax proceeds proved insufficient. The financial situation was worsened by the need to buy land, by improvements at Ward's Island, and by the general desire to provide better assistance to those it was helping. Almost every year, the reports indicate the Commission ran short of money. In particular, in many years, the Commission did not reimburse the counties in a timely fashion. In April 1853, the rate was raised to $2.00 per passenger. The abrupt decline in immigrant volume in 1855 did not help the financial situation, because the Commission needed to continue to make payments on its existing debt and the lower volume translated into a reduction in the revenue generated by the head tax.[26]

In addition to keeping sick immigrants away from the general population and helping immigrants leave the city, another motive for having a government agency assist the arriving immigrants was the presence of runners and others who would endeavor to cheat the newcomers out of their funds. To the extent the runners were successful, more individuals became stranded in New York City, increasing the burden on the city. Before 1855, the reports are filled with discussions of this issue. In August 1855, the solution was found when the Emigration Commission opened Castle Garden as an immigrant-landing depot. The Commission erected physical barriers to keep out the runners, although this procedure had to survive a court challenge. Within the confines of the landing depot, the Commission provided for the various needs of the immigrants. One year later, the Commission established a program of lending money to needy immigrants to continue their journey, although the immigrants had to leave their luggage as collateral. Upon repayment, the luggage was shipped to the immigrant. Finally, in 1857, the Commission sent an agent to Europe in an effort to keep the immigrants from being defrauded on their transatlantic tickets. Although it is unclear how successful either of these last two endeavors was, the later reports speak glowingly of the establishment of Castle Garden as providing a cure for many of the previous problems.

The establishment of the Emigration Commission and Castle Garden might explain the increase in New York City's share of total arrivals in the 1850s (Table 7.1). After staying stagnant at about 65 percent since 1835, New York's percentage increased to 75 percent between 1850 and 1860. It is possible that, by letter and word of mouth, immigrants learned of the new system and more decided to sail for New York.

[26] Commissioners of Emigration, *Annual Reports*, pp. 189–90.

The Geographic Location of the Immigrants

Upon arrival in New York City or another port, friends and family greeted many immigrants. Some, such as Johann Bauer, stayed with friends for a few months before leaving the city. Others, such as Edward Phillips, left the city immediately after arrival.[27] Both situations were not unusual. Many immigrants who did not require assistance from the Emigration Commission or another aid society stayed in the city for a while to visit friends, rest from their trip, and to gather information concerning the location of job opportunities in the United States. Others had developed more comprehensive plans before leaving Europe, often based on the advice and financial assistance of previous migrants. Many, in fact, already had tickets to get them to a waiting job in another part of the country. This discussion emphasizes that the port of arrival was not the final destination for most of the immigrants. For example, the Irish and German populations of New York City increased between 1850 and 1860 by only 70,000 and 64,000, respectively. Total Irish and German immigration during this period was 841,000 and 761,000, respectively.[28] In fact, of those immigrants arriving in New York City between 1840 and 1850, about 65 percent left within the first year and 85 percent were not there five years after arrival.[29] Although data are lacking for the other ports, presumably only a distinct minority of the arriving immigrants settled permanently in the arrival ports.

Given that most immigrants did not stay very long in the port where they arrived, the question arises as to where the immigrants relocated. No comprehensive data are available before 1850, because that year was the first one in which the census collected information on the nativity of the population. In 1850, the entire body of the foreign born comprised 11.1 percent of the free U.S. population, and the percentage rose to 15.0 percent in 1860.[30] The distribution by state and region of the three major immigrant groups in 1850 – the British, Irish, and Germans – is shown in Table 7.4. Also shown is the distribution of total manufacturing output by state in 1850, a factor that is discussed later. The importance of each group in the total population of each state in 1850, along with

[27] See Chapter 1 for information about Johann Bauer and Edward Phillips.
[28] Ó Gráda, "New York City Irish."
[29] Ferrie, *Yankeys*, p. 42.
[30] The percentage born in a European country in 1850 was 10.2%, as shown in Table 7.5.

TABLE 7.4. *Distribution of the Foreign Born and Manufacturing in 1850, by State (percent of column total)*

State	Immigrant Population				Distribution of Manufacturing Output
	Irish	British	German	All Europeans	
Maine	1.4	0.7	0.1	0.8	2.5
New Hamp.	0.9	0.5	0.0	0.5	2.3
Vermont	1.6	0.7	0.0	0.9	0.9
Massachusetts	12.1	5.6	0.8	7.1	15.0
Rhode Island	1.7	1.4	0.0	1.1	2.2
Connecticut	2.8	1.9	0.3	1.8	4.5
New York	35.7	30.6	20.7	29.6	22.7
New Jersey	3.2	3.6	1.9	2.8	4.0
Pennsylvania	15.8	14.3	13.7	14.3	15.4
NORTHEAST TOTAL	75.1	59.4	37.4	59.0	69.5
Delaware	0.4	0.3	0.1	0.3	0.5
Wash. D.C.	0.2	0.2	0.2	0.2	–
Maryland	2.0	1.3	4.7	2.6	3.2
Virginia	1.2	1.1	1.0	1.1	3.6
N. Carolina	0.1	0.4	0.1	0.1	0.9
S. Carolina	0.4	0.4	0.4	0.4	0.7
Georgia	0.3	0.3	0.2	0.3	0.7
Florida	0.1	0.1	0.1	0.1	0.1
Alabama	0.4	0.4	0.2	0.4	0.5
Mississippi	0.2	0.2	0.2	0.2	0.3
Louisiana	2.5	1.3	3.1	3.1	0.7
Texas	0.1	0.3	1.4	0.6	0.1
Arkansas	0.1	0.1	0.1	0.1	0.1
Tennessee	0.3	0.3	0.2	0.3	1.0
Kentucky	1.0	1.0	2.4	1.4	2.4
Missouri	1.5	1.7	7.7	3.5	2.4
SOUTH TOTAL	10.9	9.4	21.9	14.6	17.1
Ohio	5.4	9.7	19.4	10.4	6.2
Michigan	1.4	3.5	1.8	2.0	1.1
Indiana	1.3	1.9	5.0	2.6	1.9
Illinois	2.9	6.3	6.7	4.9	1.7
Iowa	0.5	1.3	1.2	1.0	0.4
Wisconsin	2.2	7.1	6.0	4.8	0.9
Minnesota	0.0	0.0	0.0	0.0	0.0
MIDWEST TOTAL	13.7	29.7	40.1	25.7	12.2
California	0.3	1.1	0.5	0.6	1.3
Territories[a]	0.1	0.5	0.1	0.1	–
TOTAL	961,719	379,093	573,225	2,031,867	

[a] Includes New Mexico, Oregon, and Utah Territories.

Sources: Population: Calculated from U.S. Bureau of the Census, Seventh (1850), *Seventh Census*, Table XV, p. xxxvi. Manufacturing: DeBow, *Statistical View*, Table CXCV, p. 179.

all the foreign born, is shown in Table 7.5.[31] One major similarity and a number of differences among the three groups are apparent.

The similarity is that the South was the least important destination for any of the immigrant groups. In the major cotton-producing states, immigrants typically comprised less than 2 percent of the total free population, far below their percentage in the entire U.S. population, and thus an even lower percentage of the population of these states if the slaves were included. As a whole, the South was most attractive to the Germans, but the 22 percent of German immigrants who lived in the South was small in comparison to the native born. Not including the slaves, 35 percent of the native born lived in the South in 1850. As shown in Tables 7.4 and 7.5, in both absolute terms and relative to the state's population, large numbers of Germans lived in only four southern states in 1850 – Missouri, Maryland, Louisiana, and Texas – none of which were major cotton producers. Only about 11 percent of the Irish and slightly less than 10 percent of the British lived in the South. The Irish had a fairly large presence in Louisiana and Maryland, but in no other southern state did either the Irish or the British account for more than 2 percent of the population.

Outside of the South, each of the three immigrant groups had their own distinctive geographic pattern in 1850. More than 75 percent of the Irish lived in the Northeast in 1850, but only 41 percent of the native-born, free population did. The British immigrant shares in the Northeast also exceeded that of the native-born population in 1850, although to a smaller degree than the Irish did. A smaller percentage of Germans, on the other hand, lived in the Northeast than the native-born population. Thus, the Irish, and to a lesser extent the British, were the immigrant groups most likely to live in the Northeast. Alternatively, the Germans were most likely to live in the Midwest. About 40 percent of all German immigrants lived in the Midwest in 1850, much more than the 23 percent share of the native-born, free population.[32] The Irish percentage was lower than the natives, and the British percentage was slightly larger. These differences are partly because of the sailing routes discussed in Chapter 6. Most of

---

[31] Tables similar to 7.4 and 7.5 could be constructed for 1860. All of the results discussed in this section also hold for 1860. Taylor, *Distant Magnet*, p. 173, presents a map indicating where more than 10% of the population was foreign born in 1860. Also, see Jones, *American Immigration*, pp. 100–1, who provides a brief, though good, discussion of the location of immigrants in 1860, including those groups not discussed here.

[32] Including those Germans who lived in Missouri and Kentucky with those in the Midwest would increase the German share in this slightly broader area to 50%.

TABLE 7.5. *Foreign Born in the United States in 1850, by Country of Origin and State of Location*

State	Total Population[a]	Percent Irish	Percent British	Percent German	Total Percent European Born[b]
Maine	583,169	2.4%	0.4%	0.1%	2.9%
New Hamp.	317,976	2.8%	0.6%	0.1%	3.5%
Vermont	314,120	4.9%	0.8%	0.1%	5.8%
Massachusetts	994,514	11.7%	2.1%	0.4%	14.5%
Rhode Island	147,545	10.8%	3.7%	0.2%	14.9%
Connecticut	370,792	7.2%	1.9%	0.5%	9.7%
New York	3,097,394	11.1%	3.7%	3.8%	19.4%
New Jersey	489,333	6.4%	2.8%	2.2%	11.7%
Pennsylvania	2,311,786	6.6%	2.3%	3.4%	12.6%
NORTHEAST TOTAL	8,626,629	8.4%	2.6%	2.5%	13.9%
Delaware	89,242	3.9%	1.3%	0.4%	5.7%
Wash. D.C.	48,000	4.9%	1.8%	2.9%	10.2%
Maryland	492,666	4.0%	1.0%	5.5%	10.6%
Virginia	949,133	1.2%	0.4%	0.6%	2.3%
N. Carolina	580,491	0.1%	0.2%	0.1%	0.4%
S. Carolina	283,523	1.4%	0.6%	0.8%	2.9%
Georgia	524,503	0.6%	0.2%	0.2%	1.1%
Florida	48,135	1.8%	1.0%	0.6%	4.1%
Alabama	428,779	0.8%	0.4%	0.2%	1.7%
Mississippi	296,648	0.6%	0.3%	0.4%	1.6%
Louisiana	272,953	8.9%	1.8%	6.4%	23.0%
Texas	154,431	0.9%	0.8%	5.3%	7.8%
Arkansas	162,797	0.3%	0.2%	0.3%	0.9%
Tennessee	763,154	0.3%	0.1%	0.2%	0.7%
Kentucky	771,424	1.2%	0.5%	1.8%	3.7%
Missouri	594,622	2.5%	1.1%	7.5%	11.8%
SOUTH TOTAL	6,460,501	1.6%	0.6%	1.9%	4.6%
Ohio	1,980,427	2.6%	1.9%	5.6%	10.7%
Michigan	397,654	3.4%	3.3%	2.5%	10.2%
Indiana	988,416	1.3%	0.7%	2.9%	5.3%
Illinois	851,470	3.3%	2.8%	4.5%	11.7%
Iowa	192,214	2.5%	2.5%	3.7%	10.1%
Wisconsin	305,391	6.9%	8.8%	11.3%	32.1%
Minnesota	6,077	4.5%	2.1%	2.3%	10.3%
MIDWEST TOTAL	4,721,649	2.8%	2.4%	4.9%	11.1%
California	92,597	2.6%	4.4%	3.2%	13.5%
Territories[c]	86,195	0.7%	2.1%	0.5%	3.5%
U.S. TOTAL	19,987,571	4.8%	1.9%	2.9%	10.2%

[a] White and Free Black Population only.

[b] Includes all European countries. Does not include those born in Canada, Mexico, etc.

[c] Comprised of New Mexico, Oregon, and Utah Territories.

Source: U.S. Bureau of the Census, Seventh (1850), *Seventh Census*, Table XV, p. xxxvi.

the arrivals in Boston left from Ireland, whereas most of those arriving in New Orleans left from the Continent.[33] Yet it is not clear how important the arrival ports were to explaining location, given the fact that so many immigrants moved elsewhere.

In summary, compared to both the native-born population and the other immigrant groups, the Irish located primarily in the Northeast. In fact, more than one-third of the Irish immigrants lived in New York State in 1850. Large numbers of Irish also lived in Pennsylvania and Massachusetts. Except for large contingents in the northeastern states of New York and Pennsylvania, the Germans were most numerous in a variety of Midwestern states – especially Ohio, Illinois, and Wisconsin – along with Missouri. The British, on the other hand, were most balanced. Relative to the native-born population, a larger proportion of the British immigrants lived in both the Northeast and the Midwest. Although 30 percent lived in New York, Pennsylvania was the only other state where more than 10 percent of the British immigrants lived in 1850.

Table 7.5 provides data on the combined importance of the European immigrants by state. In the Northeastern and Midwestern states, except for Indiana and those in upper New England, immigrants comprised 10 percent or more of the total population. The state with the largest immigrant presence in 1850 was Wisconsin, where one-third of the population was comprised of immigrants. Louisiana, which also included a large number of French and Spanish, had the second largest share of immigrants. New York was close behind, with almost 20 percent of its 1850 population being immigrants.[34] In other states, the proportions were smaller. However, even though the immigrant share was relatively consistent across most of the Northeastern and Midwestern states, the composition was quite different. The Irish accounted for 68 percent of all immigrants in the Northeast while the Germans accounted for 47 percent of all the immigrants in the Midwest. The British accounted for 19 percent of all the immigrants in the Northeast and 20 percent in the Midwest.

Regardless of any regional distinction among the immigrants, all of the immigrants, even the British, were much more likely than the native born to live in larger cities. Table 7.6 shows the percentages of each immigrant group and the total foreign born in fifteen of the largest cities in the United

---

[33] Jones, *American Immigration*, pp. 101–2.
[34] Because New York City was the most important arrival port and, as noted in the text, many immigrants did not leave the city immediately after arrival, the percentages for New York State in Tables 7.4 and 7.5 would be somewhat larger than the steady-state percentage.

TABLE 7.6. *Foreign-Born Population of Largest Cities in 1850*

City	Total Population[a]	Percent Irish	Percent British	Percent German	Percent Foreign-Born
Panel A: Eastern Cities					
New York	513,485	26.0	6.1	10.9	45.9
Philadelphia	408,045	17.7	5.1	5.6	29.8
Baltimore	165,983	7.3	1.6	11.7	21.4
Boston	135,625	26.0	3.0	1.3	34.4
Providence	41,434	18.4	3.5	0.2	23.4
Newark	38,883	14.3	6.1	9.8	31.7
Washington	37,812	5.4	1.9	3.3	11.3
Portland, Me	20,777	11.1	1.0	0.2	16.9
New Haven	20,338	13.6	2.4	1.4	18.2
Panel B: Western Cities					
Cincinnati	115,099	12.5	4.2	29.1	47.4
New Orleans	99,071	20.4	3.6	11.5	49.1
St. Louis	74,926	13.0	4.7	30.1	51.2
Louisville	37,540	8.3	2.5	20.0	33.2
Chicago	29,375	20.8	8.5	17.3	53.4
Milwaukee	19,963	14.1	7.3	36.4	64.0
ABOVE CITIES AS PERCENT OF U.S. TOTAL	8.8	34.3	21.3	33.7	29.7

Note: The cities in the table were the largest in the United States in 1850, with the exception of Albany and Charleston, S.C. These cities were not included because the total given as foreign born was less than the sum of the Irish, British, and Germans listed as living in each city.

[a] Total population for which nativity could be determined.

Source: U.S. Bureau of the Census, Seventh (1850), *Seventh Census*, Appendix Table III, p. 399.

States in 1850. Only 8.8 percent of the entire U.S. population, and only 6.2 percent of the native born, lived in these cities in 1850. Yet close to 30 percent of all the immigrants did, and the percentage reached one-third among the Irish and the Germans.[35] The Irish accounted for large shares of the population of cities in both the east and the west, at least partly because of the many females who worked as domestic servants.[36] The Germans were much more likely to be found in the western cities. Consequently, the western cities generally contained a larger percentage

---

[35] The situation was similar in 1860. See U.S. Bureau of the Census, Eighth (1860), *Population*, pp. 608–15.

[36] Jones, *American Immigration*, p. 104.

of immigrants, often reaching 50 percent or more, than the eastern cities, where immigrants seldom exceeded one-third of the total population. In the east, the immigrants were found in the largest proportions in or near the cities serving as ports of arrival. Other eastern cities seldom contained more than 20 percent immigrants. Two cities, one in the east and one in the west, were exceptions to these general findings. Almost half of New York's population was comprised of immigrants, presumably because New York was the major port of arrival. It is also possible that the existence of the Commissioners of Emigration of the State of New York, which assisted the immigrants by 1850, caused many to remain in the city. The other exception was Louisville, where only about one-third of the population was made up of immigrants, presumably because Kentucky was a slave state. Although New Orleans was also located in a slave state, it was an important port of arrival, a factor that led to a large immigrant population.[37]

The U.S. Occupations of the Immigrants

The economic success of the immigrants depended directly on the jobs they were able to acquire in the United States. Finding a suitable job depended partly on the skills the immigrants brought with them, that is, their backgrounds in Europe. To obtain the best job, the immigrants usually needed to leave their port of arrival – where a glut of existing and new immigrants lowered wages – but such a move was not easy for many. Thus, the geographic location of the immigrants in the antebellum United States reflected their backgrounds, their wealth, and the jobs they obtained. The next section discusses the interconnections among these factors, while this section investigates the jobs the immigrants acquired.

The U.S. Census first collected data on the occupations held by each individual in 1850. The census did not publish an occupational break-down by nativity, however, until 1870.[38] Fortunately, occupational data can be obtained beginning in 1850 from the census samples available from the Integrated Public Use Microdata Series (IPUMS), which are available online. These contain all the data that each census collected

---

[37] Smaller southern cities had a lower proportion of immigrants than either New Orleans or Louisville. The immigrant share of the population of Mobile was 30%, Memphis 22%, Nashville 12%, and Savannah 27%.

[38] These data are discussed in the appendix to this chapter. Besides not being available until 1870, the use of these data provides unclear results because black unskilled workers are included among the U.S. figures and women are included among all the groups.

on each individual, although for only a sample of the population.[39] For our purposes, the data collected by the census on each individual's place of birth and occupation were used. The IPUMS not only provides the original occupational classification used in each census but also codes this information according to the system used in 1950. The latter system classifies by skill level, reflects the system currently used by economic historians, and is thus used here. The same basic system, in fact, was used to discuss immigrant occupations in Chapter 5. The occupational distributions of the white male labor force by country of birth obtained from the IPUMS for 1850 through 1870 are shown in Table 7.7.[40]

The data in Table 7.7 imply that all groups of antebellum immigrants generally achieved success in the U.S. labor market.[41] This conclusion is supported by the data in three ways. The first is to directly compare the overall occupational distributions of the males in the three immigrant groups to that of white males born in the United States. For the British and the Germans, the percentages that had White-Collar jobs were similar to those for U.S. males, generally between one-tenth and one-seventh of the total males.[42] Similarly, about one-quarter of the German and U.S.-born white males were Unskilled workers, although this category contained

---

[39] The analysis of the 1870 census data in the appendix yields the same results as those discussed in the text. This finding emphasizes the general validity of the IPUMS, even though it represents only a sample of the entire census.

[40] Ruggles et al., *Integrated Public Use Microdata Series.* The entire 1850 and 1860 samples include 1% of the free population, and the 1870 sample 1% of the entire population. As noted in the text, I restricted my samples to white males in the labor force, which yielded data on approximately 50,000 people in 1850, 70,000 in 1860, and 90,000 in 1870. It is important to note that each sample contains different people, that is, they are not designed to follow the same individuals over time. In Table 7.7, farm laborers are classified as Unskilled rather than as Farmers.

Although the 1870 distributions include some immigrants who arrived after 1860, most of the foreign born living in the United States in 1870 had arrived before 1860. Of the total arriving from Europe between 1835 and 1869, only 30% arrived between 1860 and 1869. See Carter et al., *Historical Statistics,* series Ad91, p. 555. In any case, it is not likely that the average skill level of the arriving immigrant stream was very different in the 1860s than during the antebellum years.

[41] Using data on wages for later periods, researchers have reached a similar conclusion. For the latter years of the nineteenth century, Hatton, "How Much," finds that immigrants' wages relative to natives' wages grew by 20% in the first twenty years after arrival. Borjas, *Heaven's Door,* pp. 29–32, reaches a similar conclusion for immigrants arriving between the 1950s and the 1970s. Although it is impossible to tell with any certainty, the immigrants likely increased their income more than if they had not migrated.

[42] The United States had an advantage among Professionals. In 1850, of those born in the United States, 3.3% were Professionals. The corresponding percentages were 2.2%, 0.9%, and 1.9% for Great Britain, Ireland, and Germany, respectively.

TABLE 7.7. *White Male Occupational Distributions, 1850–1870, by Country of Birth (percentage of year total)*

Year	White Collar	Skilled	Farmers	Unskilled
United States				
1850	10.4	23.3	51.8	14.4
1860	12.9	22.0	43.0	22.1
1870	13.8	22.2	37.5	26.5
Great Britain				
1850	11.5	48.9	22.6	17.0
1860	13.1	45.4	22.7	18.8
1870	13.6	48.3	20.0	18.1
Ireland				
1850	6.6	29.3	12.4	51.7
1860	7.0	31.8	11.7	49.5
1870	8.1	34.6	13.1	44.2
Germany				
1850	10.0	44.3	21.9	23.8
1860	13.2	40.8	21.0	25.0
1870	14.8	39.7	21.8	23.7

Source: Calculated from IPUMS samples for 1850, 1860, and 1870. See Ruggles et al., *Integrated Public Use Microdata Series*. The following categorization was used for the IPUMS Occupation, 1950 variable: White-Collar – Professional, Technical; Managers, Officials, and Proprietors; Clerical and Kindred; Sales Workers; Farmers – Farmers; Skilled – Craftsmen; Operatives; Unskilled Workers – Service Workers; Farm Laborers; Laborers.

less than one in five of the British. The largest differences were in the two middle-income categories of Skilled workers and Farmers. A much larger percentage of the British and Germans were Skilled workers – about 40–50 percent – while a much larger percentage of the U.S. males were Farmers, although it declined from 50 percent in 1850 to under 40 percent by 1870.[43] The Irish, on the other hand, were clearly at a disadvantage relative to the other groups of immigrants. About half of the Irish males had Unskilled jobs, a much larger percentage than any of the other groups, while fewer than 10 percent were White-Collar workers, less than the other groups.[44] Thus, British and German immigrants had occupational

[43] The only immigrant group that had a proportion in farming similar to the United States in 1870 was the Scandinavians. See the analysis in Page, "Some Economic Aspects: II."

[44] Ferrie suggests that the skills brought by the Irish may have been a worse "fit" with the U.S. labor market. The Irish also accumulated wealth at a slower rate than immigrants from Britain or Germany. See Ferrie, *Yankeys*, pp. 97, 105–6. Also, see the comparative estimates of occupations of New York residents by nationality provided in Ó Gráda, "New York City Irish," Tables 4, 5, and 6.

distributions in the United States similar to U.S. males, although the Irish lagged.[45]

A second way of using the data in Table 7.7 is to examine changes in the occupational distributions over time. All three immigrant groups experienced a substantial increase in White-Collar workers between 1850 and 1870. Although the increase in percentage points for the British and the Irish, 2.1 and 1.5, respectively, was smaller than the 3.4 percentage point increase in the U.S. labor force, the increase for the Germans was a much higher 4.8 percentage points.[46] This change is the only trend apparent in all four distributions. The increase for the British was at the expense of the Farmer group, while the increase for the Germans was at the expense of the Skilled worker group. The major change for the United States was the decline in the Farmer category. The changes over time for the Irish, however, indicate a consistent, although not sizeable, improvement. The percentage of the Irish in the Unskilled category declined by 7.5 percentage points between 1850 and 1870, while each of the other three higher-paying categories experienced a gain. Thus, all three immigrant groups improved their average skill level over time, again implying the immigrants experienced success in the U.S. labor market.[47]

This analysis would not be accurate for a specific country if the composition of that country's arriving immigrant stream changed over time. For example, the higher skill levels observed in 1870 relative to 1850 in the census data might simply reflect an increase in the skill levels of the arrivals between 1850 and 1870. Yet the material in Chapter 5 indicates that little change likely occurred during this period. If anything, the growing use of the steamship in the late 1860s made it easier for lower-skilled

---

[45] A person's occupation broadly determined his or her income. Ferrie, *Yankeys*, Appendix D, pp. 203–8, provides estimates of annual incomes in 1850 for 157 occupational titles based on the 1850 IPUMS. For White-Collar workers, average annual incomes generally ranged from $500 to $1,300. The range was similar among Professional workers as other White-Collar groups, so the U.S. advantage in the former subcategory did not differentially affect incomes. For Skilled workers, the range was $300 to $600; for Farmers, $600 to $1,000; and for Unskilled workers, $250 to $600, although the figure for general laborers was more than $300. Taylor, *Distant Magnet*, p. 175, indicates that most skilled workers earned $1.50–$2.00 per day and laborers earned no more than $1. The figures are comparable with those derived by Ferrie, given the number of work days in a year.

[46] Because the figures from the IPUMS are based on samples of the population, technically confidence intervals should be calculated.

[47] Licht, *Working*, pp. 221–3, in his study of the railroad industry found that, by 1880, workers of Irish and German heritage held upper management positions in about the same proportion as the native born. Such was not the case before the Civil War.

immigrants to move to the United States.[48] In fact, the general improvement over time in the skill levels of the immigrant groups may have been somewhat *greater* than it appears from the data in Table 7.7. The biggest change in the average skill level of the arriving immigrant stream occurred in the 1830s, when it declined substantially (see Chapter 5). The 1850 occupational distributions, therefore, contained a number of skilled immigrants who arrived during or before the 1830s.[49] Because of deaths and continued new arrivals, these more skilled Europeans would have comprised a smaller percentage of the 1860 occupational distribution and an even smaller percentage of that for 1870. Yet in spite of the decline in the skill level of the surviving immigrant stream over time, the data recorded in the census show an increase each decade in the average skills of those born in Europe.[50] The implication is that all immigrant groups experienced a somewhat greater success over time in the U.S. labor market than indicated by the figures in Table 7.7.[51]

A third and related way of using the distributions in Table 7.7 is to directly compare them to those provided in Table 5.4 (p. 109), which showed the skill levels of the arriving male immigrants taken from the Passenger Lists. Such an exercise is complicated by three factors. The first is that the data in Table 5.4 relate to arrivals during a particular period of years, whereas that in Table 7.7 includes all immigrants surviving up to the census year. Most of the immigrants alive in 1850, however, had arrived after 1831, when the increase in volume, and the decline in skill levels, began. Thus, the various estimates in Table 5.4 for the skill levels of

---

[48] Cohn, "Transition." For the Irish, in particular, little change is evident in the occupational distribution of arrivals between 1851 and 1875. See Blessing, "Irish Emigration," Table 2.3, p. 20.

[49] Of arrivals between 1820 and 1849, 9% of the British arrived between 1820 and 1831, and 19% between 1820 and 1835. For the Irish, the percentages were 7% and 14%, and they were 2% and 10% for the Germans. See Carter et al., *Historical Statistics*, series Ad107, Ad108, and Ad111, p. 560. Although these calculations ignore arrivals between 1815 and 1819, they also ignore the fact that a larger percentage of the earlier arrivals would have died by the 1850 census year.

[50] This entire discussion bears a resemblance to the controversy between Chiswick and Borjas concerning more recent immigration to the United States. Chiswick, "Effect," found that immigrants caught up to their American counterparts over time. Borjas, "Assimilation," claimed the results were an artifact of the relative decline in the skill levels of later groups of immigrants who arrived from different countries. See the discussion in Borjas, "Economics," pp. 1671–80.

[51] Another factor complicating the analysis is that some of the immigrants who were working in each year immigrated as children. Such individuals may have had a labor market experience more similar to natives than to adult immigrants. See Friedberg, "Labor Market Assimilation."

arrivals during the latter 1830s and 1840s would be the best measure of the average skills carried by the arriving immigrant stream before 1850 or 1860. The second complicating factor is that farm laborers were included with Farmers in Table 5.4, but are included with Unskilled workers in Table 7.7. In the following discussion, therefore, Farmers and Unskilled workers are combined into one group.[52] The final factor is that, as discussed in Chapter 5, the accuracy of the occupational information taken from the Passenger Lists is not clear. Thus, the entire comparison should not be viewed as definitive.

The results of this exercise indicate that the immigrants living in the United States in 1850 (and 1860) increased their skill levels after arrival.[53] For each country, the percentages in the White-Collar group in 1850 and 1860 exceeded the percentages that had arrived with those skills. A similar result holds for Skilled workers from each country. Obviously, therefore, the total percentage of those who said they were Farmers or Unskilled workers on the Passenger Lists was larger than those found to have these jobs in the 1850 and 1860 censuses. The fact that the occupational structures in Tables 5.4 and 7.7 are broadly similar adds to the confidence that can be placed in these results. For example, the percentages of the Irish immigrants that the Passenger Lists recorded as having a White-Collar or a Skilled job was smaller than the similar percentages for either the British or the Germans. Similarly, the percentage of the Irish recorded with either of these occupations in the U.S. Census was smaller than those for the British or the Germans. As discussed in Chapter 5, the information from the Passenger Lists indicates that the Irish were clearly the least skilled immigrant group, a finding identical to that recorded in the 1850 and 1860 U.S. Censuses.

Three conclusions are evident. First, at a minimum, the European immigrants did not become worse off because of their migration. In fact, the occupational evidence presented here indicates that they prospered.[54]

---

[52] This factor probably has little effect on the results, because few immigrants were recorded in the Passenger Lists as "farm laborers." See the discussion in Chapter 5.

[53] This finding is similar to Ferrie's result that, on average, the British and Germans obtained more skilled jobs after arrival, whereas fewer Irish did. In Ferrie's view, much of the improvement occurred soon after arrival. See Ferrie, *Yankeys*, pp. 78–80.

[54] Johann Bauer became a farmer and it is thought that Edward Phillips did also. These two immigrants were introduced in Chapter 1. Bauer eventually settled outside of Kirksville, Missouri, an area with few other Germans. He became quite wealthy over time, although he did occasionally receive a little money from his parents still in Germany. In 1860, he was a farmhand working for his brother. In 1870, Bauer had a farm worth $3,000, and in 1880 he had a farm of 125 acres, twice the size of his 1870 farm.

This conclusion does not mean the immigrants did not face numerous hardships in the United States. What it does mean is, through the years, these hardships were generally overcome. Second, it is apparent the differences in the skill levels among the immigrants arriving from the different countries had long-term effects. In particular, the lower skills among the Irish arrivals were apparent as late as 1870 (and almost certainly even later). Although the Irish improved their skills in the United States between 1850 and 1870, they were still clearly the least skilled immigrant group by the latter date.[55] Third, the similarity of the occupational distributions taken from the Passenger Lists and the U.S. Census suggests that, at an aggregate level, many immigrants obtained jobs in the United States at the same general skill level as the jobs they had left in Europe.

The finding that the immigrants enjoyed success in the U.S. labor market is supported by other research, although the question remains somewhat controversial. Ferrie has completed the best study of what happened to the antebellum immigrants after arrival. He drew a sample from the Passenger Lists of individuals who arrived in New York between 1840 and 1850 and found a number of those same individuals in the 1850 and/or 1860 census materials. Thus, he was able to follow a small group of specific immigrants through their first ten to twenty years in the United States.[56] It is worth quoting his conclusion, similar to that reached here, in more detail:

The early years of antebellum immigrants' experience in the United States were years of change. From their arrival at the docks of New York until up to twenty years later, they changed their locations, their occupations, and their wealth holdings, and changed them in ways consistent with an effort to find their niche in the economy of their adopted homeland. Some groups had a more difficult time than others making these transitions: by virtually every measure, the Irish fared

See Kamphoefner et al., *News*, pp. 150–1. Phillips bought a farm in Chester County, Pennsylvania, although no further information is available on his wealth. See Erickson, *Invisible Immigrants*, p. 270.

55 The slow catch-up of the Irish is similar to what Borjas has suggested will occur with the lower-skilled immigrants who arrived in the 1980s. See Borjas, *Heaven's Door*, pp. 29–38.

56 Ferrie, *Yankeys*. Ferrie's samples, although scientifically drawn, are very small. He drew data on more than 23,000 immigrants from the passenger lists. About 1,500 immigrants were successfully linked to each of the 1850 census manuscripts and 1860 census manuscripts, with only slightly more than 500 linked to both census manuscripts. Thus, only 10.6% of those drawn from the passenger lists were successfully linked. See his discussion on p. 22. Not surprisingly, he was much more successful linking those with white-collar jobs, which accounted for between 10% and 15% of the total, a percentage much above that in arriving immigrant stream. See his Table 2–4 on p. 26.

considerably worse than the British or Germans who arrived over the 1840s. But even the Irish experienced the extensive mobility characteristic of antebellum immigrants in the years immediately after their arrival in the United States.[57]

Before the work by Ferrie, a number of other researchers had investigated the experiences of immigrants in the United States. Much of this work found little upward occupational movement for the immigrants after their arrival in the United States.[58] These studies, however, did not examine all the immigrants or even a specific group over time. Before Ferrie's work and the development of the IPUMS, the best that could be done was to examine the occupational mobility of those immigrants who remained in a specific city over a period of time. These immigrants did not experience a large amount of upward mobility. Given the assumption that those who left the city did not fare as well as those who remained, the conclusion was that immigrants achieved little overall success in the United States. Yet Ferrie's work and the less technical discussion provided here based on the IPUMS implies that the immigrants who moved must have done well. In fact, in many cases, the reason for the move was to take advantage of better economic opportunities in another location.[59]

Occupations and Geographic Location

Attempts to explain the geographic location by state of the immigrants in the United States has been the subject of a large body of empirical research for the period after the Civil War.[60] Generally, two factors have been found to be important. The first is state per capita income, and the second is the presence in the state of previous immigrants from the same country, what has been called the "friends and family" effect.[61] For the antebellum period, the former cannot explain the *differential* location in the United States of immigrants from different countries because all immigrant groups should have been equally attracted to the high income

---

[57] Ferrie, *Yankeys*, p. 185.
[58] Thernstrom, *Poverty*; Thernstrom, *Other Bostonians*; Esslinger, *Immigrants*; Griffen and Griffen, *Natives*.
[59] See the discussions in Ferrie, *Yankeys*, pp. 71–2, 144–58.
[60] For examples of this literature, see the following: Vedder and Gallaway, "Geographical Distribution"; Dunlevy and Gemery, "Role"; Gallaway et al., "Distribution"; and Dunlevy and Gemery, "Economic Opportunity." The Vedder and Gallaway article also includes 1850 but their model does not adequately explain the settlement patterns in that year.
[61] For example, Dunlevy and Gemery, "Economic Opportunity," p. 912, conclude that their "results suggest that the family and friends effect was important in determining the settlement pattern of every nationality."

states. In turn, the latter variable begs the question of what factors caused the earlier immigrants to settle where they did. Furthermore, the antebellum period saw settlement westward in the United States, so areas where "friends and family" would become important in the future were first being established. Thus, most of the literature for the postbellum period cannot be used to explain settlement patterns during the antebellum period. Instead, the argument in this section is consistent with the more recent work of Dunlevy and Saba, who find for the late nineteenth century that "differences among the migrant nationalities were important in influencing the settlement decisions."[62]

As discussed earlier, the Irish were most likely to be found in the Northeast. Although the Irish were fairly mobile, not many moved to the West.[63] A major reason was the cost of doing so.[64] The standard transatlantic fare during the antebellum years was £3 10s to £5 (see Chapter 3). Because the exchange rate at the time was $4.87 = £1, the cost in dollars was $16 to $24.[65] In 1847, moving to a westward city cost another $10–15 – about a 60 percent increase above the transatlantic fare – although Buffalo and Cleveland could be reached via water travel for about $5.[66] Given their lower levels of wealth and the relatively high cost of moving westward, most of the Irish stayed in or near their arrival port in the Northeast.[67] In fact, although as noted earlier, approximately 65 percent of the immigrants arriving in New York in the 1840s left within one year, distinct differences existed by country of origin. More than 70 percent of the German arrivals left New York within a year, as did 65 percent of the British. Yet only 57 percent of the Irish left, a reflection of the existing settlements of Irish in New York as well as their limited wealth.[68]

---

[62] Dunlevy and Saba, "Role," p. 247.

[63] In Ferrie's sample, two-thirds of all the immigrants who survived changed their county of residence between 1850 and 1860. See Ferrie, *Yankeys*, p. 138.

[64] See Ó Gráda, "New York City Irish," for a discussion of contemporary accounts of this point.

[65] The standard fares are taken from Taylor, *Distant Magnet*, p. 94. The exchange rate is from Officer and Williamson, "Computing," accessed June 19, 2006.

[66] Ferrie, *Yankeys*, pp. 56–8. In 1839, a group of two hundred Prussians paid a total of $1,500, an average of $7.50 each, for transportation from Buffalo to Milwaukee. Before the first railroad line from Albany to Buffalo was opened in 1846, it took seven to eight days to go between the cities via the Erie Canal. From New Orleans to St. Louis took a week to ten days on the Mississippi River. See Page, "Distribution," pp. 688–91.

[67] The low level of wealth among the Irish is emphasized by the fact that, in 1860, almshouses in New York City contained seven times as many Irish as German immigrants. See Page, "Distribution," p. 685.

[68] Ferrie, *Yankeys*, pp. 46–7. Also, see Page, "Some Economic Aspects: I," p. 1015–16, who says that many immigrants exhausted their financial resources simply getting to the United States.

A second factor important in explaining the location of many of the Irish immigrants was the location of manufacturing in the United States. Many of the Irish worked in factories (the Mill Workers in Table A7.1) or had other skilled manufacturing jobs (the other Artisan and Skilled categories). Table 7.4 provides data on the distribution of manufacturing output in 1850, in addition to the data on the geographic distribution of the different groups of immigrants. The simple correlation coefficient between the distribution of manufacturing output and the distribution of the immigrant population – both calculated at the state level – is 0.95 for the Irish, 0.87 for the British, and 0.69 for the Germans.[69] Thus, besides the financial problems with moving west and the location in the Northeast of many other Irish, the presence in the Northeast of the new factories and a large amount of the other types of manufacturing strengthened the Irish connection to this region during the antebellum period.

The fact that the correlation coefficient with manufacturing is the largest for the Irish is probably because of their lack of interest in working in agriculture. A number of reasons have been suggested.[70] First, their lack of wealth limited opportunities to begin or buy farms.[71] It is also likely that the Irish were not interested in jobs as agricultural laborers, given their generally unpleasant experience of renting farms in Ireland.[72] Next, having dealt almost exclusively with potato farming in Ireland, the Irish agricultural skills may not have been very useful in the United States. Because one of the main attractions of the West was agriculture, the small number of Irish in this occupation limited the number who went westward. Those Irish who did go to the West either worked in manufacturing or as part of gangs of unskilled workers who were employed to build railroads, canals, and other public works (and thus often had their way paid by their employer). Finally, many Irish women worked as servants and these jobs were located in the Northeast. As with most groups, many of the male Irish immigrants married female Irish immigrants, and

---

[69] All the coefficients are statistically significant at the 1% level. The relationship between immigration and U.S. manufacturing is discussed more extensively in Chapter 8.

[70] Page, "Distribution," pp. 686–7; Jones, *American Immigration*, pp. 103–4, 111–12.

[71] The cost of establishing a farm was quite large, in most places around $1,000 for a forty-acre farm. See the calculations in Atack and Bateman, *To Their Own Soil*, pp. 121–45. Also, see the discussions in Ferrie, *Yankeys*, pp. 57–8, and Page, "Some Economic Aspects: II," pp. 36–7. Jones, *American Immigration*, p. 102, says that most immigrants who went into farming took over established farms.

[72] Immigrants were less likely to go into farming by becoming tenants than the native born. See Atack, "Tenants," pp. 27–9.

thus had a greater tendency to remain in the Northeast.[73] Overall, a number of economic and social factors kept the majority of the Irish in the Northeast.

The British immigrants were found throughout the northern United States in 1850 for a number of reasons, one of which was the location of manufacturing. A large number of the British also found jobs in factories as Mill Workers (see Table A7.1) or had other skilled jobs. In addition, a sizeable number, especially among the Welsh, worked as miners, and mining output was included at this time with manufacturing in the census. The biggest differences between the British and the Irish were in their wealth and interest in agriculture. More than one in five of the British males were Farmers in 1850 and 1860 (Table 7.7), and about one-fourth of the British Unskilled workers were agricultural laborers. A portion of the British immigrant stream had been farmers in England, and apparently, many of these individuals were able to continue to work as farmers after their arrival in the United States.[74] Although some older farms could be purchased in the Northeast, by the late antebellum period, most agricultural activity was in the West. Other British were obviously interested in agricultural work, and working as an agricultural laborer was often an effective method of earning money to buy a farm and to learn about U.S. conditions. The British in general were also wealthier than the Irish were, and this fact allowed many more to move west. Besides the abundant farmland, the West was attractive because the social structure was less rigid and the economic opportunities were greater. An example was Chicago, where Galenson has shown that, after adjusting for occupational differences, immigrants had as much success as the native born in accumulating wealth during the 1850s.[75] The mix of British among factory workers, miners, other skilled workers, and farmers caused the British to settle throughout the northern sections of the United States.

[73] On these points, see Ó Gráda, "New York City Irish." For New York City, he finds occupations that were exclusively female contained large numbers of Irish. In total, he finds that 61% of the Irish population in New York City was female. In Philadelphia, the percentage female was 58%, while in Boston it was 51%. Somewhat surprisingly, he also finds that wages for domestic servants may have been fairly high, partly to compensate for the stigma attached to the job. Finally, he finds that most Irish marriages in New York City were of couples born in the same or neighboring counties in Ireland.

[74] A discussion of what happened to some of these farmers is contained in Van Vugt, *Britain*.

[75] Galenson, "Economic Opportunity." Ferrie finds that the wealth of immigrants who lived in the Midwest was higher. Ferrie, *Yankeys*, pp. 108–9. Not only was economic opportunity better in the western states, these states were also more liberal in extending voting privileges to immigrants. See Engerman and Sokoloff, "Evolution," pp. 898–909.

A number of factors attracted the German immigrants to the west. Their occupational distribution was least oriented toward the northeastern factory jobs during the antebellum years, probably because of the high skill levels with which they arrived. Only 1 percent of all German immigrants in 1870 were Mill Workers. Instead of factory jobs, the Germans were much more likely to be Artisans, such as tailors, bootmakers, carpenters, or White-Collar workers, especially merchants. These nonfarming jobs were located mainly in cities and, as just noted, opportunities were greater in the western cities. Furthermore, as with the British, more than one in five of the German males were Farmers in 1850 and 1860. Farming became an important reason for the Germans to settle in Ohio, Missouri, Wisconsin, Illinois, and Texas, all states with a large German influence. Most of these states also attracted Germans because of the presence of large cities. Louisiana, Maryland, New York, and Pennsylvania also contained large cities and thus plentiful jobs for which the Germans had the appropriate skills. With few workers in factories, the highest level of wealth among the immigrants, and the abundant farming and nonfarming opportunities in the West, the Germans were the group most likely to move west.

As noted earlier, immigrants were not very likely to settle in the southern states. Little agricultural opportunity was available, because so much of the production system was in the form of plantations. Buying a plantation would have been prohibitively expensive for almost all of the immigrants. The existence of slavery also meant that jobs for the immigrants as agricultural laborers were not available. Yet some immigrants did settle in the South, and the reasons were apparently identical to those in other parts of the country. In 1850, the South contained 17 percent of U.S. manufacturing, two-thirds of which was in Virginia, Maryland, Missouri, and Kentucky (Table 7.4). In the same year, these states, along with Louisiana – where some immigrants remained in the important arrival port of New Orleans – contained 75 percent of the Irish immigrants and 68 percent of the British immigrants living in the South. On the other hand, 82 percent of the German immigrants in the South in 1850 lived in Maryland, Missouri, Kentucky, and Louisiana, all states with large cities. The next most important state was Texas, which along with Missouri had many German farmers.[76] Although the

---

[76] The German influence in Texas began in the 1840s when a German society embarked on a project of peopling the state. Although the scheme ultimately failed and a number of Germans left for other states, some remained, and their numbers were increased by further colonization efforts in the 1850s. Hansen, *Atlantic Migration*, pp. 231–3, 301.

harsh southern climate may have also kept some immigrants away, it appears that the existence of the plantation system, the limited amount of manufacturing activity, and the small number of large cities provides a sufficient explanation for the lack of a large immigrant presence in the South.[77]

Another feature discussed earlier is that immigrants were much more likely to live in bigger cities. Not surprisingly, the reasons centered on the types of jobs that immigrants were able to obtain. Only a minority of the immigrants could afford to buy or begin a farm with their own wealth. Except for those who accumulated wealth through working as agricultural laborers, the others found it much easier to find a suitable job in a city, and the bigger cities had the most jobs, as well as being where many countrymen lived. For the Irish, these urban jobs were in factories or as unskilled workers. For the British, the jobs were in factories and in a number of artisan and white-collar areas. For the Germans, the jobs were primarily as merchants and artisans.

Summary

Economic historians have had a difficult time trying to explain the location of immigrants in the United States. Little has been learned beyond the fact that new immigrants located near previous migrants. The original locational patterns, however, were established during the antebellum period when immigrant volume first became large. For those with the best skills and the most wealth, such as the Germans, the movement was usually into the larger cities of the Midwest, where economic opportunity was abundant. Here, the Germans obtained jobs in a variety of skilled and white-collar areas, but few worked in factories. Other Germans had enough wealth to go into farming. Thus, the Germans were more likely to be found in the Midwest than were the other immigrant groups. The Irish, on the other hand, were the least skilled and the poorest of the antebellum

---

[77] Page, "Distribution," p. 679, discusses the role of the southern climate. Vedder and Gallaway, "Geographical Distribution," p. 31, also conclude that immigrants avoided the southern states for unknown reasons beyond the economic factors in their model. This conclusion has subsequently been challenged. See Dunlevy and Saba, "Role." In any case, these latter discussions center on the South after the Civil War, and not for the antebellum period discussed here. Dunlevy, "Regional Preferences," finds that immigrants avoided the South in 1850, but his model includes neither a manufacturing nor an urbanization variable. Furthermore, the per capita income estimates he uses are from 1840 and do not correct for regional price differences.

immigrants and the group least likely to enter agriculture in the United States. Thus, the Irish constituted the smallest immigrant presence in the Midwest. Instead, the males worked as unskilled laborers and in factory jobs in numerous cities in the Northeast. Even those Irish who lived in other sections of the United States were distributed in direct relation to U.S. manufacturing. The British, as on so many other counts, were in the middle. Many worked in U.S. factories, but sizeable numbers worked in other skilled jobs or as farmers and many also obtained white-collar jobs. Beginning in 1847, the New York Commissioners of Emigration provided various means of assistance for many immigrants to move to their desired location.

Over time, the immigrants found success in the U.S. labor market.[78] As early as 1850, if the data from the Passenger Lists are accurate, the distribution of immigrant occupations in the United States reflected a skill level at least as high as that brought by the migrants from Europe. In addition, the skill level of all the immigrant groups rose over time. For the British and the Germans, the rate of increase was similar to that for the native born. The Irish skill levels grew faster than the other groups, but their low starting level kept their overall skill level well below that of the other groups as late as 1870. Had immigrants not improved their well-being by migrating to the United States, it is doubtful, given the well-developed transatlantic communication system, that others would have continued to migrate. Yet throughout the nineteenth century, the volume of immigration continually increased, a trend fully consistent with the success found by those migrating before the Civil War.

Appendix 7.1
Occupational Data in the 1870 Census

The usefulness of the 1870 census in providing comparative data on occupations for the native born and the immigrants is complicated by three factors. The first is that, instead of by skill level, the occupational distributions are provided by industry group. These data have been reorganized by skill level and they appear in Table A7.1. The categories follow those used in Chapter 5, with the exception that farm laborers are included as Unskilled workers. A second factor is that the figures for the native

---

[78] Later in the nineteenth century, many immigrants moved back to Europe and used the wealth they earned in the United States to build large houses, which began to be called "American" houses. This trend is discussed in Wyman, *Round Trip to America*.

TABLE A7.1. *Occupational Distribution in 1870, by Country of Birth*

Country of Birth	United States	Great Britain	Germany	Ireland	Entire Labor Force
Labor Force Participation Rate	42.8%	50.9%	51.9%	53.5%	44.3%
White-Collar Workers Of Which:	9.6%	10.4%	13.5%	6.9%	9.6%
% Professional	28.6%	17.4%	11.9%	10.3%	25.3%
% Company Offs.	1.0%	0.7%	0.3%	0.6%	0.8%
% Clerks	22.8%	20.6%	16.1%	16.5%	21.6%
% Merchants	27.6%	34.0%	42.7%	38.6%	30.1%
Artisans/Other Skilled Of Which:	18.2%	47.1%	36.9%	28.0%	21.7%
% Carpenters	14.8%	7.2%	9.6%	6.3%	12.7%
% Blacksmiths	5.7%	3.6%	4.5%	4.7%	5.2%
% Bootmakers	6.1%	3.5%	9.1%	6.4%	6.3%
% Tailors	5.3%	3.4%	10.8%	6.8%	6.0%
% Mill Workers	7.5%	12.5%	2.3%	13.1%	7.8%
% Miners	3.2%	19.5%	2.8%	8.6%	5.6%
Farmers	26.6%	19.3%	20.0%	10.0%	24.3%
Unskilled Workers Of Which:	45.7%	23.2%	29.6%	55.1%	44.4%
% Ag. Laborers	60.3%	26.4%	23.1%	8.3%	52.0%
% Other Labs.	13.7%	32.6%	39.6%	44.4%	18.9%
% Servants	16.3%	18.4%	17.3%	28.0%	17.6%

Source: Calculated from U.S. Bureau of the Census, Ninth (1870), *Population*, Table XXIX, pp. 704–15. The occupational data in the 1870 census is provided by industry. The data were reclassified according to the classification given in Appendix 5.2, with the exception that "Agricultural laborers" were included as Unskilled Workers.

born are not broken down by race. Race needs to be taken into account because the antebellum immigrants were clearly not substitutes for slave labor. The third factor is that none of the country of birth figures are separated by gender.[79]

Even so, a careful analysis of the census data yield a number of interesting results. The first finding evident from Table A7.1 is the difference in the labor force participation rates. More than 50 percent of the

[79] See U.S. Bureau of the Census, Ninth (1870), *Population*, Table XXIX, pp. 704–15. The 1870 occupational data are analyzed in Page, "Some Economic Aspects: II." Although he discusses the varying skill levels, his analysis primarily follows the industry groups used in the census.

population of each of the three major foreign-born groups was working, while the figure for the U.S.-born was just under 43 percent. This difference primarily reflects the fact that most of the immigrants were between fifteen and thirty-five years old (see Chapter 5). A second finding of interest is, compared with the Germans and British, the U.S. labor force contained substantially more Unskilled workers and slightly fewer White-Collar workers. This result is because of the inability to account for race. At the time, the former slaves accounted for a large portion of the U.S. Unskilled workers who were agricultural laborers. Agricultural laborers accounted for 27.5 percent of all U.S.-born workers in 1870. If these individuals were deleted from the calculations, then only 25 percent of the U.S.-born labor force would have been Unskilled workers and more than 13 percent would have been in the White-Collar category. Of course, not all of the agricultural laborers were black, so this procedure provides an overestimate of the effect of accounting for race.

A comparison of Tables 7.7 and A7.1 indicates the large effects of limiting the U.S. labor force to white males. The Unskilled category falls for the United States and the Farmer category increases, both by a substantial amount. In addition, the Unskilled category is smaller in Table 7.7 for all immigrant groups, presumably because of the exclusion of female servants.

The complications introduced by race in comparing the occupational distribution of the U.S. labor force to those of the foreign born do not affect a comparison among the foreign born, although gender still plays a role. In 1870, the Irish were clearly the least skilled of the three major immigrant groups. More than half of the Irish immigrants were Unskilled workers, about twice the percentage for either the British or the German immigrants, although more than a quarter of the Unskilled Irish were (mainly female) servants. The Irish labor force also contained a smaller proportion of White-Collar workers than the British or the Germans. Finally, the Irish were least likely to be working in agriculture, either as Farmers or as agricultural laborers. Overall, only 17 percent of the Irish labor force had jobs as White-Collar workers or were sufficiently wealthy to have purchased land and become Farmers. This percentage is half that of the Germans and less than half that of the British.

The British and German immigrant labor forces in the United States were relatively similar at an aggregate level but less so when more specific job categories are examined. For both countries, the largest percentage was Skilled workers, followed by Unskilled workers, Farmers, and White-Collar workers. The immigrant labor force distributions were also similar for both countries in the subcategories of their Unskilled workers. Some differences are apparent, however, among the White-Collar workers. The British immigrant labor force had a substantially larger percentage who were Professionals than the German immigrant labor force, while the Germans had a larger percentage who were Merchants. The largest differences occurred in the Skilled subcategories. About one-third of the British Skilled workers were either Mill Workers or Miners, while only 5 percent of the Germans were employed in these occupations. On the other hand, about 20 percent of the German Skilled workers were tailors or bootmakers, jobs that were held by only 7 percent of the British. Thus, the similarity at the aggregate level between the British and the German immigrant occupational distributions hides substantial differences at a more detailed level. Overall, an analysis of the 1870 census data yields findings similar to those from the IPUMS.

8

The Effects of Immigration on the United States

Among other events, the antebellum years in the United States saw the rapid development of manufacturing, a huge fall in internal transportation costs, changes in the distribution of income, and the largest outbreak of nativism in U.S. history. This chapter investigates the effects of immigration on the antebellum United States from both a theoretical and an historical perspective. These effects depend directly on the skill level and size of the immigrant stream, both relative to the native labor force. Numerical estimates of each factor are presented in the first section of this chapter, and they provide a basis for a discussion of the theoretical effects of immigration on the United States. Both overall and distributional effects occur, although the distributional effects of immigration are typically more important and discussions of these are the major focus of the historical events discussed in this chapter. Given the lack of government constraints on immigration, two features of the antebellum years discussed in previous chapters – the large increase in immigrant volume and the decline in the skill level of the immigrant stream – make the period of particular interest. Overall, immigration was no less controversial at this time than it is during the present day.

The Skill Level and Rate of Immigration

This section first determines the skill level of the arriving immigrant stream and then measures the rate of immigration, both relative to the native labor force. Most discussions of the relative skill levels of the immigrants and the native born simply use skilled labor and unskilled labor. This approach – which has sometimes been used in discussing

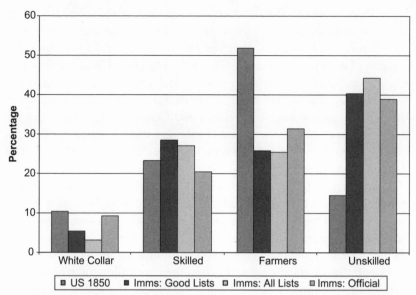

FIGURE 8.1. Immigrant Occupations Relative to Native-Born Adult White Males, 1836–1860. *Note:* All columns are the percentage of the total males in the group with that occupation. *Sources:* "U.S. 1850" is the distribution of the U.S. adult white male labor force in 1850, and is taken from Table 7.7. The next two columns are weighted averages of the distributions of the arriving immigrants between 1836 and 1860 calculated from the data in Table 5.4. The weights are the shares of the British, Irish, and Germans in total immigration from these three countries between 1836 and 1860. "Imms: Good Lists" is based on the data in rows 2–4 for England, row 6 for Ireland, and rows 2–3 for Germany. "Imms: All Lists" is based on the data in the last two rows for each country. "Imms: Official" is calculated from the data underlying Figure 5.1.

immigration during the antebellum period – is too simple to understand fully the effects of immigration before the Civil War. Indeed, previous chapters have divided labor into four categories: White-Collar, Skilled, Farmers, and Unskilled. This chapter continues to use these four categories in analyzing the relative skill level of the antebellum immigrant stream.

Comparisons of the occupational distribution of the white male native-born labor force to that of the European immigrant stream are shown in Figure 8.1. Because immigrant volume was largest between 1845 and 1855, the comparison is centered around 1850. The column on the left for each occupational category – based on data from the IPUMS reported in Table 7.7 – shows the distribution of the white male native-born labor force in 1850. The other columns provide three estimates of the occupational distribution of the immigrant stream. The first two (the two middle columns for each occupational group in Figure 8.1) are based on samples of male immigrants taken from the Passenger Lists by a variety of researchers for the period between 1836 and 1860. These were reported in Table 5.4, and the estimates in Figure 8.1 are weighted averages of the percentages for England, Ireland, and Germany.[1] One of these estimates is based only on the "good" Passenger Lists, whereas the other is based on a sample that includes data from the "questionable" lists.[2] The final column for each occupational group is calculated from the official U.S. data on immigrant occupations. Although this distribution includes females, it is not very different from the ones that include only males. Note that all three distributions of immigrant occupations are based on occupations reported in the Passenger Lists and not on the types of jobs the immigrants actually held in Europe or found in the United States.

Essentially identical results are obtained regardless of which occupational distribution is used for the immigrants. The largest differences between the native born and the immigrants were in two categories: Farmers and Unskilled Labor. The immigrant stream was relatively scarce in the former and relatively abundant in the latter. In addition, the immigrant stream was scarce in White-Collar workers and probably abundant in Skilled Labor, although the differences here are much smaller.[3] Four pertinent observations can be made. First, the results would obviously differ by country of origin. The Irish immigrants, for example, were much less skilled than the U.S. labor force. Similarly, both the individual British and German distributions would look substantially different from the average. Second, both Unskilled workers and Farmers are usually considered to be unskilled labor. If they were combined, then the occupational distributions of the immigrant stream and the native-born labor force would be similar. In fact, such a result has been found for comparisons between the two groups later in the nineteenth century.[4] Third, one of

---

[1] As discussed in Chapter 2, these three countries constituted 92% of total immigration from Europe before the Civil War. Thus, ignoring the remaining source countries has only a minor effect on the distributions shown in Figure 8.1.

[2] See Chapter 5 for a discussion of the differential quality of the Passenger Lists.

[3] The "Imms: Official" percentage for Skilled Labor would likely be larger if the females could be removed.

[4] Hill, *Economic Impact*, Table 27, p. 128. Hill calculates the skill level of the immigrants relative to the native born. With unity being equivalent skill levels, Hill finds a value of 0.97 for 1870 and 0.99 for 1880. Also, see the discussion in Carter and Sutch, "Historical Perspectives," pp. 332–4.

the questions concerning the accuracy of the occupational information on the Passenger Lists is whether many farm laborers were listed as Laborers rather than Farmers. Superficially, correcting for this factor might reduce the observed differences. In reality, however, given the expense of going into farming in the United States, European farm laborers would have had little expectation of becoming Farmers when they decided to immigrate. In addition, as presented, the distributions of both the immigrants and the native born include farm laborers in the Unskilled category.[5]

This point brings us to our fourth observation. Although the popular view is that immigrants came to the antebellum United States seeking land, that view does not appear to be correct for the late antebellum period. Instead, relative to the U.S. labor force, immigration was most abundant in non-agricultural Unskilled workers. As noted, Skilled workers were also abundant in the immigrant stream. Thus, after 1835, the United States was primarily receiving workers who would have sought a job in a sector other than agriculture. During this period, those sectors were manufacturing and transportation, therefore many of the effects of antebellum immigration should have occurred here. Because the skill level of the immigrant stream fell during the 1830s (see Chapter 5), the relationship may have been very different during the colonial and early antebellum periods. However, the volume of immigration was small during these earlier years and thus any effects were probably not large.[6]

Many of the theoretical effects of immigration are minor when the volume of immigration is small, as it was before the early 1830s (Chapter 2). The increase in volume beginning at this time – and the large numbers arriving during the 1840s and 1850s – suggest that immigration had its major effects during the latter period. Most studies of immigration discuss its size by measuring the volume of immigration relative to the

[5] In any case, reclassifying farm laborers as Farmers would probably have little effect on the relative differences shown in Figure 8.1. Farm laborers accounted for 39% of all native-born laborers in the 1850 IPUMS. Although it is not clear what fraction of those listed as Unskilled on the Passenger Lists were farm laborers, the 1850 IPUMS reports that only 22% of the laborers born in Britain were farm laborers, 13% of those born in Ireland, and 19% of those born in Germany. Although the percentages are lower in the foreign-born groups, the actual numbers of Unskilled workers among the immigrants are larger. Thus, any effect of reclassifying on the overall distribution would likely be minor.

[6] If immigration was more skilled than the native labor force during the colonial period, it may have contributed to colonial growth over the long run. To the best of my knowledge, however, no economic historian has viewed immigration as an important source of colonial growth.

existing population, a variable called the immigration rate. This work indicates the highest rate in U.S. history – more than 1.5 percent – was reached in the late 1840s and early 1850s.[7] Yet this figure is certainly an underestimate of the labor market effects of immigration for several reasons. First is that a larger proportion of the immigrants than the native population was in the fifteen- to forty-five-year-old age group, the prime working years. Next is that a larger proportion of the immigrants than the native population was male.[8] A third reason involves the slave population. Although counted as part of the U.S. population, the immigrants were hardly in competition with the slaves for jobs. Correcting for each of these factors raises the importance of immigration relative to the native labor force.

Figure 8.2 presents a series of estimates that provide a more accurate idea of the potential labor market effects of immigration. The bottom line in the figure shows the consequences of removing the slave population from the U.S. total. The effect is to raise the annual immigration rate – measured as all immigrants to the white U.S. population – to nearly 2 percent by the early 1850s. The middle line adjusts this figure by excluding all females. This line then shows the volume of male immigrants each year as a percentage of the total white males in the population. The adjustment indicates that as early as 1832, immigration was adding 1 percent to the existing male labor force each year, and the rate remained at that level for almost every year during the remainder of the antebellum period. By the late 1840s, the annual percentage rose to more than 2 percent, and it peaked at more than 3 percent during the early 1850s. Yet even this figure is an underestimate of the annual effect on the *native* labor force, because the figure for total white males includes previous immigrants. As a crude adjustment for this factor, the top line shows the effects when the white male population is reduced by 75 percent of the total number of immigrants who had arrived since 1820.[9] Now, the percentage averages 4 percent *each year* during the 1851 to 1854 period. Thus, moving to an estimate of the effects of immigration on the male labor force results in

[7] For example, see Ferrie, *Yankeys*, pp. 35–6.
[8] Kuznets, "Contribution," investigates the connection between these two factors and the growth of the U.S. population and labor force for the period from 1870 to 1940.
[9] Accurate data on the nativity of the population in the United States are not available until 1850. The 75% adjustment recognizes that some of the previous immigrants arriving since 1820 would have died. Adjusting by only 75% of the total immigrants may be too small. If so, then a more accurate adjustment would lead to a higher rate of immigration than that shown in the top line in Figure 8.2.

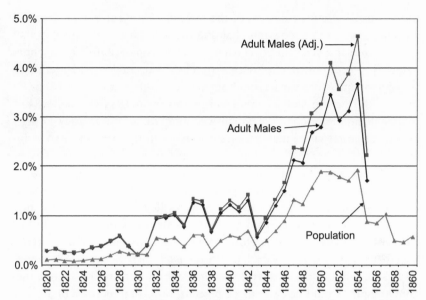

FIGURE 8.2. Immigration Relative to White Population and Labor Force, 1820–
1860. *Notes:* For each year, "Adult Males" measures male immigrants, age 15
and older, as a percentage of White Males in the population, age 15–59. "Adult
Males (Adj.)" reduces the White Male population, age 15–59, by 75 percent of
the total male immigrants between 1820 and that year, as a crude adjustment
to compare immigration to the size of the native-born labor force. "Population"
measures total immigration as a percentage of the total white U.S. population.
Sources: Adult Male immigrants, age 15 and older: Calculated from Table 2 for
each year in Bromwell, *History*. Total Immigrants, Total White Population, and
White Males, age 15–59: Carter, *Historical Statistics*, Series Ad1, Aa24, Aa 294–
305. The estimates for Total White Population in noncensus years were calculated
assuming a constant growth rate between the census years.

a minimum of a doubling of the population-based immigration rate of
1.5 percent.

The adjustments shown in Figure 8.2, however, still underestimate the
effects of immigration in certain areas of the country and in certain jobs.
The consequences of immigration probably did not extend throughout
the antebellum economy. Few immigrants, and few workers born in the
North, would have moved to the South in order to look for a job. Thus,
as distinct from recent analyses of immigration where economists assume
the effects of immigration are distributed throughout the country, the
effects during the late antebellum years were probably felt mainly outside
the South. One indicator of this fact is that few immigrants settled in

the South, less than 15 percent of the total in 1850 (Table 7.4). Because almost 29 percent of the white males in the U.S. population lived in the South in the same year, the effects of immigration on the native-born white male labor force outside the South would be about 20 percent larger than the estimate provided earlier, or about 5 percent during the early 1850s.[10] In sum, during the high immigration period from 1845 through 1854, total male immigration to the North accounted for approximately 31 percent of the total white male labor force living in this area in 1850.[11] In addition, all of these estimates are an *average* over all occupations. Given the relatively unskilled nature of the immigrant stream, the effects were larger in the lower skilled job categories. For example, about 40 percent of the immigrants arriving after 1835 were Unskilled workers, whereas only about 15 percent of the native-born males were in 1850. If only Unskilled workers are considered, therefore, immigration was adding more than 9 percent to the native-born labor force *each year* between 1851 and 1854 and, if only Unskilled workers outside the South are considered, the annual figure would be close to 12 percent, or a total increase of almost 50 percent during these four years![12] Thus, immigration during the late

---

[10] Calculated as $(1 - 0.15)/(1 - 0.29) = 1.20$.

[11] This calculation is based on data in Carter et al., *Historical Statistics*, Series Aa294, Aa296, Aa299, Aa302, and Aa305, p. 57; U.S. Census, *Historical Statistics*, Series A175, p. 16; and Bromwell, *History*, Table 2 for each year. The census counted a total of 5,537,772 white males between the ages of fifteen and fifty-nine in 1850. Of all whites (including females), 71.2% lived outside the South. Assuming the male-female breakdown was the same in the South and outside of the South, then 3,943,252 ($= 71.2\% \times 5,537,772$) white males lived outside the South in 1850. From Bromwell, total male immigrants fifteen and older who arrived between 1845 and 1854 are calculated to be 1,432,322. Because 85.4% of the immigrants settled outside of the South, then approximately 1,223,203 immigrant males would have settled outside the South. Thus, immigrant arrivals between 1845 and 1854 measured 31% ($= 1,223,203/3,943,252$) of the *total* white male labor force outside the South in 1850. Because the total white male labor force in 1850 includes the foreign born, the effects on the native-born labor force during the high immigration period were even larger.

[12] There were a total of 673,680 native-born unskilled white males tabulated in the 1850 census, according to the IPUMS. See the figures in Carter et al., *Historical Statistics*, Table Ba1140–Ba1143. From U.S. Census, *Historical Statistics*, Series 141A, I calculate there were an average of 275,153 total immigrants in the 14–44-year-old age group each year from 1851 to 1854. Because about 57.69% of immigrants were male in the period, there were approximately 158,735 ($= .5769 \times 275,153$) male immigrants in the 14–44-year-old age range each year. Of these, 40% ($= 63,494$) were Unskilled workers. Thus, considering the entire United States, immigration was increasing the number in the Unskilled labor force by 9.4% ($= 63,494/673,680$) during each of these years. Note that the calculation excludes male immigrants older than forty-four, but includes those

antebellum period was extremely large if the group being considered was Unskilled workers living outside the South.

It is unlikely that a properly measured immigration rate has ever again reached the levels experienced in the 1840s and 1850s. The volume and rate of immigration was again large in the last decade of the nineteenth century and the first fifteen years of the twentieth century. Immigrants were still less likely to settle in the South, and the immigrants were still disproportionately male. Yet a larger proportion of the native born had left agriculture and moved to manufacturing jobs, and the black labor force, although still primarily found in the South, could now be considered as a possible substitute for the immigrants.[13] Thus, adjustments to the standard immigration rate similar to those undertaken here would not have as large an effect.[14] Similarly, more recent immigration encounters a very mobile national labor market. In addition, a larger proportion of females are now members of the labor force, and immigration has a more balanced gender ratio. All of these factors suggest that the period between 1845 and 1854 saw the largest effects that immigration has ever had on the U.S. economy.

The Theoretical Effects of Immigration on the Antebellum United States

During the late antebellum period, the large volume of immigration primarily resulted in an increase in the supply of unskilled labor.[15] A basic theoretical effect would be a decline in the wages of unskilled workers

who were age fourteen and fifteen. From the 1850 IPUMS, I calculate that 68.6% of the Unskilled native-born workers lived outside the South (I include Missouri in this total), but 85% of the immigrants did. Adjusting the above calculation by this information yields a percentage of 11.7% for the effect on Unskilled workers who lived outside the South each year between 1851 and 1854.

[13] See Carter and Sutch, "Historical Perspectives," p. 337, for a brief discussion of the effects of pre-World War I immigration on keeping blacks "bottled-up" in the South.

[14] Jerome, *Migration*, Table 11, p. 52, adjusts the immigration figures for 1909 to 1921 so they relate to the labor force. The largest figure he finds is 2.93% for 1910.

[15] As in the preceding section, the term "unskilled" does not include farmers. The discussion in this section is mainly based on my reading of the following sources: Borjas, "Economics"; Carter and Sutch, "Historical Perspectives"; Friedberg and Hunt, "Immigration"; and Greenwood and McDowell, "Factor Market Consequences." For a more formal model that explicitly considers the effects of immigration on skilled and unskilled labor and other resources, but is similar in spirit to the one discussed in the remainder of this section, see Altonji and Card, "Effects."

already in the United States, thus harming native unskilled workers who
directly competed with the immigrants.[16] The fall in unskilled wages
would occur not just in areas where immigrants settled, but also in other
regions of the country.[17] Thus, if immigrants lowered real wages for
unskilled workers in the area where they settled, then some of the immigrants would have an incentive to move elsewhere. In addition, fewer
native unskilled workers would migrate to such an area. The tendency
for immigrants to leave the port cities where they arrived and the greater
concentration of immigrants than natives in cities (see Chapter 7) are both
examples of this idea. Yet, as previously noted, the effects of immigration
probably did not extend to the antebellum southern economy, which was
in many ways a separate labor market.

If sufficiently large, the decline in the wages of unskilled labor would
cause U.S. producers in many industries to adopt production processes
that used relatively more unskilled labor relative to skilled labor, at least
where existing technology made that possible. Production theory allows
for one, a few, or many possible production processes in an industry,
each relating to a different ratio of skilled labor to unskilled labor. If
only one production process existed, then the decline in unskilled wages
would not affect the skilled labor-unskilled labor ratio, although a larger
influx of workers would allow more of the product to be produced. The
transportation infrastructure was affected in this way during the antebellum period, therefore this chapter examines the connection between
this development and immigration. If more than one production method
existed, however, or if new methods could be developed, the change in
relative wages could cause the producers in an industry to change how
they produce their products. Production methods changed in manufacturing during the antebellum period so this chapter will investigate the
relationship between these changes and immigration.

Owners of other resources – skilled labor, capital, and land – were
also affected by immigration and the decline in unskilled wages. These
effects are illustrated in Panel A of Figure 8.3. The effect on the actual
wages of skilled labor, a substitute for unskilled labor, is uncertain. On
one hand, the lower wages for unskilled labor would lower the demand
for skilled labor. However, the decline in unskilled wages would lead

---

[16] Technically, new immigrants would harm all workers with directly competing skills,
including those of previous immigrants. It is, however, easier conceptually to think of
just the native-born workers as being harmed.

[17] See the discussion in Borjas, "Economics," pp. 1695–1700.

A. *Effects on Specific Resources*

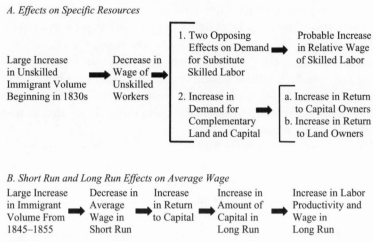

FIGURE 8.3. Theoretical Effects of Antebellum Immigration on Returns to Resources.

to an increase in output, which would increase the demand for skilled labor. Overall, what happened to the amount and the actual wages of skilled labor is then theoretically unclear.[18] It is probable, though, that skilled wages rose *relative* to the falling unskilled wages. Although capital is currently considered as a complement for skilled labor, during the antebellum period capital and unskilled labor were complements.[19] The greater use of unskilled labor thus led to an increase in the demand for capital, raising its return. Similarly, owners of land also benefited from an increased demand resulting from the larger amount of labor.[20] Overall, although the effects on skilled labor are not clear, the owners of both capital and land were beneficiaries of the antebellum immigration.[21]

A common belief is that the inflow of labor resulting from immigration depresses real wages relative to the return to capital. Although this change might happen over a short period of time, it will not be a permanent occurrence. In competitive labor markets, the average real wage in the

---

[18] See the discussion in Friedberg and Hunt, "Impact," pp. 28–9.

[19] This assumption is consistent with the discussion and findings in James and Skinner, "Resolution." For a formal discussion of this point and the reasons for the change over time, see Goldin and Katz, "Origins."

[20] Margo, "Rental Price," analyzes the effects of immigration on increasing rents in New York City during the antebellum period.

[21] Similarly, the effects of immigration on Farmers and White-Collar workers depend on the relationship of these workers to Unskilled workers.

economy can permanently decline only if the marginal product of labor falls. Over short periods, a large influx of labor will depress the marginal product of labor and lower the real wage. However, the decline in the marginal product of labor is not permanent, because the higher return to capital provides an incentive to accumulate more capital. Over time, the larger amount of capital increases the marginal product of labor, and thus reverses the short-term decline in real wages. These effects are illustrated in Panel B of Figure 8.3.

Two comments are in order. First, the volume of immigration between 1845 and 1854 was so large that we might expect, on a theoretical basis, a decline in average real wages. Second, it is likely that the distributional effects resulting from immigration were larger during the antebellum period than they are today. In modern economies, most individuals own a combination of resources, for example, a person might be a skilled worker who owns a house and has a stock portfolio. The total effect of immigration on this individual would then be the combination of the effects on the different resources. Quite possibly the positive and negative effects would offset each other, ameliorating any strong consequence from the immigration. Even around the turn of the twentieth century, about one-third of the labor force were owners of land and capital.[22] In the even earlier antebellum period, it is likely that most workers, especially those who were unskilled, owned only their labor resource. The consequence is that the effects of immigration on unskilled laborers may have been larger than in a more modern economy. This factor may have contributed to the outbreaks of nativism in the antebellum economy, especially during the latter years when immigrant volume was large.

When all groups are considered, economic theory predicts that the natives in the destination country will reap an overall static benefit from immigration.[23] Ignoring the uncertain effect on skilled labor during the antebellum period, therefore, the gains to the owners of capital and land outweighed the losses to native unskilled workers. The size of the gain does not depend on the numbers in each group, but rather depends on the difference in the resource content of the immigrant stream relative to the U.S. economy. Generally, the gain is larger if the difference

[22] Lebergott, *Manpower*, pp. 512–13.
[23] See the discussion of the "immigration surplus" in Borjas, "Economic Benefits." The theoretical material in this paragraph follows this article. The overall benefit occurs because the "(i)mmigrants increase output by more than they take home in wages." The quote is from Carter and Sutch, "Historical Perspectives," p. 323.

between the resource content of the two groups is greater. The data in Figure 8.1 indicate the difference in the resource content of the natives and the immigrants was not large, except for Farmers and Unskilled workers. Although a formal attempt to measure the immigration surplus for the antebellum period would be very complex, it is likely that the net static gain to the antebellum United States from immigration was not large.

Finally, immigration probably increased the rate of economic growth in the antebellum United States.[24] Economic growth occurs when there is an increase in per capita real incomes. At any point in time, per capita real incomes in a country are equal to the product of the labor force participation rate and average labor productivity.[25] Immigration certainly increased the overall labor force participation rate in the United States, because compared to the native labor force, the immigrants were more likely to be male and between the ages of fifteen and thirty-five.[26] In addition, immigration may have increased average labor productivity in a number of different ways. First, the immigrants probably contributed to the increase in the rate of capital formation in the United States that occurred during the nineteenth century.[27] The contribution occurred because it is likely the immigrants were heavy savers, due to their both being of prime working age and arriving in the United States with little wealth. In addition, a large part of the human capital that was required to raise the immigrants to working age was expended abroad. Thus, the United States received ready-made workers without having to pay for them. U.S. resources could thus be used elsewhere in the economy, and some of those resources would have augmented the capital stock. Second, some immigrants contributed to the rate of inventive activity in the United States. Third, immigration increased the size of the U.S.

[24] Much of the discussion in this paragraph follows Carter and Sutch, "Historical Perspectives." Evidence supporting many of the statements in this paragraph can be found in their discussion. Greenwood and McDowell, "Factor Market Consequences," pp. 1745–6, suggest the effects discussed in this paragraph occurred historically, but are less likely to hold for recent immigration.

[25] Mathematically, if Q equals real GDP, L equals the labor force, and P equals the population, then Q/P equals per capita real incomes, L/P equals the labor force participation rate, and Q/L equals average labor productivity. Then, by definition, $Q/P = L/P \times Q/L$.

[26] See the data in Table A7.1. Note that overall per capita real incomes will increase. Although it is likely that those for the native population will also increase, this result is not certain.

[27] The capital–labor ratio in the United States grew by 0.6% per year between 1800 and 1885. See Abromowitz, "Search," Table 1, p. 223.

population. By doing so, new inventions were likely to be diffused more rapidly throughout the economy and any unexploited economies of scale could be captured.

The discussion in this section provides a large number of possible effects of immigration. Not every theoretical effect has been investigated by economic historians or is able to be investigated for the antebellum economy. In many cases, the needed data are simply not extant. The remainder of this chapter, therefore, reviews the findings on a subset of the previously mentioned areas. Specifically, the following five topics are examined:

1. How did immigration affect the development of manufacturing, including its effects on the relative wages of skilled and unskilled workers?
2. How did immigration affect the development of the antebellum transportation infrastructure?
3. Did immigration affect the level of real wages during the 1840s and 1850s?
4. What was the connection between immigration and the outbreaks of nativism?
5. How did immigration affect the long-term growth potential of the United States?

Developments in Manufacturing

This section examines the connections between antebellum immigration and three aspects of antebellum manufacturing. First, this period saw considerable expansion of manufacturing in the U.S. economy. In 1810, only 3 percent of the labor force worked in manufacturing, whereas the percentage rose to 14 percent in 1850. Second, the expansion was connected to an increase in firm size in manufacturing and a change in how goods were produced. Third, one theoretical prediction is that the large amount of unskilled labor entering the United States should have led to a relative decrease in the wages of unskilled workers. Investigating these issues is complicated by the fact that events other than immigration – in particular, transportation costs fell – also affected the antebellum economy. The discussion is also complicated by the important changes that occurred in the skill level and the volume of immigration. Although explained in detail in the remainder of this section, the major developments that occurred in antebellum manufacturing are illustrated in Figure 8.4.

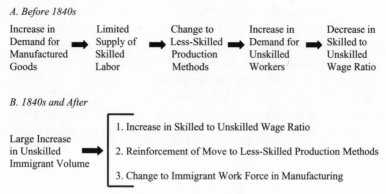

FIGURE 8.4. Developments in Antebellum Manufacturing.

To at least some extent, the expansion of manufacturing reflects higher per capita incomes because people then have money available to spend on products other than food. To actually produce more manufactured goods, however, entrepreneurs had to open new firms and find more resources that could be used in the sector. Given the high skill level of the immigrant stream before the 1840s, it is not surprising that many of the manufacturing entrepreneurs were immigrants, especially in the important textile industry. British immigrants filled about half of the new managerial and machine-making positions created between 1824 and 1831.[28] Many owners of textile firms in 1850 in the Philadelphia region were immigrants. In Kensington, forty-three of forty-five manufacturers for whom nativity could be determined were immigrants. In Germantown, the figure was twenty-seven of thirty. In Manayuank, the figure was twenty-four of thirty-three, and another five owners were sons of immigrants.[29] Because virtually all of the owners would have been in the United States for a number of years, it is apparent the early skilled immigrants played an important role in developing some of the new manufacturing firms.[30]

---

[28] Jeremy, *Transatlantic Industrial Revolution*, p. 161. The nephew of Edward Phillips, one of the immigrants introduced in Chapter 1, rented a farm in 1835 that contained a small factory for carding wool. He then made a spinning machine and a loom and manufactured the raw wool into different kinds of cloth. See Erickson, *Invisible Immigrants*, pp. 270–1.

[29] Scranton, *Proprietary Capitalism*, pp. 196, 227–8, 251.

[30] Immigration was particularly important in raising entrepreneurship in the manufacturing sector. See the comparative information in Ferrie and Mokyr, "Immigration," Table 3, p. 126. This article is discussed in more detail later in this chapter.

The increased volume of manufacturing output in the United States was associated with an increase in average firm size. During the colonial period and into the early 1800s, most market manufacturing was produced in small artisan shops. The nineteenth century witnessed a move to larger establishments that used more unskilled labor and more machinery, famous features of antebellum manufacturing. The growth of larger establishments was not caused by new power sources, because only some of the new larger firms used steam or waterpower to run their machinery. In 1850, most firms, especially those outside of the textile industry, still used human power.[31] Instead, as transportation costs fell in the U.S. economy, market areas increased so that an individual firm could sell more output. Yet producing a larger amount of output was difficult for individual artisans and, furthermore, new artisans took a period of years to train. Given the ready profits that could be achieved in manufacturing, the incentives were to increase firm size. In fact, between 1820 and 1850, average firm size in manufacturing grew by 66 percent.[32] In New York City, for example, only twelve firms hired more than 25 workers in 1820 whereas 588 firms did so in 1850.[33] Even so, many smaller firms continued to survive and most of the new larger firms were not yet factories.

The larger manufacturing firms needed to hire a large number of workers. These workers could be obtained in one of three ways. They could be attracted from the current agricultural sector; there might be resources not currently being used in the economy; or the needed resources could result from immigration. The former source was apparently used over the entire antebellum period.[34] Yet producers turned to the other two sources to complement the movement out of agriculture. Initially, with immigrants being generally skilled and the volume small, native-born women

[31] For more on this point, see Laurie and Schmitz, "Manufacture," and Ross, *Workers*, pp. 81–2. Nonhuman power was most likely to be used in textile production. The number of power looms used in the United States increased from less than 2,000 in 1820 to about 31,000 in 1831. See Jeremy, *Transatlantic Industrial Revolution*, p. 150.

[32] Sokoloff, "Was the Transition," pp. 354–5. Although some of the increase was because of the cotton textile industry, average firm size grew by 43% excluding this industry. In this article, Sokoloff also argues that over time the remaining artisan firms were found in less populated or rural areas where market sizes were smaller.

[33] These data are from Wilentz, *Chants Democratic*, pp. 31, 112, and Table 11, p. 404.

[34] See Table 7.7, which shows a consistent decrease in the proportion of Farmers in the U.S. figures after 1850. Goldin and Sokoloff, "Women," p. 746, provide estimates of the proportion employed in agriculture in the Middle Atlantic states and New England. In the former set of states, the proportion declined from 74% in 1820 to 34% in 1850. In the latter area, the decline was from 73% to 33%.

and children were used, especially in the Northeast where they were not being fully employed.[35] The proportion of the Northeastern manufacturing labor force comprised of women and children reached 30 percent by 1820 and rose to about 40 percent in the 1830s or early 1840s.[36] After this point, however, immigrants began replacing women and children in manufacturing firms, and the percentage of women and children declined to 29 percent in 1850. Some specific figures will emphasize the change. At Hamilton Company in Lowell, Massachusetts, immigrants comprised only 2.8 percent of the labor force in 1836. In 1850, the immigrant percentage was 55.2 percent. In Philadelphia in 1850, immigrants made up 38 percent of the male manufacturing labor force.[37] In 1855 in New York City, immigrants comprised more than 50 percent of the workers in a wide variety of manufacturing jobs.[38] Although other explanations are possible, the move to immigrant labor during the 1840s is consistent with the rise in immigrant volume in the early 1830s and the decline in its general skill level.[39]

In the larger firms, the change in production methods meant there was a larger demand for unskilled labor relative to the skilled artisans. Skilled labor was still used. Now, however, many of the artisans no longer ran their own shops but began working as employees in the larger firms.[40] What was different was that unskilled workers were now in higher demand, partly to run the machines and partly to do many of the minor tasks that had been done previously by the artisans.[41] Because of the difference in skills brought by the immigrants from Europe, the Irish were often found in unskilled positions in the firms, while the more skilled positions usually went to the British, the Germans, or the native

---

[35] Jeremy, *Transatlantic Industrial Revolution*, p. 161, argues that British immigration during the 1820s was large enough to fill only about 25% of the new positions in textile firms.

[36] Goldin and Sokoloff, "Women," pp. 746–7.

[37] Scranton, *Proprietary Capitalism*, pp. 27–9, 46.

[38] Ernst, *Immigrant Life*, Table 27, pp. 214–17. The data by type of manufacturing are conveniently summarized in Wilentz, *Chants Democratic*, Table 15, p. 406.

[39] Curiously, although Goldin and Sokoloff recognize the possible consequences of immigration in other articles, they do not list it as one of their possible explanatory factors for the decrease in the proportion of the Northeastern manufacturing labor force comprised of women and children. See Goldin and Sokoloff, "Women," p. 772.

[40] On the movement of artisans to larger firms, see the following: Ross, *Workers*, p. 97; Laurie and Schmitz, "Manufacture," pp. 53–5; Laurie et al., "Immigrants," pp. 99–100; and Wilentz, *Chants Democratic*, pp. 29–34, 107, 132–3, 141.

[41] Atack et al., "Skill Intensity," provide empirical evidence that deskilling occurred in manufacturing between 1850 and 1880.

born.[42] Artisans' real wages did not necessarily suffer as a result of these changes (a subject discussed in more detail later) because the presence of unskilled labor caused the artisans to be more productive. On the other hand, it became much less likely that any artisan would achieve independence, a goal of many artisans.[43] Yet overall, the larger volume of immigration beginning in the 1830s probably allowed manufacturing in the United States to expand faster than otherwise. It is difficult to imagine the manufacturing sector becoming as large as it did in the United States as quickly as it did if it had to rely primarily on the production of individual artisans or the labor of unskilled native workers.

The final issue concerning manufacturing is the effect of antebellum immigration on the relative wages of skilled and unskilled labor. Substantial controversy exists concerning this matter.[44] Many historians believe that artisans were harmed by the move to larger manufacturing firms, although some disagreement exists about whether the harm was a decline in real wages or a fall in their wages relative to unskilled workers or simply a loss of independence.[45] Alternatively, one study of Northeastern manufacturing workers during the antebellum period found that artisans' wages grew the most rapidly.[46] What happened to the real wages of artisans and other workers is addressed in the next section. Here, the changes in relative wages are discussed.

Although a number of researchers have examined this subject, Margo has done the most comprehensive work.[47] His book uses data on the wages paid by the military to hire civilian workers at military installations throughout the United States during the antebellum period. Margo provides estimates for common laborers, artisans, and white-collar workers in the major census regions. Because his annual figures are estimates partially based on regression analysis, the data from his five-year periods for common laborers and artisans has been used. Because both immigration and industrialization had its major effects in the Northeast and Midwest, only these two regions are considered. The ratio of the wage

[42] See the data provided in Laurie et al., "Immigrants."
[43] On the desire of artisans for independence, in particular see Lane, *Solidarity*, pp. 15–16, 23–4.
[44] See the brief summary discussion in Pope, "Inequality," pp. 135–6, who says no consensus is apparent.
[45] For an example, see Ross, *Workers*.
[46] Sokoloff and Villaflor, "Market." They arrive at this result by implication. Their actual result is that wages in small manufacturing shops, which presumably relied more on artisans, increased relative to those in larger firms.
[47] Margo, *Wages*.

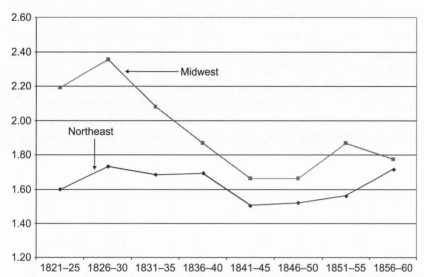

FIGURE 8.5. Ratio of Artisan Wages to Common Laborer Wages, 1820–1860.
Source: Calculated from Margo, *Wages*, Tables 3A.5 and 3A.6, pp. 67–68.

for artisans to that of common laborers in these two regions is shown in Figure 8.5.

Although the relative wage figures for the Northeast and Midwest might support other interpretations, they are consistent with the events discussed here. In both the Northeast and Midwest, artisans' relative wages show a tendency to fall into the early 1840s. During this period, immigration was not large but manufacturing was moving to less-skilled production techniques. The move to larger firms that used more machinery reduced the relative demand for artisans, and thus their relative wages. In the Midwest, the figures show a much larger downward trend into the early 1840s. The larger decline is probably due to falling transportation costs between the Northeast and Midwest. In the Midwest, the work of artisans early in the nineteenth century may have been protected by high transportation costs and the resulting small market areas, causing artisan wages to be much higher relative to those of common laborers than in the Northeast. Once transportation improved and market areas grew, it became profitable to move to larger production units in Midwestern manufacturing. Midwestern artisans thus suffered from the changes in manufacturing as well as the decline in transportation costs. Consequently, the gap in relative wages between the regions was much smaller by the late 1830s. This interpretation is consistent with the work of Ross, who finds that artisans' relative wages in Cincinnati fell after 1825. In addition, he notes that the mid-1820s and 1830s saw substantial improvement in Ohio's canal network.[48] Overall, the period into the early 1840s shows artisans' wages were falling relative to those of common laborers in both the Northeast and Midwest.

After the early 1840s, the trend in relative wages reverses in both regions.[49] This reversal is difficult to understand without accounting for immigration. After all, in many ways, the changes in manufacturing were spreading to more and more industries, and one would presume the earlier trend in relative wages would continue. The early 1840s, however, saw a rising volume of immigration, with unskilled workers now accounting for a much larger proportion of the total. As discussed earlier, theoretically this event should raise (lower) the relative wages of skilled (unskilled) workers. In fact, that is apparently what happened. It was only at this point that immigration became sufficiently large and sufficiently unskilled that it had a noticeable effect on relative wages. Indeed, immigrant volume was now so large that it completely offset the forces acting to lower the relative wages of artisans.

Overall, therefore, immigration and manufacturing were connected in many ways during the antebellum period. The high skill level of the immigrants arriving during the first thirty years of the nineteenth century likely stimulated the development of manufacturing and its move to more machine-intensive and unskilled labor-intensive methods of production. After the skill level of the immigrant stream declined, many of the larger volume of new arrivals found jobs in the manufacturing firms. In fact, the larger volume of unskilled immigration may have allowed manufacturing to continue to expand rapidly after 1840. As discussed in Chapter 7, the location of manufacturing also had an important effect on where immigrants settled. By the latter years of the 1840s, the volume of immigration was so large – and its skill level lower – that the preceding twenty-year decline in the relative wages of artisans in the Northeast and Midwest was reversed.

Developments in Transportation

One of the major economic events in the United States during the antebellum years was a drastic fall in internal transportation costs.[50] The

---

[48] Ross, *Workers*, pp. 9–17, 28–9, 137–43.

[49] Little trend exists in relative wages in the South Atlantic and South Central regions. The South, however, had relatively little manufacturing, few internal transportation improvements, and did not become the home of many immigrants.

[50] The classic work stating this case is Taylor, *Transportation Revolution*.

development of canals and then railroads was the primary cause of the decline, although the advent of the steamboat also contributed in places. Steamboats, however, were small and relatively easy to build, whereas the construction of each canal and railroad was a major undertaking. The only known method of building canals and railroads during the antebellum years required a large amount of unskilled labor. For example, to form the bed for a canal, workers had to literally dig into the existing terrain using picks and shovels and then use carts to move the resulting dirt, trees, stumps, and so on.[51] When large rock formations were encountered, blasters would use explosives to loosen the rock. Then all the rock had to be loaded onto barrows and carts and hauled away. Given that many canals ran for hundreds of miles, the unskilled labor requirements were huge. One estimate is that about thirty-five thousand workers were required by the late 1820s, and the needed volume remained at this level until the economic panic in 1837.[52] Similarly, in building railroads the construction process involved large numbers of unskilled workers who shaped the bed, laid down the track and ties, and connected the track piece by piece. Because the railroad industry became much larger than the canal industry, the unskilled labor required to build the railroads was also large.

Attempts at building both canals and railroads frequently ran into problems in getting the needed unskilled labor. Such was the case in building canals in the 1820s, when the volume of immigration was small.[53] Although the industry used some native-born workers, not many were interested given their alternatives in agriculture.[54] Thus, the canal industry could most easily satisfy its large unskilled labor needs by using immigrants. In fact, the need for unskilled labor was so great that the company building the Chesapeake and Ohio Canal in 1829 attempted to bring over a large number of Irish as indentured servants.[55] As noted in an earlier chapter, by this time the institution of indentured servitude had generally died out and the company's efforts to revive it proved unsuccessful. As the volume of immigration increased, canal companies were able to find

---

[51] See the discussion of how canals were built in Way, *Common Labour*, pp. 32, 133–43. Some of the jobs involved in building a canal required more skilled labor, such as the making of locks, although most of the jobs were unskilled.

[52] Way, *Common Labour*, p. 54. After 1837, the number of canal projects fell because of state financial problems and competition from the new railroads.

[53] Way, *Common Labour*, pp. 54–5.

[54] The native born who gravitated to the transportation industry usually took jobs running the canals and railroads rather than building them. For example, see the discussion in Licht, *Working*, p. 221.

[55] Steinfeld, *Invention*, pp. 167–9.

more workers, particularly after the panic in 1837 and the development of
the railroad reduced the number of canal projects. The companies building the railroads, however, ran into similar problems in getting sufficient
unskilled workers, a problem intensified because of the larger size of the
railroad industry. As early as 1836, the Baltimore & Susquehanna railroad complained that construction was slowed because of a lack of labor.
The Baltimore & Ohio made the same complaint in 1853.[56] The lack of
non-immigrant unskilled workers persisted even after the Civil War, when
many of the companies building the transcontinental railroads imported
Chinese labor.

In the construction of both the canals and the railroads, unskilled
immigrants – especially the Irish – formed the bulk of the unskilled labor
used. By the 1830s, most canal workers were Irish and they had a virtual
lock on the job by the 1840s.[57] An examination of a Chesapeake and
Ohio work camp in 1850 found that 380 of 407 total laborers were Irish.
Another nineteen were Germans, and only the remaining eight were native
born.[58] Although similar studies of the railroad construction market are
lacking, the accepted view is that the Irish formed the vast majority of
the unskilled construction crews.[59] Note that the effects of immigration
in the transportation industry were somewhat different from in manufacturing. In the latter sector, the increasing unskilled nature of antebellum immigration reinforced an existing trend toward using less-skilled
production techniques. In transportation, the only available production
technique required the use of a large amount of unskilled labor. Antebellum immigration thus did not change the production techniques used
here, but by increasing in size and falling in overall quality, it allowed the
transportation projects to be completed more quickly than otherwise.

Thus, antebellum immigration was extremely important in building
the transportation infrastructure. In the absence of the rising volume of
unskilled immigration, the canal and railroad system would almost certainly have been built much more slowly, because the labor problems for
the construction companies would have been much more severe. Overall,
the rising volume of, especially, unskilled immigrant labor was likely a
critical factor in causing internal transportation costs in the United States
to fall as rapidly as they did during the antebellum years.

---

[56] Licht, *Working*, pp. 60–1. Licht also says that the railroad companies did not encounter
any labor problems in running the railroads once they had been built.
[57] Way, *Common Labour*, pp. 97–100.
[58] Way, *Common Labour*, Table 7, p. 279.
[59] Thompson, *Short History*, p. 95.

Antebellum Real Wages

Economic researchers examining the antebellum period have determined that the real wages of workers were significantly higher in 1860 than in the early 1800s. For example, Margo found that between 1821–5 and 1856–60, the real wage of common laborers grew by 41 percent, those of artisans by 36 percent, and those of white-collar workers by 55 percent.[60] Williamson's and Lindert's results for the same period show an increase of 66 percent for common laborers and 120 percent for skilled labor.[61] For manufacturing workers in the Northeast, Sokoloff and Villaflor found a 60–90 percent rise in real wages from 1820 to 1860.[62] Over an even longer period, Adams determined that real wages in manufacturing in the Brandywine region of southeastern Pennsylvania rose by 62 percent between 1800–9 and 1850–60, with most of the increase coming after 1820. Furthermore, expenditures on food took 53.5 percent of a family's budget in the 1810s but only 38.3 percent in the 1850s.[63] This result is strongly consistent with the rise in real wages, because wealthier families typically spend a smaller proportion of their budget on food.

Many historians present a different view of the antebellum period. Workers are portrayed as being forced from a relatively secure nonmarket environment, usually as owners of small farms, or from an independent production situation, as the small-scale artisans previously discussed in manufacturing, to increased reliance on a market economy.[64] The implication is that the workers' level of well-being declined. Yet as just noted, all the empirical studies show that real wages generally rose for all groups. It is difficult to know whether the increased real wages sufficiently compensated workers for the reduced "security," and such a determination lies well outside the scope of this book.[65] What is relevant

---

[60] Calculated from Margo, *Wages*, Table 5.B.5, p. 118.

[61] Calculated from the presentation in Margo, *Wages*, Table 2.1, p. 21. Margo takes the data reported from Williamson and Lindert, *American Inequality*. The figures I use are those deflated by the Williamson-Lindert price index. Williamson and Lindert obtained their results after splicing together various series, causing Margo to be critical of the accuracy of their results. See the discussion in Margo, *Wages*, pp. 19–24.

[62] Sokoloff and Villaflor, "Market," p. 41.

[63] Adams, "Standard of Living," Tables 1 and 7, pp. 904–5, 915. In other papers, Adams reached similar results for a number of other regions.

[64] For examples, see Ross, *Workers*; Wilentz, *Chants Democratic*; Way, *Common Labour*; and Steinfeld, *Invention*.

[65] Some of the disparate findings can, perhaps, be reconciled. Ross, *Workers*, found that Cincinnati artisans suffered after 1825 as their wages increased more slowly than prices.

is that antebellum immigration probably contributed to the development of a market economy, that is, workers becoming a separate and distinct group from capitalists. Whatever situation they left in Europe, upon arrival in the United States the immigrants mostly needed to find jobs in the market economy. As was shown in Chapter 7, many of the available jobs were as workers in the growing manufacturing or transportation sectors, both of which were characterized by a distinct division of capital from labor. Thus, by increasing the number of "market workers" in the United States and contributing to the growth of manufacturing and transportation, immigration almost certainly hastened the move to the development of a market economy in the entire economy.

The controversy over what happened to the standard of living is tangential to our main concern. For what is apparent in virtually all of the studies cited is that real wages stagnated or fell during the latter part of the antebellum period. In Margo's figures, real wages declined between 7 percent and 13 percent for each group between 1841–5 and 1851–5. In Williamson's and Lindert's work, the fall is 7–10 percent between 1846–50 and 1851–55. Sokoloff and Villaflor have real wage figures only for 1850 and 1860, not annual, but these show little change over the decade. Adams' figures show some increase but only if 1860 is included. Otherwise, little change is evident between the mid-1840s and the late 1850s. In fact, Fogel claims the period between 1843 and 1857 saw a "hidden depression" for nonfarm workers, both laborers and skilled workers, with a real income decrease between 1848 and 1855 averaging 25–50 percent.[66] One effect of the stagnation in real wages was a sizeable increase in

Yet Cincinnati may be a special case, where artisans were protected by the city's isolation early in the nineteenth century. The improvement in western transportation would have caused artisans' real wages in Cincinnati to fall relative to those of eastern artisans. If this supposition is correct, then what happened to artisans in Cincinnati during the antebellum period is not typical of the eastern regions of the economy. Wilentz, *Chants Democratic*, p. 117, discusses a fall in real wages in manufacturing in New York City, but does not provide any data on specific groups. The context of his discussion is that average real wages fell (at least in part) because the newer less-skilled workers had lower incomes than the artisans had earned. For example, see his discussion of the Irish on p. 119, and of workers in industries that did not undergo large changes on pp. 134–41. Way, *Common Labour*, pp. 106–7, 236–46, suggests the well-being of canal workers fell after 1837. Way, however, examines only the wages paid and makes no adjustment for price changes. In any case, the canal industry was in decline after 1837. Even if canal workers were worse off, the lot of unskilled workers in general may still have been improving.

[66] Fogel, *Without Consent*, pp. 354–62. On p. 356, Fogel says that the northern nonfarm workers "suffered one of the most severe and protracted economic and social catastrophes of American history." Later comments by Fogel are found in Fogel, *Slavery Debates*, pp. 57–9.

pauperism during the 1850s. The number of individuals receiving public assistance rose from 5.8 per 1,000 population in 1850 to 10.2 per 1,000 in 1860.[67] Thus, although real wages likely rose over the entire antebellum period for nonfarm workers, the increase occurred before 1850, and probably before 1845. In the years after 1845, real wages fell, or at best stagnated.[68]

The path of real wages during the 1845–55 decade and the rise in pauperism between 1850 and 1860 are consistent with the very large volume of immigration detailed earlier in the chapter.[69] As noted, although immigration does not permanently lower real wages, a large volume in a short period of time may temporarily do so. The late 1840s and early 1850s – when immigrant volume was so large that the northern labor force increased by some 2–4 percent per year – appear to be such a period.[70] Yet the decrease in real wages and the rise in pauperism are not the entire story. Economic theory also predicts that such an occurrence will stimulate the capital stock. Indeed, although yearly figures on the capital stock are not extant, it certainly rose at increasing rates over the course of the nineteenth century.[71] Furthermore, a good deal of evidence suggests that, after about 1850, the newer techniques in manufacturing – the greater use of machinery and nonhuman power sources and the increased emphasis on unskilled labor – began to spread more rapidly throughout the American economy.[72] All of this evidence is consistent with a large volume of immigration between 1845 and 1854 temporarily lowering real wages and stimulating the growth of the capital stock. One consequence may have been a more rapid spread of manufacturing throughout the economy after 1850.

[67] Kiesling and Margo, "Explaining," p. 405. For a contemporary discussion of paupers sent from Germany, see Abbott, *Immigration*, pp. 142–4.

[68] Data on average body heights also point to a decline in well-being after 1845. See Costa and Steckel, "Long-Term Trends," pp. 50–3.

[69] Kiesling and Margo, "Explaining," pp. 409–12, use an econometric model to examine the rise in pauperism. They find that pauperism was higher in counties with a lower real unskilled wage, a higher percentage of foreign born, and a greater degree of urbanization. Because a larger percentage of foreign born in a county would probably lower the real unskilled wage and increase urbanization, immigration seems to have played the major role in increasing pauperism between 1850 and 1860.

[70] Other explanations are certainly possible. For example, food prices rose to high levels in the first half of the 1850s. Sokoloff and Villaflor, "Market," pp. 46–62, investigate the factors and conclude that immigration was the more important factor, although high food prices caused large short-term fluctuations in real wages.

[71] Abromowitz, "Search."

[72] For example, see Laurie and Schmitz, "Manufacture," Tables 3 and 7, pp. 49, 59.

Immigration and Nativism

The American colonies generally welcomed immigrants, although many citizens did not want paupers – who might become public charges – or Catholics.[73] Occasionally, however, nativist feelings surfaced. For example, about one hundred thousand Germans settled in colonial Pennsylvania between 1720 and 1750. The large influx caused some concerns about economic competition from the new workers. In addition, along with others, Benjamin Franklin worried about the Germans' willingness both to help defend the colony and to assimilate to the American culture.[74] Yet over time, these worries proved groundless. Immigration was viewed so favorably by most colonists that one of the objections listed in the Declaration of Independence against King George III was: "He has endeavoured to prevent the population of these States; for that purpose obstructing the Laws for Naturalization of Foreigners; refusing to pass others to encourage their migrations hither, and raising the conditions of new Appropriations of Lands."

After independence, immigration continued to be looked upon favorably by most Americans with a few exceptions.[75] During the early 1790s, when much of Europe was at war, Thomas Jefferson worried about the ability of immigrants who came from European monarchies to fit into a democratic America. When a number of immigrants in fact supported the Jeffersonian Republicans, in 1798 the Federalists increased the period for naturalization to fourteen years. This law was repealed in 1801 and a five-year period of naturalization was set. Some nativist feelings persisted until the end of the war period in 1815, and even later in a few cases. For the most part, however, immigration died down as a contentious issue. Important reasons were probably the small volume of arrivals throughout the 1820s and the high skill levels of the immigrants.

More organized occurrences of nativism in the United States began in the 1830s, contemporaneous with the increase in immigrant volume and the decline in skill level. In particular, as regions of Ireland outside of the north became important sources of immigration, a larger portion of the more numerous Irish immigrants were Catholic. Most native born were

---

[73] Much of the discussion in this paragraph follows Lane, *Solidarity*, pp. 13–15, Curran, *Xenophobia*, pp. 12–18, and Billington, *Protestant Crusade*, pp. 1–19.

[74] For a reproduction of Franklin's comments, see Leonard and Parmet, *American Nativism*, pp. 115–16.

[75] The discussion in this paragraph follows Leonard and Parmet, *American Nativism*, pp. 20–5.

Protestants and many became concerned about the central authority of the Pope in the Catholic religion. The Catholic share grew substantially with the potato famine and the changes in the sources of German immigration to different areas. Because immigration after the early 1830s changed in all three ways – a larger volume, lower skills, and more Catholics – it is very difficult to determine which aspect led to the outbreaks of nativism. Different researchers emphasize different factors. Yet it also needs to be stressed that most of the native born were not attracted to the nativist movements and continued to favor immigration.[76]

The decades of the 1830s and 1840s saw a variety of nativist outbreaks.[77] In 1834, Samuel Morse published an anti-Catholic book called *The Foreign Conspiracy Against the Liberties of the United States*. Two years later, an exposé of lurid events that supposedly went on in a convent was published. Between these two books, in June 1835, the Native American Democratic Association was formed in New York City. Their platform included not appointing immigrants to office and reducing encroachments by the Catholic Church. The party carried 39 percent of the vote in the November mayoral election in New York City, but it soon faded from the scene. A similar political party formed in New Orleans also did not last. A proposal to provide public support for parochial schools in New York reignited nativist feeling in the early 1840s. The American Republican Party was formed in New York City and elected the mayor in April 1844. In May and July of that same year, anti-immigrant (and anti-Catholic) riots broke out in Philadelphia. Although the American Republican Party had some success at the polls in November of that year, the outbreaks of violence caused the overt nativists to lose the support of many of the native born. Again, with minor exceptions, the nativists did not find success in electing candidates to public office.

The early 1850s saw the largest outbreak of nativism in U.S. history. The Order of United Americans formed in New York City in December 1844 and became active in New York politics in 1849. Other nativist groups formed in other states. During 1853, the nativist feeling coalesced into what became known as the Know-Nothing Party. For the only time during the antebellum period, a nativist party experienced widespread electoral success, at least partly because of the ongoing disintegration of

---

[76] Curran, *Xenophobia*, p. 21, claims that only one of three Americans joined nativist groups, although he provides no discussion concerning how he arrived at this fraction.

[77] Much of the discussion in this paragraph follows Anbinder, *Nativism*, pp. 9–13, and Leonard and Parmet, *American Nativism*, pp. 49–59.

the Whig Party. The Know-Nothings contributed to the surprise victory of the Whig candidate for mayor of Philadelphia in June 1854.[78] In the October state elections in Pennsylvania, Know-Nothing candidates won two of the three statewide offices and seventeen of the twenty-five state congressional elections. They also had success in San Francisco, Ohio, and Indiana during October. The results of the national elections in November 1854 were astounding. Know-Nothing candidates essentially swept the statewide and congressional elections in Massachusetts. In New York, their candidate for governor lost but fared well. The party did, however, elect four congressmen and had the support of seven others. Overall, about seventy-five men directly or loosely affiliated with the Know-Nothings were elected to Congress. In state elections during the spring of 1855, the Know-Nothings swept elections held in Connecticut, New Hampshire, and Rhode Island. Later in the year, the Know-Nothings won elections in Maryland, Kentucky, Delaware, and Louisiana and repeated their success in many of the states that had elections in 1854. By the end of 1855, the Know-Nothing Party's electoral success caused many neutral observers to believe they would win the 1856 presidential election. Instead, as discussed in Chapter 4, the party disintegrated during 1856 over the issue of slavery.

How much of the nativist outbreaks can be blamed on the economic consequences of immigration rather than the Catholicism of many of the new arrivals is not clear. As noted earlier, both facets of immigration changed at the same time. A few researchers have suggested economic factors were of little importance. In particular, Anbinder claims that economic nativism existed at a fairly constant level over the nineteenth century.[79] He establishes the backgrounds of the members of several Know-Nothing lodges, and finds they represented a cross-section of the labor force, except that few farmers were members.[80] He also notes that the outbreak of nativism in 1835 occurred during a period of prosperity, and the economy was beginning to recover when the 1844 riots took place. In his view, a slight downturn in 1854 cannot explain the rapid rise of

[78] The information on the election results is from Anbinder, *Nativism*, pp. 53–92, and Leonard and Parmet, *American Nativism*, pp. 93–9.

[79] Anbinder, *Nativism*, pp. 32–3. Curran, *Xenophobia*, sees religion, temperance, and the break-up of the Whig Party as the primary issues. Similarly, both Montgomery, "Shuttle," p. 411, and Feldberg, *Philadelphia Riots*, pp. 3–16, say anti-Catholicism was more important than economic factors in causing the 1844 riots in Philadelphia. Billington, *Protestant Crusade*, discusses all of the above factors along with some economic effects.

[80] Anbinder, *Nativism*, pp. 33–50.

the Know-Nothing Party from fifty thousand members in June 1854 to over one million by the end of October. "No new religious controversy emerged in these months, and the economy did not suddenly collapse."[81] In turn, he proposes that the anti-slavery and anti-liquor leanings of many of the northern Know-Nothings caused their success in 1854, at a time when the moribund Whig Party did not seem to provide an effective counter to the Democratic Party.[82]

Other researchers claim that economic matters played a more central role in the rise of nativism in the 1850s. As noted earlier, real wages fell during these years to such an extent that Fogel claims a "hidden depression" occurred over the entire 1843–57 period for native-born, nonfarm workers. In his view, the root cause was the large volume of immigration. The period from 1848 to 1855 saw rapidly rising food prices, with the real income of the native nonfarm workers declining between 25 percent and 50 percent. The worst phase of the "hidden depression" occurred from 1853 to 1855, exactly at the time the Know-Nothing movement was in full bloom.[83] The period beginning in the latter 1830s also saw the body heights of many groups of native-born males begin to fall – evidence of worsening living standards – perhaps because of a decline in nutrition levels.[84] Finally, the first few years of the 1850s saw a renewal of the trade union movement. During 1853 and 1854, about four hundred total labor strikes occurred – an exceptionally large number in a short period – with sometimes twenty-five or thirty strikes taking place at the same time.[85] Clearly, many workers during the latter half of the antebellum period found their level of economic well-being in decline.

Perhaps the issue of nativism and immigration should be looked at in a slightly different manner. Anti-Catholicism was certainly evident throughout (and before) the antebellum period. At times, this feeling led to nativist rhetoric and occasional outbreaks of violence. However, the outbreaks were not continuous nor, in spite of many attempts at forming parties and trying to get candidates elected, did the nativists have much

---

[81] Anbinder, *Nativism*, p. 43. Recall from the discussion in Chapter 4 that Industrial Production did not decline in 1854 from its level in 1853.

[82] Anbinder, *Nativism*, pp. 94–101. Per capita alcohol consumption apparently increased more than 50% between 1840 and 1860. See Curran, *Xenophobia*, p. 61.

[83] Fogel, *Without Consent*, pp. 354–69.

[84] Costa and Steckel, "Long-Term Trends," pp. 50–3. See the contrasting explanations for the fall in heights in Steckel, "Stature," and Komlos and Coclanis, "On the Puzzling Cycle."

[85] Commons et al., *History*, pp. 576–616.

political success until 1854. Many of the historical accounts of nativism see the movement as building throughout the antebellum period until it finally achieved widespread success with the Know-Nothing Party. Yet a more accurate view is that the success of the Know-Nothing Party was the outlier. Had something not changed, the nativist movement probably would have remained on the fringes of the political scene throughout the entire antebellum period. In other words, their success was not the culmination of a long period of effort on the part of committed nativists. For certain reasons, only in 1854 and 1855 were a sufficient number of voters – perhaps a majority of those in the North – willing to vote for candidates espousing nativist views.

The question then becomes what changed in the early 1850s. Given the unprecedented levels of immigration discussed earlier in the chapter, the widespread outbreak of strike activity in 1853 and 1854, the decline in body heights, and the evidence presented earlier concerning the decline of real wages in the early 1850s, it seems that economic factors must have played at least an underlying role. Although the strike activity was specific to workers, the other factors lowered the well-being of the entire native working class – common laborers, artisans, and white-collar workers. Anbinder might be correct that economic troubles were not the precipitate factor in causing the explosive rise of the Know-Nothings during 1854. Even so, the troubled economic condition of most northern workers must have made them susceptible to "solutions" that were out of the ordinary. When native workers looked for someone to blame for their troubles, the large-scale immigration after 1845 seemed an obvious factor – and one that probably was an important factor. A party based on nativism – even though the party might have also reached out to voters on other grounds – would have been more attractive to the native born in the early 1850s than at any other time. Thus, at the least, it is likely that the underlying deterioration of economic conditions for the native born, due in large part to the large volume of immigration, set the stage for the success of the Know-Nothings during 1854 and 1855. In turn, the absence of large-scale immigration both before and after the early 1850s caused the nativists to have only minor electoral success during the remainder of the antebellum period.

Immigrants, the Capital Stock, and Economic Growth

An important aspect of immigration was that a large portion of the immigrant stream was composed of adults of working age. Thus, many immigrants arrived "ready to work," where the U.S. economy did not have to expend resources raising the individuals to working age. In this way, immigration contributed to the growth of the capital stock in the United States. Neal and Uselding make the point succinctly: "This contribution, which would have been lost with a native labour supply of equal size, derives from the pool of resources released, for alternative uses, from the task of rearing children."[86] The economy could then do other things with these resources. Presumably, some portion of the freed resources would be used to undertake investment and thus increase the size of the stock of capital beyond what it otherwise would have been. With a larger capital stock, workers would be more productive and per capita incomes in the United States would increase.

Neal and Uselding estimated the contribution immigration made to augmenting the capital stock. For immigration starting in 1790, their procedure involved determining the total amount of resources the U.S. economy would have expended on raising to working age the adult immigrants who arrived, after accounting for the deaths that would have occurred before reaching working age. In order to perform these calculations, they assumed the size of the population would have been the same had immigration not occurred.[87] Neal and Uselding then estimated the fraction of these resources the economy used for investment purposes, and applied this fraction to the saved resources. Note the implicit assumption that natives and immigrants saved the same percentage of their income. Their procedure accounted not only for the direct increase in the capital stock but also for the compounding that arose from the positive gain the new capital would have provided. Their estimates indicated that the "savings" from immigration accounted for between 4.7 percent and 9.1 percent of the total size of the capital stock in 1850.[88] Because these percentages are not insubstantial, they concluded that immigration made an important contribution to the growth of the U.S. economy after 1790.

[86] Neal and Uselding, "Immigration," p. 69. Carter and Sutch, "Historical Perspectives," p. 332, refer to this gain as a "gift." Also see Uselding, "Conjectural Estimates," who provides estimates of the total amount of human capital that immigrants brought with them to the United States.

[87] The view that immigrants lowered the birth rates of natives and replaced them one-for-one is called the Walker thesis. Although few economic historians believe this view today, adopting this approach simplified the analysis and provided a lower bound for the effects of immigration on economic growth.

[88] The difference arises from whether they compounded the gains from the new capital at 3% or 6%. See Neal and Uselding, "Immigration," p. 85.

As might be expected, the data and procedures used to reach these results have not gone unchallenged. In particular, Gallman leveled a number of criticisms.[89] First, he suggests that immigrants were not perfect substitutes for the native born, especially as it came to their income levels and the percentage of their income saved. Yet Gallman is likely not correct on the latter point. Although the foreign born did have lower average income levels, they were heavy savers, at least in part because their income was low after immigrating.[90] In addition, this chapter has shown that immigrants obtained jobs at skill levels similar to those of the native born. Second, Gallman suggests that the one-for-one replacement of the native born by immigrants also had an offsetting loss, that being the welfare (as distinct from the income) that the native-born adults would have gained from having more children. The size of such an effect would be difficult to measure. Third, Gallman notes that immigrants brought infectious diseases with them, with the result that more of the native born died than would have occurred without immigration. These extra deaths obviously represented a loss to the economy. Thus, in some ways, the estimates arrived at by Neal and Uselding are too large.

Yet it should also be noted that Neal and Uselding made a number of assumptions that caused their estimates to represent a lower bound on the contribution of immigration to economic growth. Perhaps the most important one is their assumption that the total size of the population would have remained the same without immigration. If the absence of immigration more realistically had led to a smaller population, then the economy would have lost from a smaller amount of scale effects, the gains firms achieved from being able to sell in larger markets.[91] In addition, less immigration and a smaller population would cause losses for the economy from less inventive activity and similar effects described earlier in this chapter. In summary, it appears that immigration probably had an overall positive effect on the rate of economic growth during the antebellum years, although attempts to provide an accurate measurement of how large the effect was will probably always prove extremely difficult.

Another way in which the United States benefited from immigration was the effect on the level of entrepreneurial ability. Although work is quite limited in this area, one study found that immigration contributed in

---

[89] Gallman, "Human Capital."
[90] See the discussion in Carter and Sutch, "Historical Perspectives," pp. 327–30.
[91] Neal and Uselding, "Immigration," p. 72. Also see the discussion in Carter and Sutch, "Historical Perspectives," pp. 331–2.

a number of ways to entrepreneurship.[92] One source of data used was the biographies of the most successful Americans taken from the *Dictionary of American Biography*. These data showed that immigrants comprised 20–35 percent of the total born before 1849, except for those born during the low immigration period between 1784 and 1815. Other data were taken from the Passenger Lists and the IPUMS. These data indicated that immigrants were more likely to have entrepreneurial occupations than the native born. In addition, the rate of entrepreneurship for the immigrants increased over time. Finally, sons of immigrants also had higher rates of entrepreneurship than the native born. Immigration thus increased the level of entrepreneurship in the United States both before and after the Civil War. In turn, the greater entrepreneurship would have increased the rate of economic growth in the United States.

Summary

Immigration played a central role in the economic and political developments in the antebellum United States. American economic history textbooks currently do not reflect this fact. Instead, although the textbooks discuss the fall in internal transportation costs, the rise in manufacturing, and changes in the distribution of income, they do not emphasize the importance of European immigration in these areas. The key factor was the rise in the volume of immigration, especially in the number of unskilled workers. As early as the middle of the 1830s, the immigrant stream was adding more than 1 percent each year to the white male labor force. As the volume continued to rise, the annual percentage reached 4–5 percent in the North during the early 1850s. Relative to the number of unskilled workers, the percentages were substantially larger. Without the huge numbers of arriving immigrants, the antebellum economy would have developed more slowly than it did. The transportation network would have been completed more slowly. Manufacturing would have increased more slowly. The distribution of income would have changed more slowly. Thus, immigration should assume a more important place in discussions of the antebellum economy.

More generally, the antebellum years in the United States provide an excellent period to analyze the economic theory of immigration. Because of the length of the voyage, the movement of individuals was generally permanent, that is, the reason for immigration was to take advantage

---

[92] Ferrie and Mokyr, "Immigration." The material in this paragraph follows this article.

of expected long-term income differentials. In addition, the volume of immigration became sufficiently large during the latter part of the antebellum years that the theoretical effects of immigration should have been evident. Although no definitive proof has been provided in this chapter, the discussion strongly suggests that immigration's distributional effects on the antebellum United States were in line with the predictions made in standard economic models. Yet the reader should also recognize that immigration during the antebellum years had a variety of positive effects on the growth of the U.S. economy, from increasing entrepreneurship to adding to the capital stock to providing larger markets for firms. Overall, immigration affected the antebellum U.S. economy in a number of both positive and negative ways.

9

The End of Mass Migration Under Sail

The Steamship and Its Effects

The factor that led to the end of mass migration under sail was, of course, the development of the transatlantic steamship. Once Fulton demonstrated the feasibility of the steamship on the Hudson River in 1807, technological improvements were continual.[1] Although many observers believed that a steamship would never cross the Atlantic Ocean, the first two – the *Great Western* and the *Sirius* – did so in a famous race in 1838.[2] In 1839, the first important steamship company, the well-known Cunard Line, was founded. The British government subsidized the line to carry the mail, although Cunard's steamships also carried cabin passengers. Other steamship companies arose during the 1840s and early 1850s, almost all subsidized by some government to carry the mail. Throughout this period, the steamships mainly carried merchants and tourists and thus were not important in the immigrant trade.[3] The situation began to change in the 1850s. Between 1852 and 1857, the Inman Line carried some steerage passengers from Liverpool to Philadelphia. Inman changed his U.S. terminus to New York City in 1857 and increased the steerage capacities of his company's ships. A number of other steamship companies, including those operating out of Germany, rapidly followed

[1] For discussions of the technological development of the transatlantic steamship, see the following: Adams, *Ocean Steamers*; Gardiner, *Advent*; and Rowland, *Steam*.
[2] See Adams, *Ocean Steamers*, pp. 23–4. For many years, transatlantic steamships were sufficiently untrustworthy that they also had sails that could be used when necessary.
[3] Cohn, "Transatlantic U.S. Passenger Travel." In 1847, the Ocean Steam Navigation Company added second-class accommodations but the fare was still prohibitive for most immigrants. See Bowen, *Century*, p. 53.

Inman's example.[4] Thus, it was only at the end of the 1850s that steerage passage on steamships became common.

When the antebellum volume of European immigration to the United States peaked in 1854 at more than 406,000, virtually all of the passengers arrived on a sailing ship. Only about 5,300 of those arriving in New York – just 1.7 percent of the total – came on a steamship.[5] Thus, 1854 was the peak year for arrivals by sailing ship in U.S. history. Even with steerage becoming common only near the end of the decade, the number of passengers arriving in New York City on a steamship rose consistently throughout the 1850s. In 1861, arrivals by steamship had increased to 21,500. This figure accounted for almost 31 percent of the much smaller total volume of arrivals in New York City in 1861. When the Civil War ended and mass migration to the United States resumed, most passengers began arriving on a steamship, as construction began to catch up with demand. For example, more than 80 percent of the 240,000 immigrants who arrived in New York City in 1867 came on a steamship. Essentially, the period of mass migration under sail had ended.

The biggest advantage of the steamship, of course, was its speed. The trip from Europe, which took a minimum of five weeks on a sailing ship – and typically took six to seven weeks – was immediately cut to two weeks and soon fell to around ten days. The high variability in the length of the trip that existed with sailing ship travel was also drastically reduced. Besides these advantages, a steamship was easier to maneuver into and out of port, so they began to pick up passengers at more than one port. Finally, the steamships grew in size, and consequently provided the passengers a much greater degree of comfort in the transatlantic crossing. The various changes made it easier and safer to travel, therefore the average annual volume of European emigration rose to even higher levels during the postbellum period.

By shortening the trip and improving the comfort of passengers, the steamship led to a number of fundamental changes in European immigration to the United States. First, Europeans could now quickly and easily reach more foreign destinations and thus began to look at the United

---

[4] See Bonsor, *North Atlantic Seaway*.

[5] Cohn, "Transition," Table 1, p. 472, indicates that 2,989 passengers arrived on a steamship in 1852 whereas 16,628 did in 1858. The number cited in the text is interpolated between these figures. The figure for arrivals in 1855 is not used because a number of steamships that year were being used to transport troops to the Crimea. Note the percentage is based on arrivals in New York City, not total immigration. The other figures given in this paragraph are from the same source.

States as simply another one. Immigration to the United States lost the uniqueness it held during the antebellum era. Second, immigrants from more distant parts of Europe – those in the south and east – had a shorter trip to an overseas destination. Along with the spread of the railroad network, the steamship integrated more areas of Europe into the developing world migration system. Third, the shorter trip meant it was much easier for workers to move to the United States (or elsewhere) on a temporary basis. In fact, although the data are not very good, it appears the percentage of Europeans who migrated to the United States and then returned to Europe increased consistently after the Civil War.[6] Fourth, the U.S. business cycle became a more important factor in determining the volume of immigration, perhaps because the steamship better integrated the U.S. and European economies. Finally, the steamship lowered the costs of migration not only in terms of time saved but also reduced the time immigrants were confined in an enclosed environment. Thus, deaths resulting from the outbreak of epidemics aboard the ships fell substantially. Due to both this factor and the shorter trip, the overall death rate underwent a sizeable decline.[7]

In a number of other ways, the analysis of immigration after the Civil War remains the same as that before the Civil War. First, the immigrants were still mainly unskilled workers. In fact, as the agricultural sector became smaller in the United States and the urban and manufacturing sectors larger, the skill level of the arriving immigrants became even more similar to that of the native-born labor force.[8] Second, a large share of the immigrants continued to enjoy success in the U.S. labor market, even though many decided to return to Europe to live. Third, nativism in the United States continued to be an important force but was never again an important factor in the founding of a successful political party.

---

[6] See the discussion and estimates presented in Keeling, "Transportation Revolution," Table 3, p. 51, and Kamphoefner, "Volume." Most estimates after the Civil War put the percentage of migrants who returned to Europe as between 15% and 40%, with differences by country of origin. For example, Keeling calculates an overall return migration rate of 13% between 1875 and 1884, with it rising to 37% between 1905 and 1914. As noted in Chapter 1, Kamphoefner estimates a return migration rate for Germans arriving during the 1850s at around 1%.

[7] Jones, "Transatlantic Steerage Conditions," pp. 60–5. Deaths continued to occur as a result of wrecks, although precise comparative data with the sailing ship era are not available. For a list of steamships lost between 1840 and 1892, see Maginnis, *Atlantic Ferry*, Table No. 7. He counts more than 120 steamship "disasters" during this period with a loss of almost 6,400 lives.

[8] Hill, *Economic Impact*, Table 1, p. 31.

Instead, the U.S. government began adopting quantitative restrictions against immigrants from certain areas. Before World War I, restrictions were adopted against both the Chinese and the Japanese, and then after World War I, the United States restricted immigration from southern and eastern Europe. A final factor concerns the data available to study immigration. The data become better but remain incomplete. For example, the issue of comprehensiveness is important before the Civil War, but after the Civil War one confronts the complications resulting from return migration. Even today, researchers have the issue of illegal immigration that confounds estimates of the total volume of immigration.

What We Know and Could Still Learn

The findings of this book can be summarized in following eleven ideas.

1. The total number of immigrants from Europe derived from the U.S. Passenger Lists and published in *Historical Statistics* for the antebellum period is probably accurate, but only if the large number of passengers currently listed as "Other or unknown" or "Country, Not Specified" are reclassified as Europeans. Doing so provides a total of 4.84 million immigrants having arrived directly from Europe between 1820 and 1860. If arrivals through Canada and arrivals between 1815 and 1819 are included, the total increases to 5.2 million. If arrivals from other countries are also included, the grand total for the antebellum period reaches 5.4 million. Although this overall total appears to be fairly accurate, the annual totals currently listed for specific countries, especially the breakdown between Great Britain and Ireland before 1847, are definitely not accurate.

2. Although the British constituted the largest portion of colonial immigration, arrivals from northern Ireland and southwest Germany increased substantially during the early part of the antebellum period. These areas had two factors in common that caused them to send immigrants to the United States. Both areas had very high population densities, among the highest in Western Europe. Both areas also had limited opportunities for their occupants to earn seasonal income that would allow them to remain at home. The Protestants from northern Ireland did not want to compete with the Catholic Irish working in Great Britain, whereas individuals in southwest Germany lived in an area where there was little

demand for seasonal work. Immigration to the United States thus became an early outlet for both groups.

3. A secular increase in immigration began in the late 1820s and early 1830s. Average annual immigrant volume had increased very slowly during the previous two centuries. The sudden increase in volume was caused by a number of factors: high population growth in Europe pressured the standard of living; transatlantic transportation costs fell due to improvements in the shipping market; European governments reduced their restrictions on emigration; a large increase occurred in the volume of remittances and prepaid tickets; and Industrial Production in the U.S. economy began to grow more rapidly in the early 1830s. All of these factors combined to change what had been a consistent, although small, annual immigration into the beginnings of mass migration.

4. Although the annual volume of immigration rose substantially from the early 1830s through 1854, it did not increase in a consistent fashion. The antebellum downturns in volume are only partially explained by downturns in the U.S. business cycle, with other events, such as changes in the European economies, being important in some years. In particular, during two years – 1843 and 1855 – immigration underwent substantial declines with no corresponding downturn in the U.S. economy. No complete explanation exists for the decline in the former year. The latter decline was related to the widespread outbreak of nativism in the United States during the early 1850s in conjunction with the worst effects of the potato famine having passed.

5. The transatlantic passenger trade followed the established routes for the freight trade. Thus, the percentages of ships arriving in each major U.S. port – New York, New Orleans, Boston, Philadelphia, and Baltimore – from each major European port – Liverpool, Le Havre, Bremen, Hamburg, and London – differed significantly. Over the antebellum period, New York City grew in importance as the major arrival port for the Europeans. This trend reflected the geographical advantages of New York City as a port, the city's capture of a larger share of the freight trade, the opening of the Erie Canal, and the existence of immigrant assistance after the establishment of the Commissioners of Emigration of the State of New York.

6. The European immigrants who arrived before the secular increase in the late 1820s and early 1830s were highly skilled for the times,

almost certainly more skilled than either their country's labor force or the existing U.S. labor force. With the various changes making the opportunity cost of immigrating smaller, the immigrant stream from each of the major source countries became much less skilled after the early 1830s. On a comparative basis, immigrants from Germany were more skilled than those from Great Britain, who in turn were more skilled than those from Ireland. This ordering reflected differences in travel time to the embarkation ports, in income levels and the availability of remittances, and in language.

7. Of those immigrants traveling directly to the United States, about 1.5 percent of the immigrants leaving Europe died on the voyage or soon after arrival. This death rate was about five times higher than among nonmigrants of the same age. On most voyages, the death rates were not very large. On some voyages, however, an outbreak of an infectious disease, usually cholera or typhus, led to a much higher death rate. Beginning in 1847, immigrants arriving in New York City were met by agents of the Commissioners of Emigration of the State of New York. This agency worked in a variety of ways to assist the immigrants, and eventually established the first landing depot in the United States at Castle Garden.

8. Only a small percentage of the immigrants arriving in the United States settled in their port of arrival. In general, by 1850 immigrants were found disproportionately in the bigger cities, almost certainly due to greater job opportunities. German immigrants were found disproportionately in the Midwest, the Irish more in the Northeast, and the British were the most scattered. The geographic pattern reflected differences among the immigrant groups in their skill levels and preferences for working in agriculture, in factories, and as servants. The differential financial resources of the immigrants from the different source countries also affected the geographic pattern. Over time, newer arrivals moved close to their countrymen and reinforced the antebellum settlement pattern.

9. Overall, the immigrants experienced success in the U.S. labor market. The occupational skill level of the immigrants as recorded in the U.S. Census materials some years after arrival was at least as high as that recorded at arrival, and probably higher. The skill levels of the German and British immigrants became similar to those of the native-born labor force, with the exception that a larger percentage of the native born were farmers and a larger percentage of these immigrant groups were skilled workers. The Irish were clearly less

skilled than the native born. However, foreign-born males from all countries, including Ireland, increased their skill levels over time and did so at a rate similar to that of the native born.

10. Compared to the U.S. labor force, the immigrant stream in 1850 was abundant in unskilled nonfarm labor and scarce in farmers. The two groups had relatively equal percentages who were white-collar workers and skilled workers. At the time, farmers and unskilled labor were both considered to be unskilled workers, so the overall skill contents of the native-born labor force and the immigrant stream were relatively equal. The arriving immigrants, however, were mainly young and of working age, so the United States benefited from not having to expend resources to raise these individuals to working age. Particularly during the early antebellum years, the United States also gained from the more skilled immigration that included many individuals who became entrepreneurs in the new manufacturing sector.

11. In the early 1850s, immigrant volume was at unprecedented levels, adding about 4 percent per year to the northern male native labor force, and around 10 percent per year to the number of native unskilled urban workers. The huge influx of immigrants led to a general stagnation or decrease in the level of real wages in the United States. The fact that the immigrants were disproportionately unskilled urban workers led to an increase in the skilled to unskilled wage ratio outside of agriculture. Other effects were that manufacturers continued to adopt methods that used the less skilled labor force more intensively, so the importance of independent artisans declined, and the transportation network was completed more rapidly. Finally, the large influx led to the most extensive outbreak of nativism in U.S. history, with the nativists enjoying unprecedented political success.

The summary just provided indicates that quite a bit is known concerning antebellum immigration. What else, however, could be done? First and foremost, this book has suggested in a number of places that putting the original Passenger Lists in a form where they could be computer-analyzed would greatly add to our knowledge. There are four suggested areas where gains could be made, although others certainly exist. First, the accuracy of the published volume of immigration from each country could be checked. In particular, a computerized database would provide a starting point to deriving more accurate numbers of those who arrived from Great Britain and Ireland before the 1850s. The database could also check the supposition that many of the immigrants who did not have their country of origin listed came from the smaller European countries. Second, although the numbers of immigrants leaving each European port and the number arriving at each U.S. port have been presented, the number going from a specific European port to a specific U.S. port is not known. Third, a variety of issues could be further evaluated which, at the moment, can be addressed only with samples from the Passenger Lists. These issues include the occupations of the immigrants by country of origin and the mortality suffered on the voyage. Fourth, researchers could further study what happened to the immigrants in the United States, because the Passenger List data could more easily be linked with existing census data. As discussed in Chapter 6, Ferrie has done work along these lines, but connecting individuals in the two sources is currently very difficult and time consuming.

The study of antebellum immigration also suffers from a scarcity of time-series data, beyond that for the volume of immigration. The evidence we currently have suggests that transatlantic fares showed no long-run tendency to increase or decrease after about 1830. Yet clearly the fares fluctuated from year to year, although no consistent data exist on this fact. Presumably, we would expect the yearly (monthly?) volume of immigration to depend inversely on the fare, because immigrants could often choose when to migrate. Remittances are another area where time-series data are lacking. This book has suggested these played an important role in antebellum immigration, yet until the late 1840s or 1850s, the available data on the volume of remittances are actually quite sparse. In both cases, the data that are available have been obtained from occasional newspaper articles, a company's records, government reports, or immigrant letters. A more comprehensive approach to developing the data – if possible – could support or contradict a number of the arguments presented in this book.

Immigration is an important issue in the world and has been one at least since the substantial increase in volume that occurred around 1830. This book has presented a case study of immigration and its effects during a unique period in the history of world immigration. The uniqueness arose from the fact that, during the antebellum period, a large number of individuals moved to the United States by a long sailing-ship voyage, therefore the movement was expected to be permanent. The antebellum years are perhaps the one period in world history that most closely fits the classic economic theory of immigration, which typically assumes that immigration is motivated by economic factors and is permanent. In a broad sense, the findings of this book support the established economic view of how immigration affects the immigrants, the country from which they left, and the country to which they moved. As a group, the European immigrants improved their standard of living by moving to the United States. By moving in large numbers, the immigrants relieved the economic pressure on workers in Europe that resulted from rapid population growth, at least to some extent. Remittances sent home by the immigrants also helped those who remained in the source countries, and these funds along with prepaid tickets and letters of advice helped others to leave. The economic effects on the destination country – the United States in this case – are more complex. Although the United States received some overall benefits, the distributional effects were much larger, with some specific groups gaining while others lost. During the antebellum period, the large increase in volume and the decline in immigrant skill levels made all of the distributional effects very evident. As a result, immigration became very controversial in the United States and it has remained so to the present day.

References

Abbott, Edith, *Immigration: Select Documents and Case Records*. Chicago: University of Chicago Press, 1924.

Abramowitz, Moses, "The Search for Sources of Growth: Areas of Ignorance, Old and New." *Journal of Economic History* 53 (June 1993): 217–43.

Adams, Donald R., "The Standard of Living during American Industrialization: Evidence from the Brandywine Region, 1800–1860." *Journal of Economic History* 42 (December 1982): 903–17.

Adams, John, *Ocean Steamers: A History of Ocean-going Passenger Steamships, 1820–1970*. London: New Cavendish Books, 1993.

Adams, W. F., *Ireland and Irish Emigration to the New World from 1815 to the Famine*. New Haven: Yale University Press, 1932.

Albion, Robert Greenhalgh, *The Rise of New York Port (1815–1860)*. Boston: Northeastern University Press, 1984. Reprint of 1939 edition.

Albion, Robert Greenhalgh, *Square-Riggers on Schedule: The New York Sailing Packets to England, France, and the Cotton Ports*. Princeton: Princeton University Press, 1938.

Altonji, Joseph G., and David Card, "The Effects of Immigration on the Labor Market Outcomes of Less-Skilled Natives." In John M. Abowd and Richard B. Freeman, eds., *Immigration, Trade, and the Labor Market*. Chicago: University of Chicago Press, 1991, pp. 201–34.

Anbinder, Tyler, *Nativism and Slavery: The Northern Know-Nothings and the Politics of the 1850s*. New York: Oxford University Press, 1992.

Anderson, Michael, *Population Change in North-Western Europe*. London: Macmillan, 1988.

Armengaud, Andre, "Population in Europe, 1700–1914." In Carlo Cipolla, ed., *The Fontana Economic History of Europe, Vol. 3: The Industrial Revolution*. London: Collins, 1973, pp. 22–76.

Atack, Jeremy, "Tenants and Yeomen in the Nineteenth Century." *Agricultural History* 62 (Summer 1988): 6–32.

Atack, Jeremy, and Fred Bateman, *To Their Own Soil: Agriculture in the Antebellum North*. Ames, IA: Iowa State University, 1987.

Atack, Jeremy, Fred Bateman, and Robert A. Margo, "Skill Intensity and Rising Wage Dispersion in Nineteenth-Century American Manufacturing." *Journal of Economic History* 64 (March 2004): 172–92.

Atack, Jeremy, and Peter Passell, *A New Economic View of American History from Colonial Times to 1940*. New York: W. W. Norton and Company, 1994. Second edition.

Bade, Klaus J., *Migration in European History*. Oxford: Blackwell Publishing, 2003. Translated by Allison Brown.

Baily, Samuel L., *Immigrants in the Lands of Promise: Italians in Buenos Aires and New York City, 1870–1914*. Ithaca, NY: Cornell University Press, 1999.

Bailyn, Bernard, *Voyagers to the West*. New York: Alfred A. Knopf, 1986.

Baines, Dudley, *Emigration from Europe, 1815–1930*. London: Macmillan, 1991.

Baines, Dudley, "European Emigration, 1815–1930: Looking at the Emigration Decision Again." *Economic History Review* 47 (August 1994): 525–44.

Baines, Dudley, *Migration in a Mature Economy: Emigration and Internal Migration in England and Wales, 1861–1900*. New York: Cambridge University Press, 1985.

Baker, Jean H., *Ambivalent Americans: The Know-Nothing Party in Maryland*. Baltimore: The Johns Hopkins University Press, 1977.

Benz, Ernest, "Population Change and the Economy." In Sheilagh Ogilvie, ed., *Germany: A New Social and Economic History, Vol. 2, 1630–1800*. New York: St. Martin's Press, Inc., 1996, pp. 39–62.

Berkner, Lutz K., and Franklin F. Mendels, "Inheritance Systems, Family Structure, and Demographic Patterns in Western Europe, 1700–1900." In Charles Tilly, ed., *Historical Studies of Changing Fertility*. Princeton: Princeton University Press, 1978, pp. 209–23.

Billington, Ray Allen, *The Protestant Crusade, 1800–1860: A Study of the Origins of American Nativism*. Chicago: Quadrangle Books, 1964. Reprint of 1938 edition.

Blessing, Patrick J., "Irish Emigration to the United States, 1800–1920: An Overview." In P. J. Drudy, ed., *Irish Studies: Volume 4–The Irish in America: Emigration, Assimilation and Impact*. Cambridge, UK: Cambridge University Press, 1985, pp. 11–37.

Bogart, Dan, "Turnpike Trusts and the Transportation Revolution in 18th-Century England." *Explorations in Economic History* 42 (October 2005): 479–508.

Bonsor, N. R. P., *North Atlantic Seaway*. 3 volumes. New York: Arco Publishing Co., 1975.

Borjas, George J., "Assimilation, Changes in Cohort Quality, and the Earnings of Immigrants." *Journal of Labor Economics* 3 (October 1985): 463–89.

Borjas, George J., "The Economic Benefits from Immigration." *Journal of Economic Perspectives* 9 (Spring 1995): 3–22.

Borjas, George J., "The Economics of Immigration." *Journal of Economic Literature* 32 (December 1994): 1667–1717.

Borjas, George J., *Heaven's Door: Immigration Policy and the American Economy*. Princeton: Princeton University Press, 1999.

Borjas, George J., "National Origin and the Skills of Immigrants in the Postwar Period." In George J. Borjas and Richard B. Freemand, eds., *Immigration and the Work Force: Economic Consequences for the United States and Source Areas*. Chicago: University of Chicago Press, 1992, pp. 17–47.

Bowen, Frank C., *A Century of Atlantic Travel, 1830–1930*. Boston: Little, Brown, and Co., 1930.

Bromwell, William J., *History of Immigration to the United States*. New York: Arno Press, 1969. Reprint of 1856 edition.

Browne, Gary Lawson, *Baltimore in the Nation, 1789–1861*. Chapel Hill, NC: The University of North Carolina Press, 1980.

Bukowczyk, John J., "Migration, Transportation, Capital, and the State in the Great Lakes Basin, 1815–1890." In John J. Bukowczyk, Nora Faires, David R. Smith, and Randy William Widdis, eds., *Permeable Borders: The Great Lakes Basin as Transnational Region, 1650–1990*. Pittsburgh: University of Pittsburgh Press, 2005, pp. 29–77.

Canny, Nicholas, "English Migration into and across the Atlantic during the Seventeenth and Eighteenth Centuries." In Nicholas Canny, ed., *Europeans on the Move: Studies on European Migration, 1500–1800*. Oxford: Clarendon Press, 1994, pp. 39–75.

Canny, Nicholas, ed., *Europeans on the Move: Studies on European Migration, 1500–1800*. Oxford: Clarendon Press, 1994.

Carrier, N. H., and J. R. Jeffery, *External Migration: A Study of the Available Statistics, 1815–1950*. London: Her Majesty's Stationery Office, 1953.

Carter, Susan B. et al., *Historical Statistics of the United States: Earliest Times to the Present–Millennial Edition*. Volume 1: *Population*. New York: Cambridge University Press, 2006.

Carter, Susan B., and Richard Sutch, "Historical Perspectives on the Economic Consequences of Immigration into the United States." In Charles Hirschman, Philip Kasinitz, and Josh DeWind, eds., *The Handbook of International Migration: The American Experience*. New York: Russell Sage Foundation, 1999, pp. 319–41.

Chiswick, Barry R., "Are Immigrants Favorably Self-Selected? An Economic Analysis." In Caroline B. Brettell and James F. Hollifield, eds., *Migration Theory: Talking Across Disciplines*. New York: Routledge, 2000, pp. 61–76.

Chiswick, Barry R., "The Effect of Americanization on the Earnings of Foreign-Born Men." *Journal of Political Economy* 86 (October 1978): 897–921.

Cohn, Raymond L., "A Comparative Analysis of European Immigrant Streams to the United States during the Early Mass Migration." *Social Science History* 19 (Spring 1995): 63–89.

Cohn, Raymond L., "Corrigendum: The Determinants of Individual Immigrant Mortality on Sailing Ships, 1836–1853." *Explorations in Economic History* 25 (July 1988): 337–8.

Cohn, Raymond L., "The Determinants of Individual Immigrant Mortality on Sailing Ships, 1836–1853." *Explorations in Economic History* 24 (October 1987): 371–91.

Cohn, Raymond L., "Maritime Mortality in the Eighteenth and Nineteenth Centuries: A Survey." *International Journal of Maritime History* 1 (June 1989): 159–91.

Cohn, Raymond L., "Mortality on Immigrant Voyages to New York, 1836–1853." *Journal of Economic History* 44 (June 1984): 289–300.

Cohn, Raymond L., "Nativism and the End of the Mass Migration of the 1840s and 1850s." *Journal of Economic History* 60 (June 2000): 361–83.

Cohn, Raymond L., "Occupational Evidence on the Causes of Immigration to the United States, 1836–1853." *Explorations in Economic History* 32 (July 1995): 383–408.

Cohn, Raymond L., "The Occupations of English Immigrants to the United States, 1836–1853." *Journal of Economic History* 52 (June 1992): 377–87.

Cohn, Raymond L., "Passenger Mortality on Antebellum Immigrant Ships: Further Evidence." *International Journal of Maritime History* 15 (December 2003): 1–19.

Cohn, Raymond L., "Transatlantic U.S. Passenger Travel at the Dawn of the Steamship Era." *International Journal of Maritime History* 4 (June 1992): 43–64.

Cohn, Raymond L., "The Transition from Sail to Steam in Immigration to the United States." *Journal of Economic History* 65 (June 2005): 469–95.

Coleman, Terry, *Going to America*. New York: Pantheon Books, 1972.

Commissioners of Emigration of the State of New York. *Annual Reports of the Commissioners of Emigration of the State of New York from the Organization of the Commission, May 5, 1847, to 1860*. New York, 1861.

Commons, John, David J. Saposs, Helen L. Sumner, E. B. Mittleman, H. E. Hoagland, John B. Andrews, and Selig Perlman, eds., *History of Labour in the United States*. New York: The Macmillan Company, 1921.

Costa, Dora, and Richard H. Steckel, "Long-Term Trends in Health, Welfare, and Economic Growth in the United States." In Richard H. Steckel and Roderick Floud, eds., *Health and Welfare during Industrialization*. Chicago: University of Chicago Press, 1997, pp. 47–89.

Cousens, S. H., "Emigration and Demographic Change in Ireland, 1851–1861." *Economic History Review* 14 (1961): 275–88.

Cousens, S. H., "The Regional Pattern of Emigration during the Great Irish Famine, 1846–51." *Transactions and Papers (Institute of British Geographers)* 28 (1960): 119–34.

Cousens, S. H., "The Regional Variation in Emigration from Ireland between 1821 and 1841." *Transactions of the Institute of British Geographers* 37 (Dec. 1965): 15–30.

Cullen, L. M., "The Irish Diaspora of the Seventeenth and Eighteenth Centuries." In Nicholas Canny, ed., *Europeans on the Move: Studies on European Migration, 1500–1800*. Oxford: Clarendon Press, 1994, pp. 113–49.

Curran, Thomas J., *Xenophobia and Immigration, 1820–1930*. Boston: Twayne Publishers, 1975.

Davie, Maurice R., *World Immigration*. New York: Macmillan Company, 1936.

Davis, Joseph H., "An Annual Index of U.S. Industrial Production, 1790–1915." *Quarterly Journal of Economics* 119 (November 2004): 1177–1215.

Davis, Joseph H., "An Improved Annual Chronology of U.S. Business Cycles since the 1790s." *Journal of Economic History* 66 (March 2006): 103–21.

DeBow, J. D. B., *Statistical View of the United States*. Washington, DC: Beverley Tucker, Senate Printer, 1854.

Doerries, Reinhard R., "German Transatlantic Migration from the Early 19th Century to the Outbreak of World War II." In Klaus J. Bade, ed., *Population, Labour, and Migration in 19th- and 20th-Century Germany*. New York: St. Martin's Press, 1987, pp. 115–34.

Dunlevy, James A., "Regional Preferences and Migrant Settlement: On the Avoidance of the South by Nineteenth Century Immigrants." In Paul Uselding, ed., *Research in Economic History*. Volume 8. Greenwich, CT: JAI Press, 1982, pp. 217–51.

Dunlevy, James A., and Henry A. Gemery, "Economic Opportunity and the Responses of 'Old' and 'New' Migrants to the United States." *Journal of Economic History* 38 (December 1978): 901–17.

Dunlevy, James A., and Henry A. Gemery, "The Role of Migrant Stock and Lagged Migration in the Settlement Patterns of Nineteenth-Century Immigrants." *Review of Economics and Statistics* 59 (May 1977): 137–44.

Dunlevy, James A., and Richard P. Saba, "The Role of Nationality-Specific Characteristics on the Settlement Patterns of Late Nineteenth-Century Immigrants." *Explorations in Economic History* 29 (April 1992): 228–49.

Eltis, David, "Free and Coerced Transatlantic Migrations: Some Comparisons." *American Historical Review* 88 (April 1983): 251–80.

Engerman, Stanley L., and Kenneth L. Sokoloff, "The Evolution of Suffrage Institutions in the New World." *Journal of Economic History* 65 (December 2005): 891–921.

Erickson, Charlotte J., "Emigration from the British Isles to the U.S.A. in 1831." *Population Studies* 25 (1981): 175–97.

Erickson, Charlotte J., "Emigration from the British Isles to the U.S.A. in 1841: Part I. Emigration from the British Isles." *Population Studies* 43 (Nov. 1989): 347–67.

Erickson, Charlotte J., "Emigration from the British Isles to the U.S.A. in 1841: Part II. Who Were the English Emigrants?" *Population Studies* 44 (March 1990): 21–40.

Erickson, Charlotte J., *Invisible Immigrants: The Adaptation of English and Scottish Immigrants in Nineteenth-Century America*. Coral Gables, FL: University of Miami Press, 1972.

Erickson, Charlotte J., *Leaving England: Essays on British Emigration in the Nineteenth Century*. Ithaca, NY: Cornell University Press, 1994.

Erickson, Charlotte J., "The Uses of Passenger Lists for the Study of British and Irish Emigration." In Ira A. Glazier and Luigi De Rosa, eds., *Migration across Time and Nations*. New York: Holmes & Meier, 1986, pp. 318–35.

Erickson, Charlotte J., "Who Were the English and Scots Emigrants to the United States in the Late Nineteenth Century?" In D. V. Glass and R. Revelle, eds., *Population and Social Change*. New York: Edward Arnold, 1972, pp. 347–81.

Ernst, Robert, *Immigrant Life in New York City, 1825–1863*. New York: King's Crown Press, 1949.

Esslinger, Dean R., *Immigrants and the City: Ethnicity and Mobility in a Nineteenth-Century Midwestern Community*. Port Washington, NY: Kennikat, 1975.

Feldberg, Michael, *The Philadelphia Riots of 1844: A Study of Ethnic Conflict*. Westport, CT: Greenwood Press, 1975.

Ferenczi, Imre, *International Migrations*. Vol. 1. New York: Arno Press, 1970.

Ferrie, Joseph P., "A New View of the Irish in America: Economic Performance and the Impact of Place of Origin." Unpublished Manuscript, Northwestern University, 1997.

Ferrie, Joseph P., *Yankeys Now: Immigrants in the Antebellum United States, 1840–1860*. New York: Oxford University Press, 1999.

Ferrie, Joseph P., and Joel Mokyr, "Immigration and Entrepreneurship in the Nineteenth-Century U.S." In Herbert Giersch, ed., *Economic Aspects of International Migration*. Berlin: Springer-Verlag, 1994, pp. 115–38.

Fertig, Georg, "Transatlantic Migration from the German-Speaking Parts of Central Europe, 1600–1800: Proportions, Structures, and Explanations." In Nicholas Canny, ed., *Europeans on the Move: Studies on European Migration, 1500–1800*. Oxford: Clarendon Press, 1994, pp. 192–235.

Fitzpatrick, David, "Emigration, 1801–1870." In W. E. Vaughan, ed., *A New History of Ireland, Vol. V: Ireland under the Union, I, 1801–1870*. New York: Oxford University Press, 1989, pp. 562–622.

Flayhart, William Henry III, *The American Line: 1871–1902*. New York: W. W. Norton, 2000.

Fogel, Robert William, *The Slavery Debates, 1952–1990*. Baton Rogue: Louisiana State University, 2003.

Fogel, Robert William, *Without Consent or Contract: The Rise and Fall of American Slavery*. New York: W. W. Norton and Co., 1989.

Friedberg, Rachel M., "The Labor Market Assimilation of Immigrants in the United States: The Age at Arrival." Working Paper, Brown University, 1992.

Friedberg, Rachel M., and Jennifer Hunt, "Immigration and the Receiving Economy." In Charles Hirschman, Philip Kasinitz, and Josh DeWind, eds., *The Handbook of International Migration: The American Experience*. New York: Russell Sage Foundation, 1999, pp. 342–59.

Friedberg, Rachel M., and Jennifer Hunt, "The Impact of Immigrants on Host Country Wages, Employment, and Growth." *Journal of Economic Perspectives* 9 (Spring 1995): 23–44.

Galenson, David. W., "Economic Opportunity on the Urban Frontier: Nativity, Work, and Wealth in Early Chicago." *Journal of Economic History* 51 (September 1991): 581–603.

Galenson, David W., *White Servitude in Colonial America: An Economic Analysis*. New York: Cambridge University Press, 1981.

Gallagher, Thomas, *Paddy's Lament, Ireland, 1846–1847: Prelude to Hatred*. New York: Harcourt Brace Jovanovich, 1982.

Gallaway, Lowell E., and Richard K. Vedder, "Emigration from the United Kingdom to the United States: 1860–1913." *Journal of Economic History* 31 (December 1971): 885–97.

Gallaway, Lowell E., Richard K. Vedder, and Vishwa Shukla, "The Distribution of the Immigrant Population in the United States: An Economic Analysis." *Explorations in Economic History* 11 (Spring 1974): 213–26.

Gallman, Robert E., "Human Capital in the First 80 Years of the Republic: How Much Did America Owe the Rest of the World." *American Economic Review* 67 (February 1977): 27–31.

Gardiner, Robert, ed., *The Advent of Steam: The Merchant Steamship before 1900.* Washington, DC: Naval Institute Press, 1993.

Gayer, Arthur D., W. W. Rostow, and Anna Jacobson Schwartz, *The Growth and Fluctuation of the British Economy, 1790–1850.* Oxford: Clarendon Press, 1953.

Gemery, Henry A., "The White Population of the Colonial United States, 1607–1790." In Michael R. Haines and Richard H. Steckel, eds., *A Population History of North America.* New York: Cambridge University Press, 2000, pp. 143–90.

Glazier, Ira A., Deidre Mageean, and Barnabus Okeke, "Socio-Demographic Characteristics of Irish Immigrants, 1846–1851." In Klaus Friedland, ed., *Maritime Aspects of Migration.* Cologne: Böhlau Verlag, 1989, pp. 243–78.

Goldin, Claudia, and Lawrence F. Katz, "The Origins of Technology-Skill Complementarity." *Quarterly Journal of Economics* 113 (August 1998): 693–732.

Goldin, Claudia, and Kenneth Sokoloff, "Women, Children, and Industrialization in the Early Republic: Evidence from the Manufacturing Censuses." *Journal of Economic History* 42 (December 1982): 741–74.

Gould, J. D., "European Inter-Continental Emigration 1815–1914: Patterns and Causes." *Journal of European Economic History* 8 (1979): 593–679.

Grabbe, Hans-Jürgen, "European Immigration to the United States in the Early National Period, 1783–1820." *Proceedings of the American Philosophical Society* 133 (1989): 190–214.

Grabbe, Hans-Jürgen, *Vor der großen Flut: Die europäische Migration in die Vereinigten Staaten von Amerika, 1783–1820.* Stuttgart: Steiner, 2001.

Greenwood, Michael J., and John M. McDowell, "The Factor Market Consequences of U.S. Immigration." *Journal of Economic Literature* 24 (December 1986): 1738–72.

Griffen, Clyde, and Sally Griffen, *Natives and Newcomers: The Ordering of Opportunity in Mid-Nineteenth-Century Poughkeepsie.* Cambridge: Harvard University Press, 1978.

Grubb, Farley, "Colonial Immigrant Literacy: An Economic Analysis of Pennsylvania-German Evidence, 1727–1775." *Explorations in Economic History* 24 (Jan. 1987): 63–76.

Grubb, Farley, "The End of European Immigrant Servitude in the United States: An Economic Analysis of Market Collapse, 1772–1835." *Journal of Economic History* 54 (Dec. 1994): 794–824.

Grubb, Farley, "German Immigration to Pennsylvania, 1709 to 1820." *Journal of Interdisciplinary History* 20 (Winter 1990): 417–36.

Grubb, Farley, *Immigration and Servitude in the Colony and Commonwealth of Pennsylvania: A Quantitative and Economic Analysis.* Ph.D. Thesis, University of Chicago, 1984.

Grubb, Farley, "The Long-Run Trend in the Value of European Immigrant Servants, 1654–1831: New Measurements and Interpretations." *Research in Economic History* 14 (1992): 167–240.

Guillet, Edwin C., *The Great Migration: The Atlantic Crossing by Sailing-ship Since 1770*. Toronto: University of Toronto Press, Second Edition, 1963. First Edition 1937.

Guinnane, Timothy W., "Population and the Economy in Germany, 1800–1990." In Sheilagh Ogilvie and Richard Overy, eds., *Germany: A New Social and Economic History, Vol. 3: Since 1800*. New York: Oxford University Press, 2003, pp. 35–70.

Guinnane, Timothy W., *The Vanishing Irish: Households, Migration, and the Rural Economy in Ireland, 1850–1914*. Princeton, NJ: Princeton University Press, 1997.

Günther, Markus, *Auswandererlisten und Passenger Lists, 1855–1864: Eine Vergleichende Quellenkritik als Methodischer Beitrag zur Auswanderungforschung*. M.A. Thesis (History), Ruhr Universität Bochum, 1992.

Haines, Robin, and Ralph Shlomowitz, "Explaining the Modern Mortality Decline: What Can We Learn from Sea Voyages." *Social History of Medicine* 11 (1998): 15–48.

Hansen, Marcus L., *The Atlantic Migration, 1607–1860*. Cambridge, MA: Harvard University Press, 1940.

Harper, Marjory, ed., *Emigrant Homecomings: The Return Movement of Emigrants, 1600–2000*. Manchester and New York: Manchester University Press, 2005.

Hatton, Timothy J., "How Much Did Immigrant 'Quality' Decline in Late Nineteenth-Century America?" In Klaus F. Zimmermann and Amelie Constant, eds., *How Labor Migrants Fare*. Berlin: Springer-Verlag, pp. 37–54.

Hill, Peter Jensen, *The Economic Impact of Immigration into the United States*. New York: Arno Press, 1975.

Hochstadt, Steve, "Migration and Industrialization in Germany, 1815–1977." *Social Science History* 5 (Autumn 1981): 445–68.

Hochstadt, Steve, "The Socioeconomic Determinants of Increasing Mobility in Nineteenth-Century Germany." In Dirk Hoerder and Leslie Page Moch, eds., *European Migrants: Global and Local Perspectives*. Boston: Northeastern University Press, 1996, pp. 141–69.

Hoerder, Dirk, *Cultures in Contact: World Migrations in the Second Millennium*. Durham: Duke University Press, 2002.

Hoffmann, Walther G., *Das Wachstum der Deutschen Wirtschaft seit der mitte des 19. Jahrhunderts*. Berlin, 1965.

Holt, Michael F., "The Antimasonic and Know Nothing Parties." In Arthur M. Schlesinger, Jr., ed., *History of U.S. Political Parties, Volume 1: 1789–1860: From Factions to Parties*. New York: Chelsea House Publishers, 1973, pp. 575–620.

Horn, J., "'To Parts Beyond the Seas': Free Emigration to the Chesapeake in the Seventeenth Century." In I. Altman and J. Horn, eds., *"To Make America": European Emigration in the Early Modern Period*. Berkeley, CA: University of California Press, 1991, pp. 85–130.

Hughes, Jonathan, and Louis P. Cain, *American Economic History*, Sixth Edition. New York: Addison Wesley, 2003.

Hutchins, John G. B., *The American Maritime Industries and Public Policy, 1789–1914*. New York: Russell and Russell, 1969 (reissue of 1941 edition).

Hutchinson, E. P., "Notes on Immigration Statistics of the United States." *Journal of the American Statistical Association* 53 (1958): 963–1025.

Hvidt, K., *Flight to America: The Social Background of 300,000 Danish Emigrants*. New York: Academic Press, 1975.

Jackson, James Jr., and Leslie Page Moch, "Migration and the Social History of Modern Europe." In Dirk Hoerder and Leslie Page Moch, eds., *European Migrants: Global and Local Perspectives*. Boston: Northeastern University Press, 1996, pp. 52–69.

James, John A., and Jonathan S. Skinner, "The Resolution of the Labor-Scarcity Paradox." *Journal of Economic History* 45 (September 1985): 513–40.

Jeremy, David J., *Transatlantic Industrial Revolution: The Diffusion of Textile Technologies between Britain and America, 1790–1830s*. Cambridge, MA: The MIT Press, 1981.

Jerome, Harry, *Migration and Business Cycles*. New York: National Bureau of Economic Research, 1926.

Jewish Women's Archive. "JWA–Emma Lazarus–Introduction." Accessed December 28, 2007, at http://www.jwa.org/exhibits/wov/lazarus/index.html.

Jones, Maldwyn Allen, *American Immigration*. Chicago: University of Chicago Press, 1992, second edition.

Jones, Maldwyn A., "Aspects of North Atlantic Migration: Steerage Conditions and American Law, 1819–1909." In Klaus Friedland, ed., *Maritime Aspects of Migration*. Cologne: Böhlau Verlag, 1989, pp. 321–31.

Jones, Maldwyn A., "The Background to Emigration from Britain in the Nineteenth Century." *Perspectives in American History* 7 (1973): 1–92.

Jones, Maldwyn A., "Transatlantic Steerage Conditions from Sail to Steam, 1819–1920." In Birgit Flemming Larsen, Henning Bender, and Karen Veien, eds., *On Distant Shores*. Aalborg, Denmark: Danes Worldwide Archives, 1993, pp. 59–82.

Kamphoefner, Walter D., "The Volume and Composition of German-American Return Migration." In Rudolph Vecoli and Suzanne M. Sinke, eds., *A Century of European Migrations, 1830–1930*. Urbana: University of Illinois Press, 1991, pp. 293–311.

Kamphoefner, Walter D., *The Westfalians: From Germany to Missouri*. Princeton: Princeton University Press, 1987.

Kamphoefner, Walter D., Wolfgang Helbrich, and Ulrike Sommer, *News from the Land of Freedom: German Immigrants Write Home*. Ithaca: Cornell University Press, 1991.

Kapp, Friedrich, *Immigration and the Commissioners of Emigration*. New York: Arno Press, 1969 (reprint of 1870 edition).

Keeling, Drew, *The Business of Transatlantic Migration between Europe and USA, 1900–1914*. Ph.D. Thesis, University of California, Berkeley, 2005.

Keeling, Drew, "The Transportation Revolution and Transatlantic Migration, 1850–1914." *Research in Economic History* 19 (1999): 39–74.

Kelly, James, "The Resumption of Emigration from Ireland after the American War of Independence: 1783–1787." *Studia Hibernica* 26 (1992): 61–88.

Kenwood, A. G., and A. L. Lougheed, *The Growth of the International Economy, 1820–1990: An Introductory Text.* New York: Routledge, 1992, Third Edition.

Kerr, Barbara M., "Irish Seasonal Migration to Great Britain, 1800–1838." *Irish Historical Studies* 3 (1942–3): 365–80.

Kiesling, L. Lynne, and Robert A. Margo, "Explaining the Rise in Antebellum Pauperism, 1850–1860: New Evidence." *Quarterly Review of Economics and Finance* 37 (Summer 1997): 405–17.

Köllmann, W., and P. Marschalck, "German Emigration to the United States." *Perspectives in American History* 7 (1973): 499–554.

Komlos, John, and Peter Coclanis, "On the Puzzling Cycle in the Biological Standard of Living: The Case of Antebellum Georgia." *Explorations in Economic History* 34 (October 1997): 433–59.

Kuznets, Simon, "The Contribution of Immigration to the Growth of the Labor Force." In Robert W. Fogel and Stanley L. Engerman, eds., *The Reinterpretation of American Economic History*. New York: Harper & Row Publishers, 1971, pp. 396–401.

Lane, A. T., *Solidarity or Survival?: American Labor and European Immigrants, 1830–1924*. New York: Greenwood Press, 1987.

Laurie, Bruce, Theodore Hershberg, and George Alter, "Immigrants and Industry: The Philadelphia Experience, 1850–1880." In Theodore Hershberg, ed., *Philadelphia: Work, Space, Family, and Group Experience in the Nineteenth Century*. New York: Oxford University Press, 1981, pp. 93–119.

Laurie, Bruce, and Mark Schmitz, "Manufacture and Productivity: The Making of an Industrial Base, Philadelphia, 1850–1880." In Theodore Hershberg, ed., *Philadelphia: Work, Space, Family, and Group Experience in the Nineteenth Century*. New York: Oxford University Press, 1981, pp. 43–92.

Laxton, Edward, *The Famine Ships: The Irish Exodus to America*. New York: Henry Holt and Co., 1996.

Lebergott, Stanley, *The Americans: An Economic Record*. New York: W. W. Norton, 1984.

Lebergott, Stanley, *Manpower in Economic Growth*. New York: McGraw-Hill, 1964.

Leonard, Ira M., and Robert D. Parmet, *American Nativism, 1830–1860*. New York: Van Nostrand Reinhold Co., 1971.

Licht, Walter, *Working for the Railroad: The Organization of Work in the Nineteenth Century*. Princeton: Princeton University Press, 1983.

Lindstrom, Diane, *Economic Development in the Philadelphia Region, 1810–1850*. New York: Columbia University Press, 1978.

Lucassen, Jan, *Migrant Labour in Europe, 1600–1900*. London: Croom Helm, 1987. Translated by Donald A. Bloch.

MacDonagh, Oliver, *A Pattern of Government Growth, 1800–1860*. London: MacGibbon & Kee, 1961.

Mageean, Deidre, "Nineteenth-Century Irish Emigration: A Case Study Using Passenger Lists." In P. J. Drudy, ed., *Irish Studies: Volume 4–The Irish in America: Emigration, Assimilation and Impact*. Cambridge, UK: Cambridge University Press, 1985, pp. 39–61.

Maginnis, Arthur J., *The Atlantic Ferry: Its Ships, Men, and Working*. London: Whittaker and Co., 1892.

Margo, Robert A., "The Rental Price of Housing in New York City, 1830–1860." *Journal of Economic History* 56 (September 1996): 605–25.

Margo, Robert A., *Wages and Labor Markets in the United States, 1820–1860*. Chicago: The University of Chicago Press, 2000.

Marschalck, Peter, *Deutsche Überseewanderung im 19. Jahrhundert*. Stuttgart: Ernst Klett Verlag, 1973.

Massey, Douglas S., Joaquin Arango, Graeme Hugo, Ali Kouaouci, Adela Pellegrino, and J. Edward Taylor, "Theories of International Migration: A Review and Appraisal." *Population and Development Review* 19 (September 1993): 431–66.

McClelland, Peter D., and Richard J. Zeckhauser, *Demographic Dimensions of the New Republic: American Interregional Migration, Vital Statistics, and Manumissions, 1800–1860*. Cambridge: Cambridge University Press, 1982.

McInnis, Marvin, "The Population of Canada in the Nineteenth Century." In Michael R. Haines and Richard H. Steckel, eds., *A Population History of North America*. New York: Cambridge University Press, 2000, pp. 371–432.

Menard, Russell R., "British Migration to the Chesapeake Colonies in the Seventeenth Century." In Lois Green Carr, Philip D. Morgan, and Jean B. Russo, eds., *Colonial Chesapeake Society*. Chapel Hill: The University of North Carolina Press, 1988, pp. 99–132.

Menard, Russell R., "Migration, Ethnicity, and the Rise of an Atlantic Economy: The Re-Peopling of British America, 1600–1790." In Rudolph J. Vecoli and Suzanne M. Sinke, eds., *A Century of European Migrations*. Urbana: University of Illinois Press, 1991, pp. 58–77.

Miller, Kerby A., *Emigrants and Exiles: Ireland and the Irish Exodus to North America*. Oxford: Oxford University Press, 1985.

Mitchell, B. R., *European Historical Statistics, 1750–1970*. New York: Columbia University Press, abridged edition, 1978.

Mitchell, Wesley C., *Business Cycles: The Problem and its Setting*. NBER Studies in Business Cycles, vol. 1. New York: NBER, 1927.

Moch, Leslie Page, "Dividing Time: An Analytical Framework for Migration History Periodization." In Jan Lucassen and Leo Lucassen, eds., *Migration, Migration History, History: Old Paradigms and New Perspectives*. New York: Peter Lang, 1997, pp. 41–56.

Moch, Leslie Page, "The European Perspective: Changing Conditions and Multiple Migrations, 1750–1914." In Dirk Hoerder and Leslie Page Moch, eds., *European Migrants: Global and Local Perspectives*. Boston: Northeastern University Press, 1996, pp. 115–40.

Moch, Leslie Page, *Moving Europeans: Migration in Western Europe since 1650*. Bloomington: Indiana University Press, 1992.

Moe, Thorvald, *Demographic Developments and Economic Growth in Norway, 1740–1940: An Econometric Study*. New York: Arno Press, 1977.

Mokyr, Joel, *Why Ireland Starved: A Quantitative and Analytical History of the Irish Economy, 1780–1850*. London: George Allen & Unwin, paperback edition, 1985.

Moltmann, Gunter, "The Pattern of German Emigration to the United States in the Nineteenth Century." In Franz Trommler and Joseph McVeigh, eds., *America and the Germans: An Assessment of a Three-Hundred Year History– Volume 1: Immigration, Language, Ethnicity*. Philadelphia: University of Pennsylvania Press, 1985, pp. 14–24.

Montgomery, David, "The Shuttle and the Cross: Weavers and Artisans in the Kensington Riots of 1844." *Journal of Social History* 5 (Summer 1972): 412–46.

Morawaska, Ewa, "Labor Migrations of Poles in the Atlantic World Economy, 1880–1914." *Comparative Studies in Society and History* 31 (1989): 237–72.

Mustafa, Sam A., *Merchants and Migrations: Germans and Americans in Connection, 1776–1835*. Aldershot, England: Ashgate, 2001.

Nash, Gary B., *First City: Philadelphia and the Forging of Historical Memory*. Philadelphia: University of Pennsylvania Press, 2002.

Neal, Larry, "Cross-Spectral Analysis of Long Swings in Atlantic Migration." *Research in Economic History* 1 (1976): 260–97.

Neal, Larry, and Paul Uselding, "Immigration, a Neglected Source of American Economic Growth: 1790 to 1912." *Oxford Economic Papers* 24 (March 1972): 68–88.

New York Tribune, issues of November 19, 22, 26, and December 3, 1853.

North, Douglass C., "The United States Balance of Payments, 1790–1860." In National Bureau of Economic Research, *Trends in the American Economy in the Nineteenth Century*. Studies in Income and Wealth, vol. 24. Princeton: Princeton University Press, 1960, pp. 573–627.

Northrup, David, *Indentured Labor in the Age of Imperialism, 1834–1922*. Cambridge: Cambridge University Press, 1995.

Norton, Desmond, *Landlords, Tenants, Famine: The Business of an Irish Land Agency in the 1840s*. Dublin: University College Dublin Press, 2006.

Nugent, Walter, *Crossings: The Great Transatlantic Migrations, 1870–1914*. Bloomington and Indianapolis: Indiana University Press, 1992.

O'Connor, Thomas H., *Bibles, Brahmins, and Bosses: A Short History of Boston*. Boston: Trustees of the Public Library of the City of Boston, 1983. Second Edition: Revised.

O'Connor, Thomas H., *The Hub: Boston Past and Present*. Boston: Northeastern University Press, 2001.

Officer, Lawrence H., and Samuel H. Williamson, "Computing 'Real Value' Over Time with a Conversion from British Pounds to U.S. Dollars, or Vice Versa." Economic History Services, Accessed on September 2005, at http://www.eh.net/hmit/exchange/.

Ogilvie, Sheilagh, "The Beginnings of Industrialization." In Sheilagh Ogilvie, ed., *Germany: A New Social and Economic History, Vol. 2: 1630–1800*. New York: St. Martin's Press, Inc., 1996, pp. 263–308.

Ó Gráda, Cormac, "Across the Briny Ocean: Some Thoughts on Irish Emigration to America, 1800–1850." In T. M. Devine and David Dickson, eds., *Ireland and Scotland, 1600–1850*. Edinburgh: John Donald Publishers, 1983, pp. 118–30.

Ó Gráda, Cormac, *Black '47 and Beyond: The Great Irish Famine in History, Economy, and Memory*. Princeton: Princeton University Press, 1999.

Ó Gráda, Cormac, "Demographic Adjustment and Seasonal Migration in Nineteenth-Century Ireland." In L. M. Cullen and F. Furet, eds., *Ireland and France: Towards a Comparative Study of Rural History*. Paris: 1981, pp. 181–93.

Ó Gráda, Cormac, "The Famine, the New York Irish, and their Bank." In Antoin E. Murphy and Renee Prendergast, eds., *Contributions to the History of Economic Thought: Essays in Honour of R. D. C. Black*. New York: Routledge, 2000, pp. 227–48.

Ó Gráda, Cormac, *The Great Irish Famine*. London: Macmillan, 1989.

Ó Gráda, Cormac, *Ireland: A New Economic History, 1780–1939*. New York: Oxford University Press, 1994.

Ó Gráda, Cormac, "The New York City Irish in the 1850s." In Cormac Ó Gráda, *Ireland's Great Famine: Interdisciplinary Perspectives*. Dublin: University College Dublin Press, 2006, pp. 143–74.

Ó Gráda, Cormac, "A Note on Nineteenth-Century Irish Emigration Statistics." *Population Studies* 29 (March 1975): 143–9.

Ó Gráda, Cormac, "Some Aspects of Nineteenth-Century Irish Emigration." In L. M. Cullen and T. C. Smout, eds., *Comparative Aspects of Scottish and Irish Economic and Social History, 1600–1900*. Edinburgh: John Donald Publishers, Limited, 1976, pp. 65–73.

Ó Gráda, Cormac, and Kevin O'Rourke, "Migration as Disaster Relief: Lessons from the Great Depression." *European Review of Economic History* 1 (April 1997): 3–25.

Olson, Sherry H., *Baltimore: The Building of an American City*. Baltimore: The Johns Hopkins University Press, 1980.

Olssen, Nils William, *Swedish Passenger Arrivals in New York, 1820–1850*. Stockholm: Kungl. Boktryckeriet P. A. Norstedt & Soner, 1967.

Osmond, Jonathan, "Land, Peasant, and Lord in German Agriculture since 1800." In Sheilagh Ogilvie and Richard Overy, eds., *Germany: A New Social and Economic History, Vol. 3: Since 1800*. New York: Oxford University Press, 2003, pp. 71–105.

Page, Thomas Walker, "The Distribution of Immigrants in the United States Before 1870." *Journal of Political Economy* 20 (July 1912): 676–94.

Page, Thomas W., "Some Economic Aspects of Immigration Before 1870: I." *Journal of Political Economy* 20 (December 1912): 1011–28.

Page, Thomas W., "Some Economic Aspects of Immigration Before 1870: II." *Journal of Political Economy* 21 (January 1913): 34–55.

Page, Thomas W., "The Transportation of Immigrants and Reception Arrangements in the Nineteenth Century." *Journal of Political Economy* 19 (November 1911): 732–49.

Pawson, Eric, *Transport and Economy: The Turnpike Roads of Eighteenth-Century Britain*. New York: Academic Press, 1977.

Pope, Clayne, "Inequality in the Nineteenth Century." In Stanley L. Engerman and Robert E. Gallman, eds., *The Cambridge Economic History of the United States, Volume II: The Long Nineteenth Century*. New York: Cambridge University Press, 2000, pp. 109–42.

Post, John D., *The Last Great Subsistence Crisis in the Western World*. Baltimore: The Johns Hopkins University Press, 1977.

Quigley, John Michael, "An Economic Model of Swedish Emigration." *Quarterly Journal of Economics* 86 (February 1972): 111–26.

Rezneck, Samuel, *Business Depressions and Financial Panics*. New York: Greenwood Publishing Corporation, 1968.

Richards, Eric, "Migration to Colonial Australia." In Jan Lucassen and Leo Lucassen, eds., *Migration, Migration History, History: Old Paradigms and New Perspectives*. New York: Peter Lang, 1997, pp. 153–61.

Rosenberg, Charles E., *The Cholera Years: The United States in 1832, 1849, and 1866*. Chicago: University of Chicago Press, 1987.

Ross, Steven J., *Workers on the Edge: Work, Leisure, and Politics in Industrializing Cincinnati, 1788–1890*. New York: Columbia University Press, 1985.

Rowland, K. T., *Steam at Sea: A History of Steam Navigation*. New York: Praeger Publishers, 1970.

Ruggles, Steven, Matthew Sobek, Trent Alexander, Catherine A. Fitch, Ronald Goeken, Patricia Kelly Hall, Miriam King, and Chad Ronnander, *Integrated Public Use Microdata Series: Version 3.0* [Machine-readable database]. Minneapolis: Minnesota Population Center [producer and distributor], 2004, http://www.ipums.org.

Runblom, H., and H. Norman, eds., *From Sweden to America: a History of the Migration*. Minneapolis: University of Minnesota Press, 1977.

Scally, Robert, "Liverpool Ships and Irish Emigrants in the Age of Sail." *Journal of Social History* 17 (Fall 1983): 5–30.

Schelbert, Leo, "On Becoming an Emigrant: A Structural View of Eighteenth- and Nineteenth-Century Swiss Data." *Perspectives in American History* 7 (1973): 441–95.

Scranton, Philip, *Proprietary Capitalism: The Textile Manufacture at Philadelphia, 1800–1885*. New York: Cambridge University Press, 1983.

Searight, Sarah, *New Orleans*. New York: Stein and Day Publishers, 1973.

Shlomowitz, Ralph, Lance Brennan, and John McDonald, *Mortality and Migration in the Modern World*. Brookfield, Vermont: Variorum, 1996.

Shlomowitz, Ralph, and John McDonald, "Babies at Risk on Immigrant Voyages to Australia in the Nineteenth Century." *Economic History Review* 44 (February 1991): 86–101.

Sieglerschmidt, Jörn, "Social and Economic Landscapes." In Sheilagh Ogilvie, ed., *Germany: A New Social and Economic History, Vol. 2: 1630–1800*. New York: St. Martin's Press, Inc., 1996, pp. 1–38.

Sjaastad, Larry A., "The Costs and Returns of Human Migration." *Journal of Political Economy* 70 (October 1962): 80–93.

Skeen, C. Edward, "'The Year Without a Summer': A Historical View." *Journal of the Early Republic* 1 (Spring 1981): 51–67.

Smith, Walter Buckingham, and Arthur Harrison Cole, *Fluctuations in American Business, 1790–1860*. New York: Russell & Russell, 1969 (reissue of 1935 edition).

Sokoloff, Kenneth L., "Was the Transition from the Artisanal Shop to the Non-mechanized Factory Associated with Gains in Efficiency?: Evidence from the U.S. Manufacturing Censuses of 1820 and 1850." *Explorations in Economic History* 21 (October 1984): 351–82.

Sokoloff, Kenneth L., and Georgia C. Villaflor, "The Market for Manufacturing Workers during Early Industrialization: The American Northeast, 1820 to 1860." In Claudia Goldin and Hugh Rockoff, eds., *Strategic Factors in Nineteenth-Century American Economic History*. Chicago: University of Chicago Press, 1992, pp. 29–65.

Steckel, Richard H., "Stature and the Standard of Living." *Journal of Economic Literature* 33 (December 1995): 1903–40.

Steinfeld, Robert J., *The Invention of Free Labor: The Employment Relation in English and American Law and Culture, 1350–1870*. Chapel Hill: The University of North Carolina Press, 1991.

Swierenga, Robert P., "Dutch International Migration Statistics, 1820–1880: An Analysis of Linked Multinational Nominal Files." *International Migration Review* 15 (Fall 1981): 445–70.

Swierenga, Robert P., *Faith and Family: Dutch Immigration and Settlement in the United States*. New York: Holmes and Meier, Ellis Island Series, 2000.

Szostak, Rick, *The Role of Transportation in the Industrial Revolution: A Comparison of England and France*. Montreal: McGill-Queen's University Press, 1991.

Taylor, George Rogers, *The Transportation Revolution, 1815–1860*. New York: Rinehart & Company, 1958.

Taylor, Philip, *The Distant Magnet*. New York: Harper & Row, 1971.

Thernstrom, Stephan, *The Other Bostonians: Poverty and Progress in the American Metropolis, 1880–1970*. Cambridge: Harvard University Press, 1973.

Thernstrom, Stephan, *Poverty and Progress: Social Mobility in a Nineteenth-Century City*. Cambridge: Harvard University Press, 1964.

Thistlethwaite, Frank, "Migration from Europe Overseas in the Nineteenth and Twentieth Centuries." *Rapports du XIe Congrès International des Sciences Historiques*, vol. 5, *Histoire Contemporaine*. Stockholm, 1960. Reprinted in Rudolph J. Vecoli and Suzanne M. Sinke, eds., *A Century of European Migration, 1830–1930*. Urbana: University of Illinois Press, 1991, pp. 17–49.

Thomas, Brinley, *Migration and Economic Growth: A Study of Great Britain and the Atlantic Economy*. Second Edition. London: Cambridge University Press, 1973.

Thomas, Dorothy Swaine, *Social and Economic Aspects of Swedish Population Movements, 1750–1933*. New York: Macmillan, 1941.

Thompson, Slason, *A Short History of American Railways Covering Ten Decades*. Freeport, NY: Books for Libraries Press, 1925. Reprinted 1971.

Thorp, Willard Long, *Business Annals*. NBER General Series, no. 8. New York: NBER, 1926.

Tilly, Charles, "Transplanted Networks." In Virginia Yans-McLaughlin, ed., *Immigration Reconsidered: History, Sociology, and Politics*. New York: Oxford University Press, 1990, pp. 79–95.

Tipton, Frank B., "Government and the Economy in the Nineteenth Century." In Sheilagh Ogilvie, ed., *Germany: A New Social and Economic History, Vol. 3: Since 1800*. New York: Oxford University Press, 2003, pp. 106–51.

Tomaske, John A., "The Determinants of Intercountry Differences in European Migration: 1881–1900." *Journal of Economic History* 31 (December 1971): 840–53.

Torpey, John, *The Invention of the Passport: Surveillance, Citizenship and the State*. New York: Cambridge University Press, 2000.

Tucker, George, *Progress of the United States in Population and Wealth*. New York: Nation Press, 1870.

U.S. Bureau of the Census, Seventh (1850), *Seventh Census of the United States*. Washington, DC: Government Printing Office, 1853.

U.S. Bureau of the Census, Eighth (1860), *Population of the United States*. Washington, DC: Government Printing Office, 1864.

U.S. Bureau of the Census, Ninth (1870), *Population of the United States*. Washington, DC: Government Printing Office, 1872.

U.S. Bureau of the Census, *Historical Statistics of the United States: Colonial Times to 1970*. Washington, DC: Government Printing Office, 1976.

U.S. Bureau of Immigration, *Annual Report of the Commissioner General of Immigration, Report for 1926*. Washington, DC: Government Printing Office, 1926.

U.S. Congress, *Report of the Select Committee on the Sickness and Mortality on Board Emigrant Ships*. 33rd Congress, 1st Session, Senate Reports (#386), 1854.

U.S. Treasury, Bureau of Statistics, *Arrivals of Alien Passengers and Immigrants in the United States from 1820 to 1892*. Washington, DC: Government Printing Office, 1893.

U.S. Treasury, Bureau of Statistics, *Monthly Summary of Finance and Commerce of the United States: Immigration into the United States*, 57th Congress, 2nd Session, House Reports, Document 15, No. 12, Series 1902–3, June 1903.

U.S. Treasury, Bureau of Statistics, *Special Report on Immigration; Accompanying Information for Immigrants*. Washington, DC: Government Printing Office, 1872.

Uselding, Paul, "Conjectural Estimates of Gross Human Capital Inflows to the American Economy: 1790–1860." *Explorations in Economic History* 9 (Fall 1971): 49–61.

Van Vugt, William E., *Britain to America: Mid-Nineteenth-Century Immigrants to the United States*. Urbana: University of Illinois Press, 1999.

Van Vugt, William E., "Prosperity and Industrial Emigration from Britain during the Early 1850s." *Journal of Social History* 22 (1988): 339–54.

Van Vugt, William E., "Running from Ruin?: The Emigration of British Farmers to the U.S.A. in the Wake of the Repeal of the Corn Laws." *Economic History Review* 41 (Aug. 1988): 411–28.

Vedder, Richard K., and Lowell E. Gallaway, "The Geographical Distribution of British and Irish Emigrants to the United States after 1800." *Scottish Journal of Political Economy* 19 (February 1972): 19–35.

Wabeke, Bertus H., *Dutch Emigration to North America, 1624–1860*. Freeport, NY: Books for Libraries Press, 1970.

Walker, Mack, *Germany and the Emigration, 1816–1885*. Cambridge, MA: Harvard University Press, 1964.

Walton, Gary M., and Hugh Rockoff, *History of the American Economy*. Tenth Edition. New York: Thomson South-Western, 2002.

Way, Peter, *Common Labour: Workers and the Digging of North American Canals, 1780–1860*. New York: Cambridge University Press, 1993.

Wegge, Simone, "Chain Migration and Information Networks: Evidence from Nineteenth-Century Hesse-Cassel." *Journal of Economic History* 58 (December 1998): 957–86.

Wegge, Simone, "The Hesse-Cassel Emigrants: A New Sample of Transatlantic Emigrants Linked to their Origins." *Research in Economic History* 21 (2003): 357–405.

Wegge, Simone, "Occupational Self-Selection of European Emigrants: Evidence from Nineteenth-Century Hesse-Cassel." *European Review of Economic History* 6 (December 2002): 365–94.

Wegge, Simone, "To Part or Not to Part: Emigration and Inheritance Institutions in Nineteenth-Century Hesse-Cassel." *Explorations in Economic History* 36 (January 1999): 30–55.

Wegge, Simone, "Push and Pull Migration in the Mid-Nineteenth Century." Unpublished manuscript, 2005.

Wikipedia, specific entries used are at: http://en.wikipedia.org/wiki/Epidemic_typhus; http://en.wikipedia.org/wiki/Cholera; and http://en.wikipedia.org/wiki/Ward's_Island. Accessed on November 22, 2006.

Wilentz, Sean, *Chants Democratic: New York & the Rise of the American Working Class, 1788–1850*. New York: Oxford University Press, 1984.

Wilkinson, Maurice, "European Migration to the United States: An Econometric Analysis of Aggregate Labor Supply and Demand." *Review of Economics and Statistics* 52 (August 1970): 272–9.

Williamson, Jeffrey G., "Migration to the New World: Long-Term Influences and Impact." *Explorations in Economic History* 11 (Summer 1974): 357–89.

Williamson, Jeffrey G., and Peter H. Lindert, *American Inequality: A Macroeconomic History*. New York: Academic Press, 1980.

Winchester, Simon, *Krakatoa, The Day the World Exploded: August 27, 1883*. New York: Harper Collins, 2003.

Wittke, Carl, *We Who Built America: The Saga of the Immigrant*. Cleveland: Press of Western Reserve University, 1967, revised edition.

Wokeck, Marianne S., *Trade In Strangers: The Beginnings of Mass Migration to North America*. University Park: The Pennsylvania State University Press, 1999.

Woodham-Smith, Cecil, *The Great Hunger: Ireland, 1845–1849*. New York: Harper & Row, 1962.

Wright, Gavin, "The Origins of American Industrial Success, 1870–1940." *American Economic Review* 80 (September 1990): 651–68.

Wyman, Mark, *Round-Trip to America: The Immigrants Return to Europe, 1880–1930*. Ithaca, NY: Cornell University Press, 1993.

Zimmerman, Gary, and Marion Wolfert, *German Immigrants: Lists of Passengers Bound from Bremen to New York, 1863–1867 With Places of Origin*. Vol. 3. Baltimore: Genealogical Publishing Co., 1988.

Zolberg, Aristide R., "International Migration Policies in a Changing World System." In William H. McNeill and Ruth S. Adams, eds., *Human Migration: Patterns and Policies*. Bloomington: Indiana University Press, 1978, pp. 241–86.

Index